English Vocabulary Elements

English Vocabulary Elements

Keith Denning
William R. Leben

New York　Oxford
OXFORD UNIVERSITY PRESS
1995

Oxford University Press

Oxford   New York
Athens   Auckland   Bangkok   Bogotá   Buenos Aires   Calcutta
Cape Town   Chennai   Dar es Salaam   Delhi   Florence   Hong Kong   Istanbul
Karachi   Kuala Lumpur   Madrid   Melbourne   Mexico City   Mumbai
Nairobi   Paris   São Paulo   Singapore   Taipei   Tokyo   Toronto   Warsaw

and associated companies in
Berlin   Ibadan

Copyright © 1995 by Keith Denning and William R. Leben

Published by Oxford University Press, Inc.,
198 Madison Avenue, New York, New York 10016-4314
http://www.oup-usa.org

Oxford is a registered trademark of Oxford University Press

Library of Congress Cataloging-in-Publication Data

English vocabulary elements /
Keith Denning and William R. Leben.
p. cm.
Includes bibliographical references (p.) and index.
ISBN 0-19-506609-X
1. Vocabulary.
I. Denning, Keith.
II. Leben, William Ronald, 1943– .
III. Title.
PE1449D424   1995   428.1—dc20   94-18224

9 8 7

Printed in the United States of America
on acid-free paper

Preface

This book is intended for use either independently or in courses at the advanced high school and college levels. It is especially recommended for those interested in preparing for educational aptitude tests and other postsecondary admissions tests (including the PSAT, SAT, ACT, GRE, LSAT, MCAT, MAT) that test vocabulary skills. Part or all of the text may also be used to good effect in English for Foreign Students (EFS) and English as a Second Language (ESL) courses. The book may provide preparation for those considering majors in the natural sciences (e.g., biology, chemistry, engineering, premedical study, and physics), the social sciences (e.g., psychology, sociology, and linguistics), and the humanities (e.g., literature, classics, modern languages, philosophy, and history). If this list seems broad, it is because we feel that the skills one may acquire through the study of these materials are valuable for nearly every field of study or work which requires a facility for comprehension or expression in the English language. This list is, of course, not meant to exclude those who are merely afflicted with the kind of curiosity about language that has motivated many an amateur and professional linguist in the course of a lifetime of joyful pursuit.

The book is designed primarily to expand vocabulary skills by teaching the basic units of written English vocabulary. It also touches on a number of other areas equally important to an effective understanding of learned, specialized, and scientific vocabulary, and to the explanation of many otherwise puzzling or problematic aspects of the structure of the English language. Included here are introductions to important facets of the history of English and language change and basic phonetics. This material is intended to facilitate, supplement, and enrich the study of vocabulary elements.

The book is structured to allow for flexibility in its application to any of several kinds of curriculums with differing time constraints and differing degrees of intensiveness and scope. It may serve as the core for courses in English vocabulary (either specialized, scientific, or general), verbal aptitude examination preparation, the history of English, English grammar (for native speakers or ESL students), or scientific writing.

USING THIS BOOK

In reading each chapter, the student should focus on the key concepts and, in particular, on terminology (shown in boldface type, e.g. **morpheme, gloss**) and definitions.

After each assigned reading (or on some kind of periodic basis), the student should memorize any associated list of morphemes (i.e. meaningful word elements) and their glosses (i.e. the thumbnail definitions of their meanings) and complete the exercises assigned by the instructor. The exercises for each chapter will assume a knowledge of the morphemes, glosses, and skills covered up to that point. It is therefore advisable for students to master the material as it is encountered rather than to save memorization until the end. The following abbreviations are used throughout the text:

A = adjective N = noun V = verb

Different typefaces are used to distinguish various levels:

- Cited morphemes, words, and phrases are ordinarily written in italics (e.g. *pre-, invasion, Angela sings beautifully*).
- When the discussion deals with spelling alone, letters, words, and phrases are underlined (e.g. the letter s, traveller vs. traveler, cat's-paw and catspaw).
- If meaning (rather than sound or spelling) is the focus, a word or phrase appears within single quotes (e.g. Greek *cosmos* 'order', Old English *tunge* 'tongue').
- When it is necessary to focus the reader's attention on part of a cited form, it may be written in boldface (e.g. *Angela sings **beautifully***).

VOCABULARY-BUILDING TECHNIQUES

Mnemonics. As a mnemonic device (i.e. an aid to memorization), each **morpheme** (i.e. word element) assigned in the course is accompanied by one or more simple or familiar English words containing that morpheme and illustrating its meaning. For *narco* 'sleep', for example, one possible mnemonic is *narcotic* (i.e. a drug that causes sleep or dreaminess). It is not necessary to memorize these mnemonic words. They are intended only to allow students to put the morpheme in a frame rather than requiring them to learn an abstract, unassociated form. Sometimes the student will think of a better alternative to the mnemonic supplied and should certainly use it if it helps in learning the morpheme.

Flashcards and similar devices. Although each individual must find the most effective way to learn morphemes and their meanings, several of our students have found it helpful to create flashcards for each morpheme with the morpheme on one side and the gloss on the other, just as they would in foreign language study.

Another method (which saves some writing) is to cover one side of the list of morphemes and glosses and, going from top to bottom and then from bottom to top, to try to recall the morpheme for each gloss and then the gloss for each morpheme. Other approaches to the task of self-drilling for memorization include repeating morphemes and glosses to yourself until you cannot internally "hear" one without the other, or finding a rhyme or mental "picture" which helps to associate morphemes and their glosses (e.g. "*aster* reminds me of the flower having the same name, which looks like a <u>star</u>," or "*viv* reminds me of my friend Vivian, who is very <u>liv</u>ely").

USING A DICTIONARY

We strongly recommend that every student following the course of study outlined in this book have on hand as a supplement a dictionary designed for the collegiate level or above (i.e. one containing 150,000 or more entries), such as *The American Heritage Dictionary of the English Language* or *Merriam Webster's Collegiate Dictionary* (10th ed.). It may also be necessary to consult a larger dictionary like the *Oxford English Dictionary*, (OED) or *Webster's Third New International Dictionary*, or such specialized dictionaries as *Dorland's Illustrated Medical Dictionary*. Many of these are available in high school, college, and public libraries, as well as at bookstores selling new and used books.

Using a dictionary effectively is a skill which must be learned. It is important to become familiar with the basic layout of any dictionary you use. Most good dictionaries make this task easier by presenting explanations of entries, lists of abbreviations, and so forth, in the introductory pages. We recommend that students take the time to read this material before trying to use a new dictionary, thereby avoiding frustration later on.

One of the best ways to attack the sometimes bewildering variety of English vocabulary is to refer to a collegiate-level dictionary when you confront unfamiliar, difficult, or interesting words. When you come across an unfamiliar word or morpheme, it is a good idea either to make a note of it for later reference or to take a moment to look it up. Learning to look for and recognize the morphemes and words you learn in the course (as well as those you acquire on your own) will eventually minimize the time you will spend with a dictionary—unless, of course, you enjoy reading dictionaries, in which case you may find yourself spending more time on other words than on the one you originally meant to look up!

MOVING BEYOND THE FINAL CHAPTER

More comprehensive lists of Latin and Greek word elements than those provided in the glossary can be found in the works by Smith, Borror, and Hogben listed at the end of this book. These works list morphemes according to different principles, but the student can, with a little searching, use them to find and identify many less frequently used word elements not found in our glossary. Through the use of such guides, inquisitive exploration, and acquisition of the principles presented here, students may continue to expand their vocabulary-analysis skills far beyond their current capabilities.

We are indebted to our students and teaching assistants over the years for their many helpful and insightful suggestions relating to this book as well as the course upon which it was based. In particular, we are grateful to R. M. R. Hall, John J. Ohala, J. David Placek, and Robert Vago for reading an earlier version of this text and for providing extremely valuable comments and recommendations.

Ypsilanti, Mich.   K. D.
Stanford, Calif.   W. R. L.
July 1994

Contents

Pronunciation Guide

The following symbols are used in the text when a pronunciation must be precisely described. The words beside each symbol illustrate the current English pronunciation. The phonetic symbols used here are widely employed by American linguists. (Some alternative symbols not used in this book but employed elsewhere are shown in parentheses.)

VOWELS*		CONSONANTS	
symbol	as in	symbol	as in
a	father	b	boy
æ	cat	č (tʃ)	chip
ai (aʸ, aʲ)	ride	d	dog
au (aʷ, aᵛ)	town	ð	they
e (ɛⁱ, ɛʲ)	fiancé, raid, made	f	fat
ʌ	cut	g	go
ə	about	h	hot
ɛ	pet	ǰ (dʒ)	jump
i	machine	k	kiss
ɪ (ι)	pit	l	left
o (ɔʷ, ɔᵛ)	rose	m	mark
ɔ	call, court	n	new

ɔi (ɔʸ, ɔʲ)	noise		ŋ	singer
u	prune		p	pot
ʊ (ω)	put		r	run
			s	sit
			š (ʃ)	shape
			t	top
			θ	thigh
			v	vote
			w	worm
			y (j)	yell
			x	yech! (German: Bach)
			z	zoo
			ž (ʒ)	azure

*Many Americans do not distinguish between certain pairs of vowel sounds. For example, the words *hock* and *hawk* may sound identical to you, or you may only barely distinguish the vowels of *cut* and *about* or those of *court* and *rose*.

When the precise pronunciation of a sound or word must be indicated, that sound or word will be enclosed in square brackets. For example, 'the word *bathe* is pronounced [beð]' or 'the sound [ž] occurs at the end of the *rouge*'.

Note that at some points it will be necessary to indicate a sound's length, and this will be done by writing a colon (:) immediately after a long sound. This might be the case, for example, when we wish to carefully contrast the vowel sounds in *pit* and *Pete* (*i.e.* [pɪt] and [pi:t], respectively). In the second of these words the vowel is not only different in sound but also takes approximately twice as long to pronounce.)

When it is necessary to indicate where the primary stress in a word's pronunciation occurs, the stressed syllable will be printed in bold face. For example, in**ter** and *converse* have different meanings from **inter**- and **converse**; and the pronunciation of *hasidim* is [xa **si** dɪm].

English Vocabulary Elements

1

Introduction: The Wealth of English

WORD POWER AND A WORLD POWER

In the number of speakers who learn it as a first or second language, and in its range of uses and adaptability to general and specific tasks, English is the world's most important language today. It is the mother tongue of several hundred million people. Its rich verbal art, great works in science and scholarship, and major role in international commerce and culture have made English the most frequently taught second language in the world.

English is not the first language of as many individuals as Mandarin Chinese. But it is spoken over a much vaster area. In North America, Europe, Asia, Africa, and elsewhere, it is the official language of many nations, including some where English is not most people's first language.

A history of political importance as well as a certain linguistic suppleness have endowed English with an enormous vocabulary. *Webster's Third New International Dictionary* contains 460,000 words, and these do not include the many technical terms that appear only in specialized dictionaries for particular fields, or recent **neologisms** (new words), not to mention all the regular plural forms of nouns, the different present and past tense forms of verbs, and other words derived from these words. No other language comes close to English in a count of general vocabulary. German runs a poor second with under 200,000 words. According to Robert Claiborne, in *Our Marvelous Native Tongue: The Life and Times of the English Language* (New York: Times Books, 1983), the largest dictionary of French has about 150,000 words, and a Russian dictionary maybe 130,000.

The size of the English vocabulary has some wonderful advantages. While it may be true that any concept can be expressed in any language, a language can make the process easier or harder by providing or not providing appropriate words. Thanks to the well-developed word stock of English, English speakers have a head start over speakers of other languages in being able to express themselves clearly and concisely.

Whether one uses this head start to advantage or not is, of course, up to the individual, but speakers with a good command of vocabulary can say things in more subtly different (and, hence, often more effective) ways than others can, and this ability is noticed.

- We refer to our friends and acquaintances as good talkers, fast talkers, boring conversationalists, etc.
- College board and aptitude test scores depend very heavily on vocabulary knowledge.
- A job or school application or interview often turns on how adept at using language the interviewee is.
- We find that we can overcome many sorts of individual and group handicaps to the extent that we become established as a "good communicator."

In cases like these, the difference between success and failure often amounts to how well we have mastered the ability to speak and comprehend speech, and to read and write. The expressive power of language is enormous, and every time a word acquires a new shade of meaning—a common development, as we will see—the richness of the language is enhanced. This may make you wonder why people complain so much about novel uses of language. Some seem to react to each new twist that comes into the language as a sign of decline, but a view of language change as growth deserves serious consideration.

The enormous size of the English vocabulary also has its disadvantages, as we are reminded each time we have to use a dictionary to look up a word we don't know, or because we were tricked by the alluring picture on the front cover of a book into thinking that the language inside would be easily within our grasp. A language as rich in its vocabulary as English is full of surprises, and however wonderful it may be in some ways that this richness is always increasing, it places a potentially painful burden on us when we first learn words and their meanings.

To sum up, English is extraordinarily well endowed with words. As versatile as the language already is, the supply of words is ever on the rise, with their meanings shifting in time to reflect new uses. These are the facts that we will deal with in this book.

ON THE ATTACK

In the face of a challenge of such large proportions, a well-organized attack is called for. While we cannot expect the language always to oblige us in our quest for shortcuts to an enhanced vocabulary, we fortunately will uncover signs that some of the work has already been done for us. This is mainly due to the fact that most of the complex words in the language have similar structures. If we learn the rules that reveal the structure of a certain kind of word, it will relieve us of some of the burden (and, perhaps, boredom) of learning all the words of this type individually.

We must divide and then conquer. We will find that some aspects of the study of word structure (known as **morphology**) are helpful in analyzing words into their parts and in understanding how the parts contribute to the meaning of the whole. It will also come in handy to understand how English came to be the way it is and to learn some of the linguistic characteristics of the principal languages that English has drawn on to reach its present position.

PRECISION AND ADAPTABILITY

One significant result of the size of the English vocabulary is the degree of precision it allows. The wealth of words that are nearly synonymous but yet embody subtle shades of difference in meaning makes English the only major language which often requires the use of a thesaurus—an organized listing of words that helps a writer capture a precise tone and sense by providing exactly the right word. Most languages get by with a single word, whereas the skillful use of English requires special consideration to make the appropriate choice between two or more similar words (what the French call *le mot juste* 'the precise word'). For example, deciding between the words *paternal* and *fatherly* in the following sentences involves sensitivity to a distinction few other languages make.

> *paternal* or *fatherly?*
> a. *The judge's decision restricted Tom's _____ rights.*
> b. *George gave Kim a _____ smile and then went back to reading.*

You would probably choose to use *paternal* in the first sentence and *fatherly* in the second. Certainly *fatherly* and *paternal* share the same basic meaning or **denotation,** and we could have used *fatherly* in the first sentence and *paternal* in the second, but the opposite choice is preferred because of matters of **con-**

notation, the subtler secondary associations of a word. Connotation includes factors like style, mood, and level of familiarity. *Paternal* is a more stylistically formal choice (and therefore appropriate to a legal context like that in the first sentence) while *fatherly* is less formal in style. *Fatherly* strongly connotes the idealized qualities of fatherhood (especially those of personal warmth and love); *paternal* does not.

Not only does the wealth of choices offered by English vocabulary make such subtle distinctions possible, but its adaptability provides a ready means for creating new words as they are needed. Even if the dictionary does not list an appropriate word, we often create one to fill the need for, say, a verb meaning 'correct in advance' (which we may form by adding the **word element** *pre-*, which means 'before', to the existing verb *edit,*) and then use it in a sentence: The *author must pre-edit the manuscript.*

Similarly, the element *-like* (either with or without a preceding hyphen, as in *childlike* or *tree-like*) may be affixed to a huge number of nouns to create such new words as *tentacle-like, cup-like,* and so on. If we invent a device for examining veins and recognize that in many words *ven* means 'vein' (as in *venopuncture* 'the use of a needle to inject liquids into or draw blood from a vein') and that *scope* means 'a viewing device' (as in *microscope* 'a device for examining very small things'), we may call the new device a *venoscope,* a word never before recorded in the dictionary. The creation (or **coining**) of neologisms is commonplace in English; almost any new idea can be expressed by combining English words or their parts in new ways.

Such adaptability means that even the largest dictionaries can't capture every possible word in the language. The number of possible combinations of word elements like *pre-, veno,* and *scope,* and the immeasurable amount of speaking and writing done in English requires that dictionary editors restrict themselves to listing only the most frequent words in a language, and even then, only those used over a substantial period of time. Dictionaries are therefore always at least slightly out of date and inaccurate in their descriptions of the language's stock of words. In addition, the use of many words is restricted to specific domains. For example, medical terminology involves a tremendous number of words unfamiliar to those outside the medical community. Many of these terms never enter general dictionaries of the language and can only be found in specialized medical dictionaries.

THE CONSTANTLY EVOLVING NATURE OF ENGLISH VOCABULARY

Change and innovation are integral to English, as they are to every living language. The productivity of the language has brought in new words using the element *-ize* meaning roughly 'to make' as *finalize, standardize,* and *prioritize.* Although some of these words have been singled out as 'corruptions' by certain writers and teachers of English, all of them have established firm footholds in the language and are unlikely to be the subject of debate in coming generations.

Taste and style are often matters of personal discretion and are also subject to change. In the course of this book we hope to build a greater sense of security about language use. We all like to think of ourselves as making informed decisions about the acceptability of particular words or usages for particular circumstances. We all would like to move freely between the informal, formal, and technical domains of spoken and written English.

WHY ENGLISH IS SO RICH

Modern English is the product of a long and complex process of historical development. Consequently, we can expect to find clues to its character in the past. Indeed, English has a history as rich as its vocabulary. The most important historical factor in the growth of the English vocabulary has been the ease with which it has **borrowed** words from other languages and adapted them to its own uses. The word *clique,* which is partially synonymous with the **native** (i.e. nonborrowed, inherited) English word *group,* for example, was taken into English from French around the year 1700. Since that time, *clique* has become a familiar English word. It has been incorporated into the language to such an extent that it participates in processes which originally applied only to native vocabulary, with the result that today we have many words that have been **derived** from *clique.* (One word is derived from another by adding other word elements to it and/or by changing its part of speech—e.g. from noun to verb or from adjective to noun.) These include *cliquish, cliquishness, cliquy, cliqueless,* the verb *to clique* and others, as Otto Jespersen notes in *Growth and Structure of the English Language.* (Compare this to the way words which were not borrowed from other languages, such as *red,* are the basis for derived forms like *reddish, reddishness, redden,* etc.)

English has been so ready to take words from foreign sources that more than seventy-five percent of modern English vocabulary has either been borrowed or formed from borrowed elements. Understanding why English vocabulary is as rich and diverse as it is gives us an important aid in learning to master it. (Chapter 2 will deal in depth with the historical development of English vocabulary.) The reason that English has two words with such similar meanings as *fatherly* and *paternal* is that it retained a native word (*fatherly*) while borrowing from Latin a near synonym (*paternal*). This in a sense allowed *fatherly* to 'share' its duties with *paternal*. This is the general pattern with native and borrowed synonyms: the native word is more familiar or more basic and (usually) shorter while the borrowed word is more formal or more technical and longer. A few additional synonym pairs serve to illustrate this point.

native	borrowed
tell	inform
spin	rotate
pretty	attractive

In each of these pairs the first member is more appropriate for everyday use, more conversational, and less formal or technical than the second. The first member of each pair is native while the second is borrowed.

But the choice between familiar and formal words is only one small part of the picture. With its wealth of native and foreign resources, English vocabulary has tremendous freedom to expand. Specialized and technical terminology, which generally involve the use of elements borrowed from Latin and Greek, are the most frequent sites of vocabulary innovation.

PNEUMONOULTRAMICROSCOPICSILICOVOLCANOCONIOSIS

This forty-five letter word is listed in the *Guinness Book of World Records* as the longest word in English. It is the name of a lung disease caused by the inhalation of extremely fine particles of volcanic silicon dust. Admittedly an extreme case, it illustrates the lengths to which innovation using foreign word elements may be taken. Although perhaps bewildering at first, this monstrous word is not as difficult to handle as it might seem. It is made up a number of elements, many of which are already familiar to you by themselves or as they appear as parts of other words. These include *pneumon* (which is also part of the name for the lung disease *pneumonia*), *ultra* 'extremely' (as in *ultraconservative*), *microscopic*, *silic* (as in the word *silicon*), *volcan*, and *-osis* (as in *tuberculosis* or *neurosis*) meaning 'medical condition' or 'disease'. The most unfamiliar element of the word is *coni*, which is found in two other specialized words in which it also means 'dust': *conidium* and *koniology*. (It is also related to the element *cin* 'ashes' in *incinerate*.) So *pneumon/o/ultra/microscopic/silic/o/volcan/o/coni/osis* literally means 'lung-microscopic-silicon-volcanic-dust-disease' or (to rearrange things a bit more sensibly) 'lung disease (caused by) microscopic (i.e. extremely small or fine) volcanic silicon dust'. (Incidentally, *microscopic* could itself be broken down into three elements: *micro* 'small', *scop* 'view', and *ic*, which makes the word an adjective.) Notice that the meaning 'caused by' is not carried by any particular elements in the word but must be inferred from the relationship of the other meanings.

To approach such special words, we thus need the ability to **parse** (i.e. analyze, break down, or take apart) the word into its proper components, and we need to know the meanings of the components. The same system that we use to parse and interpret words also applies to the coining of words.

The remainder of this book deals with specific methods and rules that will put this ability and knowledge into our hands. Long words need not be intimidating. (In fact, the longer a word, the more likely it is that we can take it apart and figure out its meaning from the sum of its parts.) You may or may not want to use your new-found skills to impress your family and friends, but you will definitely find that you have some powerful tools that will open up the worlds of technical and specialized vocabulary.

THE HISTORY HIDDEN IN WORDS

English words encode interesting and useful historical information. For example, compare the words

> *captain*
> *chief*
> *chef*

These three words all derive historically from *caput,* which is the Latin word for 'head'. (It is also found in a slightly different form in the words *capital, capitol, decapitate,* and others). It is easy to see this if you consider the three words to mean 'the head of a vessel or military unit', 'the leader or head of a group', and 'the head of a kitchen', respectively.

They were borrowed into English during three successive periods in the evolution of Latin's linguistic descendant, French. Between the first and the second of these periods, certain [k] sounds (spelled with a c̲) and [p] sounds (as in *captain*) became [č] and [f] sounds, respectively (as in *chief*). Between the second and third periods, [č] sounds further changed to become [š] sounds (as in *chef*).

Two other 'word triplets' which follow the same [k] to [č] to [š] pattern are *candle–chandler* ('candle maker')–*chandelier* (originally an elaborate *candle* holder) and *cant* ('sing*song* intonation', 'jargon'; also visible in *incantation*)– *chant–chantey* (as in *sea chantey*).

The history and relationship is diagramed in table 1.1.

Table 1.1. Changes in Sound Over Time in Latin and French and Their Results in Borrowings

Latin or French sound			English borrowings with these sounds		
Period 1		[k], [p]	captain	candle	cant
	↓				
Period 2		[č], [f]	chief	chandler	chant
	↓				
Period 3		[š], [f]	chef	chandelier	chantey

Another example of a historical correspondence of sounds can be seen by comparing the originally Latin form *semi-* (as in *semicircle*) and the Greek *hemi-* (as in *hemisphere*). Both *semi-* and *hemi-* mean 'half'. This correspondence of h in one to s in the other results from the fact that Greek and Latin are **related** languages, that is, they share a common ancient vocabulary (including a single morpheme meaning 'half'). Over a long period of time, the two languages came to differ in certain respects, including the pronunciation of the first sound of this morpheme. (We will discuss the nature of language relationships and sound changes in detail in later chapters.)

Such correspondences between the sounds of words borrowed from related languages such as French, Latin, and Greek give us a way to organize information about English words. Knowing something about their historical development can provide useful cues to meanings and word relationships. In later chapters we will show exactly how to use sound correspondences to learn new word elements.

ADDITIONAL GOALS

While the main goal of the book is to teach new word elements, we should keep in mind an important secondary aim: to develop a set of powerful techniques and concepts that will place the student on a path of vocabulary growth which will continue for a lifetime.

The book should serve other purposes as well. As we come across examples in which English pronunciations and words have changed over time, we will also run into reactions that may involve resistance to change and will have to consider whether change in general or in specific cases amounts to linguistic enrichment, linguistic corruption, or something between these two poles. We will also note that usage varies greatly between one geographical area and another, and even between different speakers in the same area, and we will become aware of attitudes and prejudices (others' and our own) based on this variation. We will confront the issue of how to use sophisticated vocabulary properly for effective communication and understanding.

In the process of developing techniques for word analysis, we also introduce some of the principal areas of modern linguistics. We will treat phonetics and phonology (the study of speech sounds and how they function in language), morphology (the study of word structure), diachronic linguistics (the study of language history and change over time), lexical semantics (the study of word meaning), and sociolinguistics (the study of social factors in language variation and change).

A final goal is spelling improvement. Word structure often correlates with standard spelling. For example, if you realize the words *pyromaniac* and *antipyretic* both contain the word element *pyr* 'fire, fever', you will automatically know that there is a *y* (rather than an *i*) between *p* and *r*. Similarly, if you know that *consensus* contains the root *sens* 'feel, think', you will remember that it has an *s* where many people mistakenly put a *c*. Even though *accommodate* is one of the most frequently misspelled words in the language (often found misspelled in government documents, magazines, memos from college administrators, and in other professional writing, you will have no problem remembering that this word has two <u>c</u>s and two <u>m</u>s once you know that it has the structure *ac/com/mod/ate*, with each of its elements contributing to its meaning.

See appendix II for Morpheme (i.e. word element) set 1. Do the exercises after memorizing the list of word elements for this chapter.

EXERCISES

1. Go through the following list of borrowed words and for each one try to give a native synonym—in a single word, if possible; in a phrase, if not. (The native word will generally be less formal.) If there are words here with which you are not familiar, use the dictionary to help you find the native synonyms.

a. in**ter**	_____	g. terminate	_____
b. depart	_____	h. con**verse**	_____
c. velocity	_____	i. donate	_____
d. rapid	_____	j. injure	_____
e. decay	_____	k. prevaricate	_____
f. illumination	_____	l. rotate	_____

2. a. Indicate which is the native English word and which is the borrowed word in each of the following pairs marked a through m.

b. Besides the etymological information (i.e. facts on the historical sources of the words) contained in your dictionary, what kinds of clues to their origins do the form and structure of the words themselves provide?

a.	wordy	————	verbose	————
b.	chew	————	masticate	————
c.	vend	————	sell	————
d.	malady	————	sickness	————
e.	answer	————	respond	————
f.	old	————	antique	————
g.	tell	————	inform	————
h.	watch	————	observe	————
i.	durable	————	hardy	————
j.	eat	————	consume	————
k.	emancipate	————	free	————
l.	deadly	————	mortal	————
m.	sad	————	dejected	————

3. Following and expanding on the discussion in this chapter of the words *fatherly* and *paternal,* suggest when and why one might choose to use *pyromaniac* rather than *firebug.*

4. What are the characteristics (if any) that differentiate a *chronometer* from a *watch?*

5. Given what you've learned from Morpheme set 1, what do you think the word *nomize* might mean? (You won't find this word in a dictionary.) Explain your answer.

6. What are the denotational and connotational differences between the words used in the following pairs of sentences? (Use specific information from the dictionary as well as your own sense of the meanings of individual word choices in your response.)

1.a. Whenever I ingest crustaceans I am nauseated.
1.b. Whenever I eat shellfish I am sick to my stomach

2.a. Paul reported that Jill injured Mark rather severely.
2.b. Paul said that Jill hurt Mark pretty badly.

3.a. Discovering a new species of insect invariably disconcerted Jean.
3.b. Finding a new kind of bug always bothered Jean.

7. Fill in the blank spaces with the forms of the appropriate **morphemes** (i.e. word elements) and **all glosses** (i.e. thumbnail definitions) you have memorized. In the example below you'd write <u>pseud</u> and '<u>color</u>'. Then spell out the **full** word you have written, including any 'extra' letters (like the <u>o</u> and <u>e</u> you are given for <u>pseud**o**chrom**e**</u>).

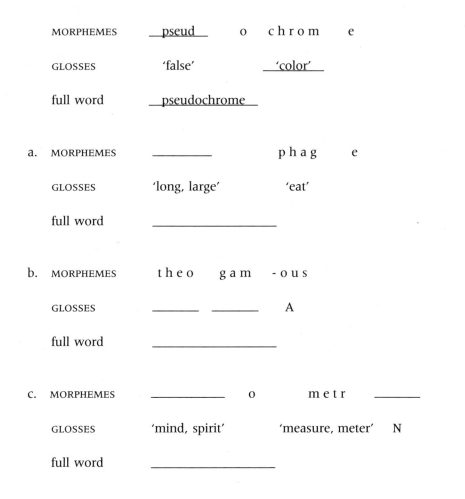

MORPHEMES   <u> pseud </u>   o   c h r o m   e

GLOSSES   'false'   <u> 'color' </u>

full word   <u> pseudochrome </u>

a.   MORPHEMES   _____   p h a g   e

      GLOSSES   'long, large'   'eat'

      full word   _____

b.   MORPHEMES   t h e o   g a m   - o u s

      GLOSSES   _____   _____   A

      full word   _____

c.   MORPHEMES   _____   o   m e t r   _____

      GLOSSES   'mind, spirit'   'measure, meter'   N

      full word   _____

d. MORPHEMES   _____   a n t h r o p   e

    GLOSSES   'hate'   _____

    full word: _____

e. MORPHEMES   d e -   p o r t

    GLOSSES   _____   'carry'

    full word   _____

f. MORPHEMES   _____   o   _____   - y

    GLOSSES   'bad'   sound, speech sound   _____

    full word   _____

2

History of English and Sources of English Vocabulary

This chapter looks at the major historical events that have shaped the English language, paying special attention to the forces that introduced massive numbers of foreign elements. This will help to explain some of the diversity of our language, particularly the words of Latin and Greek origin that have been entering the language nonstop since its beginnings. It should also serve to dispel some unsophisticated notions about why English is unusual and clarify vague ideas about the hybrid ('melting-pot'-like) character of the language.

When we use the phrase 'English language' we are really referring to something that is at the same time 'the American language', 'the Australian language', 'the Canadian language', 'the language of England, Scotland, and Wales', and so on. English today is the native tongue of more than 350 million people in many independent nations. It is also a major second language, primary, or alternative official language for an even larger number of people in places as distant and diverse as India, Nigeria, China, Germany, Singapore, South Africa, and Japan. So, what is it that's 'English' about this major world language? Certainly not its vocabulary, since as we shall see, most of this was borrowed from other languages. What is most English about the language is its history, because for almost a thousand years it was spoken almost only in England.

As we look at historical events, we will see that they have had a variety of linguistic repercussions, and we may ask what English would have been like if its history had been even slightly different.

MAJOR STAGES IN THE HISTORY OF ENGLISH

Continental Germanic (Before the Sixth Century C.E.)

The immediate ancestor of what we call English was a member of the **Germanic language family.** The languages in this family were originally spoken only on the European continent, not in the British Isles. Because these languages were typically not written, some of the earliest information about them comes from foreigners, especially a Roman historian of the first century B.C.E. named Tacitus, who tells of customs and tribal subdivisions of Germanic (also called **Teutonic**) peoples and a few words of their language (e.g. *glesum* meaning 'amber', source of the modern words *glass* and *glaze*). English is part of the **West Germanic** division of the Germanic languages, as shown in figure 2.1.

During much of the time (from approximately 1000 B.C.E. to 449 C.E.) which we will call the **Continental Germanic** period, Germanic peoples were influenced linguistically by their powerful Roman neighbors, who spoke **Latin,** a language from which many words were borrowed over these centuries. Among the earliest words borrowed from Latin are the practical, familiar terms *wine, street, mile, cheese, chalk, candle, kitchen,* and *mint* (both the plant and the place money is coined), all words for things or concepts new to the Germanic peoples.

Early History in Britain

Meanwhile, from the reign of Julius Caesar until about 449 C.E., what we now know as England was ruled by the Romans and inhabited by **Celts** or **Britons,**

Figure 2.1. Branches of the Germanic Language Family and Major Modern Languages in Each († = extinct).

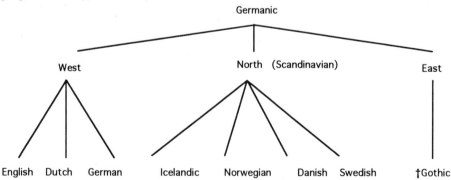

who spoke non-Germanic **Celtic** languages that leave descendants in modern **Welsh, Irish (Scots), Gaelic,** and **Breton** (spoken in Brittany in France). With the dissolution of the Roman Empire in the fifth century, the Romans withdrew, leaving Britain. But self-rule did not last for long.

The Anglo-Saxon Invasions

Internal struggles followed, with northerners and westerners attacking the Romanized Celts in the east, who called for help from the **Saxons,** a Germanic tribe on the European mainland. The Saxons actually invaded, either conquering or pushing Celtic-speaking peoples to the extreme north and western edges of Britain. Saxons were joined by others from what is today northwestern Germany and Denmark, the best known being **Angles, Frisians,** and **Jutes.** These confederated groups are often called the **Anglo-Saxons.**

This onslaught from the East was a huge success (at least for the Anglo-Saxons). In a short time the invaders had settled and established themselves as the major ethnic and linguistic group on the island. The island came to be called **England** (from *Engla land,* meaning 'land of the Angles'). The distinct language which had developed there as of the late seventh century is known as **Old English.**

Old English (Seventh to Eleventh Centuries C.E.)

Old English is the direct ancestor of the English spoken today and serves as the source of some of the most basic elements of English vocabulary. While it may at first appear quite alien to the modern reader, closer examination shows its deep resemblance to modern English.

In Old English the sentence *He has a white tongue* would have been written He hafaþ hwite tungan and pronounced, roughly, [he **ha**-vaθ **hwi**-tɛ **tʋŋ**-gan](Refer to the pronunciation guide for the sound values of these symbols.) We see that some things haven't changed much since Old English, while others are rather different. Alongside the obvious differences in pronunciation are differences in spelling—e.g. Old English f̣ for the v̪ sound, ǫ for the th (i.e. [θ]) sound. Note also the Old English **inflectional endings** -*aþ*, -*e,* and -*an* on these words. All of these disappeared on the way to twentieth-century English. These endings marked such things as the **grammatical function** of nouns, so that for example the ending -*an* on the word *tungan* 'tongue' indicated that it was the direct object of the verb *hafaþ* 'has'. Only one of these endings is likely to seem familiar to a speaker of modern English. It is -*aþ*, which is an

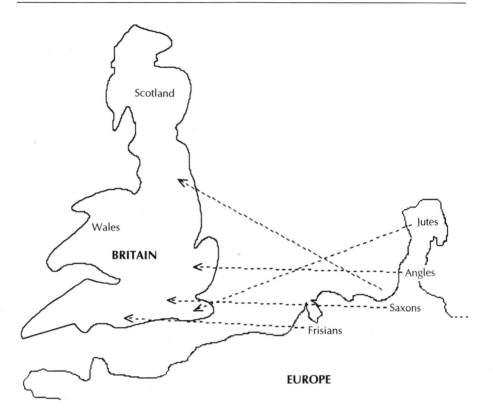

Figure 2.2. Paths of the Anglo-Saxon Invasion of Britain

earlier form of the ending -*eth* in words like Shakespearean *holdeth* 'holds'. The -*aþ* verb ending marked the **person** and **number** of the subject of the verb, which in our sentence is the third person singular pronoun *he* 'he'. In Present-Day English the ending -*s* has replaced -*eth* to mark the third person singular subject of a verb like *sings* in the sentence *Angela sings beautifully*.

One of the most important periods in the development of Old English was the reign of Alfred the Great in the ninth century. Because England was born out of conquests by separate groups of invaders, Alfred needed to devote special attention to uniting the country. He managed to bring this about in large part by linguistic means, specifically by fostering English language and literacy. Under Alfred, English came to be used in schools. Texts that had previously existed only in Latin were translated into English. This not only made the language more prestigious and more useful but also helped to make England a single nation, illustrating how language can be used as a political tool.

From the ninth to the eleventh centuries the Anglo-Saxon language and culture were among the most vibrant and active of the Western world. With every new cultural, material, technological, religious, scholarly, or artistic development, the language grew and changed, especially in vocabulary. The more sweeping the change, the more dramatic the influence on the language would be. It was during the early Old English period that England was converted to Christianity. Latin, the official language of the church, provided not only ecclesiastical vocabulary (e.g. *altar, candle, offer, mass, priest*) but also a surprising number of everyday words (e.g. *port, tower, cap, radish, school*). These were added to the stock of Latin words that earlier had passed to the Continental Germanic ancestors of the English during the period of the pre-Christian Roman Empire. (English also borrowed a few words from the Celtic languages with which it had contact during the Old English and later periods.)

Throughout the ninth and tenth centuries and into the eleventh, **Vikings** invaded and settled large parts of England. The language again responded by borrowing words, this time from the **Scandinavian** tongues of the invaders. (These languages were the ancestors of modern Danish and Icelandic, among others, and are sometimes referred to as early varieties of Old Norse or Old Icelandic.) This created an interesting mixture, because Old English was related to the Scandinavian languages, which also belonged to the Germanic language group. Words mutually inherited from the ancestral language **proto-Germanic** (*proto-* meaning 'earliest, first') are known as **cognates** (literally, 'together originated', i.e. related because they share the same ultimate source). A fair number of words borrowed from the Scandinavian language closely resembled ones that already existed in Old English, but they often had somewhat different pronunciations and meanings. These pairs of native and borrowed cognates are called **doublets.** A few English-Scandinavian doublets are illustrated in the word pairs:

Native (OE)		Scandinavian
shirt	≈	skirt (both name a garment open at the bottom)
no	≈	nay (as in *nay-sayer*)
bench	≈	bank
lend	≈	loan
whole	≈	hale (as in *hale and hearty*)

Many other Scandinavian words for which there existed no native English cognates were also incorporated into Old English (e.g. *ill, scowl, flat, rake, guess, bull*).

Middle English (Twelfth to Fifteenth Centuries C.E.)

The most important single event in the history of English was probably the **Norman Conquest** of 1066. The monumental changes that this invasion produced in the shape of English society had matching effects in the structure of the language.

The Norman conquest was primarily a political defeat and involved very little bloodshed. It once again subjected England to rule by a group of Germanic invaders. But there was a difference. The Normans (whose ancestors had been Vikings—i.e. Norsemen) came from France, under the leadership of William the Conqueror. These people had settled along the northern coast of France and had abandoned their Scandinavian language and much of their heritage in favor of the French language and culture.

After their victory, the Normans quickly assumed leadership and privilege in England. The Norman dialect of French hence was the language of the upper class while English was relegated to use by the losers of the Battle of Hastings in 1066 and the masses of peasants. As a result, the English language assimilated a multitude of French words, especially those dealing with areas of life in which French language and culture were dominant. These included government (where we find French borrowings like *court, duke, baron, county, crown, trial, village*), war *(peace, enemy, arms, battle, moat)* and 'the finer things' *(gown, robe, emerald, sapphire, feast, taste, cream, sugar).*

French (like its linguistic cousins, Spanish, Italian, Portuguese and Romanian) is a **Romance** language, a descendant of the Latin spoken during the time of the Roman Empire). Because of this, much of the vocabulary borrowed from French closely resembles words from Latin, and it is sometimes difficult to tell from a word's appearance whether it came directly into English from Latin (which was still used for many secular and religious purposes during the European Middle Ages) or indirectly by way of French. It will, therefore, sometimes be convenient to refer to words which entered English from Latin, Norman French, Old French, Middle French, or Modern French by a single label: **Latinate** vocabulary.

Middle English differed from Old English not only in vocabulary but also in its grammatical structure. It lost most of the inflectional endings of Old English and became in many respects a new language. The following lines from Geoffrey Chaucer, the greatest and most renowned of Middle English writers, illustrate some of these changes.

> Now shul ye understonde what is Confessioun, and wheither it oghte nedes be doon or noon and whiche thynges been covenable to verray Confessioun.
>
> "The Parson's Tale," in the *Canterbury Tales*

We can make this passage more understandable by substituting the modern forms of the Middle English words while keeping the Middle English word order:

Now shall ye understand what is confession, and whether it ought
needs be done or none and which things be 'convenable' to very
confession.

(Note that the words *confessioun* / *confession, covenable* / *"convenable"* and *very*
are all borrowed from French.) Understanding the passage is made easier still
when we substitute modern translations of the Middle English words and
adopt modern word order:

Now you shall understand what confession is and whether it should
be done or not and which things are appropriate to true confession.

While this passage is relatively easy to follow even in its original written form,
hearing it spoken would be quite another matter, for it was probably pronounced as follows.

[nu: shʊl ye: ʊn-dɛr-stɔn-dɛ hwɑt ɪz kɔn-fɛ-sɪ-u:n ɑnd hwɛ-ðɛr ɪt
ɔx-tɛ ne:-dɛs be: do:n ɔr no:n ɑnd hwɪ-čɛ thɪŋ-gɛs be:n kɔ-vɛn-ɑb-
lɛ to vɛr-re: kɔn-fɛ-sɪ-u:n]

As the Middle English period progressed, the influence of French dimin-
ished. In 1204, the Normans lost their foothold in France. Though they retained their ascendancy in England, the weakened link with France reduced
the impact of French on Middle English. That impact was further weakened as
a result of the Hundred Years' War, which was actually a series of wars lasting
for more than a hundred years, from 1337 to 1453. England was the loser and
was forced to give up essentially all of its French possessions; for a while this
ended the influence of French on English.

Present-Day English (Sixteenth Century C.E. to the Present)

The development of the language from the Middle English period to **Present-
Day English** (from approximately the year 1500 to the present) is marked by
continued spread in the use of the language and borrowing of foreign elements.
Thanks to the advent of movable type in England just before 1500, there began
massive printings of books in English, leading to greater standardization of the
language and to its acceptance as a major language. The English Renaissance
added great numbers of Latin and Greek words into English, along with continued borrowings from French.

One of the most extensive linguistic changes in the history of English is known as the **Great Vowel Shift,** which marks the transition from Middle English to Present-Day English. These major sound changes affected the pronunciation of **long vowels.** These changes are basically as follows.

The older sound [i:] became [ai] so that the word written *fine* in Middle English (ME) and pronounced [fi:nɛ] became *fine* [fain] in Present-Day English (PDE);*

the older sound [e:] became [i] so that the word written *clene* in ME and pronounced [klenɛ] became *clean* [klin] in PDE;

the older sound [ɑ:] became [e] so that the word written *name* in ME and pronounced [nɑmɛ] became PDE *name* [nem];

the older sound [u:] became [au] so that the word written *hus* in ME and pronounced [hus] became *house* [haus] in PDE;

the older sound [o:] became [u] so that the word written *moone* in ME and pronounced [mo:nɛ] became *moon* [mun] in PDE;

the older sound [ɔ:] became [o] so that the word written *gote* in ME, pronounced [gɔtɛ], became *goat* [got] in PDE.

By Shakespeare's time (the late sixteenth and early seventeenth centuries), the Great Vowel Shift was complete. Here is an example of the written language of that period.

The king hath on him such a countenance as he had lost some province and a region loved as he loves himself.
The Winters Tale, I.ii.369

Few if any of these words are hard to recognize. They were pronounced then very much as they would be today in American English, and even words like *hath* which have dropped out of general use may still be familiar if, for example, you are familiar with readings in the King James Version of the bible. The presence of such French loan-words as *countenance, province* and *region* is testimony to the continued importance of the additions of vocabulary which took place throughout the Middle English period.

External influences continued to enrich English vocabulary during this final period. The European **Renaissance** opened a new age for art and science in England and Europe. Along with many new words from French and Latin, Greek words now began to make their greatest impact. The scholarly disci-

---

*The unstressed final [ɛ] sound was lost during roughly the same period.

plines owe much of their vocabulary to **classical** Latin and Greek. Among the first contributions to Present-Day English from Latin were *exterior, appendix, delirium, create, exterminate,* and *disk.* At about the same time, Greek provided *tonic, catastrophe, anonymous, lexicon,* and *skeleton.*

As the English colonial empire expanded throughout the world over the last three hundred years, English borrowed words from many other languages. Among these words are names for animals and places *(moose, skunk, woodchuck, Michigan, Chicago, Manhattan)* from American Indian languages encountered by English settlers; food terms *(yam, gumbo, banana)* from African languages spoken where the foods originate; new species and technologies *(kangaroo, koala, boomerang)* from Australian languages; unusual weather phenomena and customs *(typhoon, kowtow)* from Chinese; and many others.

Still, English continues the traditions of the Renaissance in its heavy reliance on Latin and Greek. This is fortunate, since it means that the systematic study of scientific and other special vocabulary can concentrate on these two languages out of the many that English has drawn from in its history. Because the Latin of ancient Rome itself borrowed words from Greek, many Greek words entered English indirectly through Latin. As a result, the three major sources of English borrowed vocabulary—French, Latin, and Greek—have contributed to the language along the paths illustrated in figure 2.3.

The period during and after the Renaissance saw not only heavy borrowing of actual words from Latin and Greek but also the use of parts of older borrowings, resulting in the **innovation** of words that never existed in Latin and Greek when they were 'living' languages (i.e. the first languages or mother tongues spoken by children as they grew up). This process of innovation remains alive in English today and is one way that the material can be so valuable. Anyone can 'cannibalize' the elements of borrowed words to say (or write) a word like *phrenolatry* 'the act of worshipping the mind' or *somniferous* 'sleep bearing' or *steatocephalic* 'having a fatty head'. This is because English not only borrowed huge numbers of words but, in effect, also borrowed the rules

Figure 2.3. Major Paths of Borrowing from Greek and Latinate Sources into English

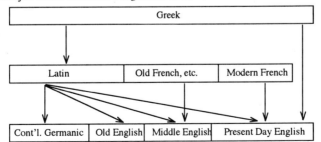

by which those forms were related to each other. For example, Latin (and subsequently French, its 'descendant') had a special rule that applied to a verb stem with a final <u>d</u> (such as *vad*, the key morpheme in *invade*) when it was turned into a noun with the meaning 'act of <u>VERB</u>-ing' (where <u>VERB</u> is a word element with verbal meaning) by adding the suffix *-ion*. In these words the final *d* of the stem became an *s* (as in *invasion* or *invasive*). So, when English borrows word pairs like *invade* and *invasion/invasive* or *erode* and *erosion*, it also borrows the relationship that holds between their forms (i.e. the rule that states "<u>d</u> becomes <u>s</u> before the suffix -<u>ion</u>").

SUMMARY

As we have seen, different historical events and political and cultural factors have left their linguistic traces on the development of English. The language has undergone a series of basic changes in grammatical structure and pronunciation. Its original Germanic word stock has been enhanced by copious borrowings from many languages, most notably Latin, Greek, and French. This makes its vocabulary more diverse than any other known language. The major stages of word borrowing into English are listed below.

Continental Germanic (before c. 500 C.E.): Borrowings from Latin. Native Germanic vocabulary is still represented in the most basic (and often formally simplest) words of Present-Day English: *sun, moon, lamb, life, death, mother, health, god*. Derived words end in *-ness, -ly, -some, -ship, -hood, -ton*, and so on.

Old English (c. 500–1100): Borrowings from Latin (especially ecclesiastical terms) and Scandinavian; a few borrowings from Celtic languages

Middle English (c. 1100–1500): Heavy borrowing from the Norman dialect of French (especially terms from law, government, the military, and the 'finer' things in life). Such words as *mortal, divine, veal, vital, sane*. Most words in *-ence, -ance, -ity, -ville, -ion*, and so on.

Present-Day English (c. 1500–present): Heavy influx of scientific vocabulary including many neologisms based on elements from Latin and Greek. Examples of borrowings and neologisms include such scientific terms as Greek *cardiac, stethoscope, pneumonic*, and Latin *cervix, dental, occiput*. Borrowings from many other languages with which English has had contact in Europe, Asia, Australia, Africa, and the Americas.

The complexity of developments in borrowing and neologism can be seen in the path taken by an ancient word (and, later, word element) meaning

Table 2.1 Developments Involving Word Elements Meaning 'Wine' Up to PDE

Source	Borrowed by	Represented in PDE
? qwin ?	Latin	
Latin *vinum* 'wine' ↓	Continental Germanic	*wine, winery,* etc.
Inherited in Old French *vinetier*	ME	*vintner* 'wine seller or grower'
"" in Old French *vinaigre*	ME	*vinegar* 'a wine derivative
"" in Modern French *vinaigrette*	PDE	*vinaigrette* 'vinegar sauce'
"" in Modern French *vin*	PDE	*coq au vin* 'chicken in wine sauce'
"" in Italian and Spanish as *vino*	PDE	*vino* 'wine'
Latin *vineus* 'of or from wine' ↓		
Inherited in Old French *vigne*	ME	*vine, vineyard, vinery,* etc.
Latin *vinaceus* 'wine grape pulp'	PDE	*vinaceous* 'wine-colored'
? gwin ?	Greek	
Greek *oin(os)* 'wine'	PDE	*oenin* 'the pigment in red grapes'
		oenologist 'wine expert'
		oenophile 'wine lover', etc.

'wine', which was borrowed from an unknown source by both Ancient Greek and Latin during the first millennium B.C.E., from which it was in turn borrowed by Continental Germanic and English at several points in its history. (The symbol ↓ indicates descent within a language over time.)

We have largely focused our attention here on the sources of vocabulary, but there are other mechanisms of linguistic change as well. For example, words can acquire new meanings. The word *hope* used to mean 'expect' and the word *edify* used to mean 'build'. We will examine many similar developments in the chapter on semantic change. Borrowing often also results in the incorporation of new relationships involving sounds (and sometimes even completely new sounds) into a language. The sound symbolized by [t] at the end of words like *democrat* and *pirate* becomes an [s] in *democracy* and *piracy* because of a related change that took place in Latin. Changes in meaning and sound will be discussed more fully in subsequent chapters.

See appendix II for Morpheme set 2.

EXERCISES

1. Which part or parts of the verb in the sentence *She perspires in the heat* marks the person and number of the subject?

2. Look up the following words in your dictionary. On the basis of the etymologies given there, state for each one

a. whether it is a native Germanic word (i.e. one present in Old English with no evidence of borrowing from any non-Germanic language) and
b. if it is not native, indicate:
  i. what language it was borrowed from and
  ii. when it was borrowed (i.e. whether during the Continental Germanic, Old English, Middle English, or Present-Day English period).

Note: In order to answer these questions, you may have to read the introductory material in the dictionary to learn how to interpret the **etymologies** (word histories) in individual word entries. Another important note: if the entry for a word refers only to Old English, Middle English and/or related Germanic languages, the word is probably native, since Modern English <u>inherits</u> from its ancestors or <u>shares words</u> also <u>inherited</u> by its close relatives. A language is only said to 'borrow' from another language which is not in its immediate line of descent. To illustrate: if human relationships were like language relationships, a child's 'native' or genetic characteristics would be those inherited from its parents and grandparents (and also shared with some or all of its siblings and cousins). These genetic traits would include such things as eye and hair color. Nongenetic traits would include such acquired behaviors as wearing a particular brand of sunglasses or a short haircut, which might be described as 'borrowed' rather than 'inherited' since they originate from somewhere other than mom's or dad's genetic characteristics (perhaps from personal life experience or the influence of a peer group).

a. time	g. chant	m. barn	s. sweet
b. face	h. critic	n. great	t. grain
c. want	i. wise	o. joke	u. crown
d. canoe	j. stigma	p. taste	v. tomato
e. finger	k. vest	q. bazaar	w. poem
f. theology	l. corn	r. please	x. canine

3. What is the meaning of the element *ver* in the Middle English word *verray*, which appears in the excerpt from Chaucer's *Canterbury Tales* in this chapter? What is the form (i.e. spelling) and meaning of the descendant of ME *verray* in Present-Day English? Does the modern form belong to the same part of speech

(i.e. noun, adjective, verb, adverb, etc.) as *verray* did? (You may want to refer to a special etymological dictionary such as the *Oxford English Dictionary* or one of the others listed in the appendix to confirm your answer.)

4. Using the pronunciation guide and recalling the discussion in this chapter, fill in the blanks in the chart below. In the first column of blanks give the symbol that represents the Present-Day English pronunciation of each word's main vowel. In the next column fill in blanks to give the Middle English pronunciation. Finally, complete the spelling of PDE words that would rhyme with the ME pronunciation of the word. (E.g. PDE *played* [pled] or [ple:d] roughly rhymes with ME *reed* [re:d], since both have [e].) Note that in ME, final *e* would have been pronounced as the English word *a* usually now is, as [ə].

PDE word	phonetic symbol	ME word	phonetic symbol	ME would roughly rhyme with PDE
reed	_i_	reed	_e_	p l a̱y̱e d
take	_____	take	_____	l _____ c k a
shoe	_____	shoo	_____	s_____
hone	_____	hoone	_____	p_____n a
shine	_____	shine	_____	s_____n a
town	_____	toun	_____	s_____n

5. After studying Morpheme set 2, test your knowledge of the morphemes by following the example and filling in the remaining blanks in the following words. With the aid of a dictionary, give a brief definition that partly or fully reflects the meaning of the individual morphemes. If you cannot find the word in your dictionary, you may find portions of it that will allow you to guess what it might mean.

a. MORPHEMES   _extra_   corpor   e   -al

   GLOSSES   'outside'   _____   ADJECTIVE

   FULL WORD   _____

   DEFINITION   _____

b.   MORPHEMES   _____   ent   -ate

       GLOSSES   'powerful'   _____   _____

       FULL WORD   _____   [It rhymes with <u>late</u>.]

       DEFINITION   _____

c.   MORPHEMES   contra   _____   t   -ion

       GLOSSES   _____   'come', 'bring'   ____

       FULL WORD   _____

       DEFINITION   _____

3
Morphology: Analyzing Complex Words

THE BASICS OF MORPHOLOGY

By and large, the words we deal with in this course are complex. Unlike such simple words as *eat, pray, cone,* and *people,* complex words can be parsed into two or more major components. There are three categories of components: prefixes (elements added to the beginnings of words), roots (the bases of words), and suffixes (elements added to the ends of words).

Prefixes, roots, and suffixes are elementary meaningful units or **morphemes** (i.e. 'form units'). We call morphemes elementary meaningful units because these are the basic elements of words; that is, words cannot be divided into smaller meaningful parts.

In the word *contemporary,* the root is *tempor,* which means 'time'. It has approximately the same meaning in other words as well, e.g. *temporal, extemporaneous.* The fact that morphemes occur in a variety of words in which they carry the same approximate meaning is what makes a course in the structure of English words both possible and potentially useful.

The morpheme *tempor* cannot be divided further into smaller meaningful parts. *Tempor* can be divided, say, into the sequence of individual sounds denoted by the letters *t, e, m, p, o,* and *r.* It can also be divided into the syllables *tem* and *por.* But none of these individual sounds or syllables has its own meaning within the morpheme *tempor.*

The word *contemporary* consists of the root *tempor* with a prefix, *con-,* and a suffix, *-ary.* (Notice that prefixes have hyphens after them and suffixes have hyphens in front of them. The hyphens indicate where they attach to the word.)

The prefix *con-* occurs at the beginning of a variety of words, including the verbs *concur, contract,* and *confuse*. Dictionaries give the basic meaning of the morpheme *con-* as 'together, with'. For example, the meaning of the verb *concur* 'agree' comes from its parts, *con-* 'together' and *cur* 'run', giving *concur* the literal meaning 'run together'. Similar are *contract* ('pull together', said, for example, of a muscle) and *confuse* (literally 'blend together').

Each word of the language can be analyzed as containing a root and sometimes one or more prefixes and suffixes as well. The word *confer* consists of a prefix and the root *fer*. The word *consolidate* has a prefix, a root *solid*, and a verb-forming suffix *-ate*.

We might diagram a few of the examples mentioned thus far in the following way:

Table 3.1 Words Parsed into Prefixes, Roots, and Suffixes

word	prefix	root	suffix
contemporary	con-	tempor	-ary
contract	con-	tract	
temporal		tempor	-al
second		second	
secondary		second	-ary

Every adjective, noun, and verb in English contains at least one root. In morphologically simple words, the root makes up the entire word (e.g. *second*). On the other hand, one or more prefixes may precede and one or more suffixes may follow the root of a word. Table 3.2 shows words containing multiple prefixes, suffixes, and even multiple roots.

Table 3.2 Words Parsed into Prefixes, Roots, and Suffixes

word	prefix	root	suffix
predisposed	pre-, dis-	pos	-ed
historical		histor	-ic, -al
photography		phot, graph	-y
mailman		mail, man	

MORE ABOUT MORPHEMES AND MEANING

The idea that the morpheme is a meaningful element has to be refined a bit. Morphemes are seldom as well behaved as the simple glosses above might lead one to expect. We have to adjust our definition of morphemes to reflect their sometimes complicated behavior. An example is the morpheme *cur*, glossed above as 'run'. The fact that this morpheme doesn't literally mean 'run' in the word *concur* may not be too troublesome, since it is easy enough to see the connection between the actual meaning of *concur* and the image 'run along with'. This example shows that recognizing literal meanings is only a first step in understanding morphemes. Instances of the morpheme *cur* in words other than *concur* may present new images, related in other ways to the literal meaning 'run'. In *recur*, whose prefix means 'again', there is normally no running in the literal sense. But the running action denoted by the basic meaning of the root *cur* makes for a more picturesque image of the bland event 'happen'.

Very often the use of morphemes relies on our ability to see ways in which one thing stands for another. In *astronomy*, the form *astro* is a variant of *aster* 'star'. This strikes us as entirely appropriate, even though we view astronomy as the study of all heavenly bodies, not just stars. The 'point' designated by the root *punct* in *punctuation* refers to a variety of marks (and, we suppose, blank spaces). In *punctual* the connection with a literal point is different. In the remainder of this chapter and in chapter 7 we will explore the ways in which morphemes depart from their literal meanings.

Prefixes and suffixes often present special meaning problems. Prefixes usually modify the root's meaning in a way similar to the way that adverbs and prepositions modify verbs. For example, consider again the root *cur*. In *concur* and *recur* the basic meaning 'run' is modified by the adverbs 'together' and 'again'. In *incur*, the preposition 'into' modifies the root meaning.

Suffixes function differently. They generally determine what part of speech a word belongs to and often add to meaning as well. For example, *-ity* creates nouns and often adds the meaning of 'quality or state of being' to the adjective or root it is attached to. Thus, *sincerity* means 'the quality of being sincere', and *ability* means 'being able'. Some *-ity* nouns designate objects characterized by a certain quality: examples are *monstrosity* ('something monstrous') and *oddity* ('something odd').

The endings *-like, -ish, -esque,* and *-y* all form adjectives such as *childlike, yellowish, picturesque,* and *risky*. These four suffixes are in fact all somewhat similar semantically; they help to describe a property in terms of its resemblance to some object. But there are also differences between them. *Childlike* can be used in flattering ways (as in *We found his childlike manner disarming*), but *childish* tends to have negative connotations (*Your childish behavior has to stop*). *Sponge-like* and *spongy* refer to the same noun to get their meaning, but the meaning is somewhat different. Something *sponge-like* is going to be similar to a sponge but something spongy may simply be *springy* but not really *sponge-like*. Thus, it is probably good for a cake to be spongy but bad for it to be sponge-like. (Different individuals may have slightly different senses of the subtler aspects of such distinctions of meaning.)

Suffixes like these show that different morphemes exhibit different degrees of variation in meaning. The meaning of the ending -*like* is quite uniform from example to example, while -*y* varies in meaning from 'like' (as in *yellowy*) to 'containing an appreciable amount of' (as in *meaty*). Sometimes, in fact, a suffix has a number of distinct meanings and/or functions. Such cases are best regarded as accidental resemblances. For example, besides the adjective-forming suffix -*y*, there is a noun-forming suffix -*y*, which appears in *monogamy*, *democracy*, and *comedy*, and also a diminutive noun-forming suffix -*y*, as in *kitty*, *Billy*, etc. These three separate occurrences of -*y* obviously have very different meanings.

Since morphemes are defined as combining form with meaning, we can see that the three separate uses and meanings of -*y* must in fact be separate morphemes, which only coincidentally have the same spelling and pronunciation. But sometimes the meaning of a morpheme is a good deal more elusive than this, making it difficult to apply meaning as the chief criterion for determining whether two forms represent the same morpheme. For example, the meaning of the suffix -*ary* in *disciplinary* is difficult to express precisely. Something like 'pertaining to' seems roughly appropriate. (This would make the word mean 'pertaining to discipline'.) But consider other English adjectives ending in this suffix, such as *secondary*, *momentary*, and *stationary*. Here, even this vague definition doesn't fare very well. The meaning of *secondary* is not 'pertaining to (the) second'. Rather, -*ary* turns *second* into an adjective meaning roughly 'in second place or a less important position'. Similarly, *momentary* is an adjective meaning 'lasting for a moment', and *stationary* is an adjective meaning 'fixed in position'. We wouldn't want to conclude that all of these instances of -*ary* are different morphemes that just happen to resemble one another in form. Still, how are we to distinguish the case of -*ary* from the case of the three different suffixes of the form -*y*? The major difference is that in the case of the three -*y* morphemes, we were able to separate their functions and ranges of meaning. For -*ary*, this is not possible. The different effects of this suffix do not fall into separate categories of meaning. Therefore, -*ary* really is a single morpheme whose meaning varies considerably from word to word. Its general function is simply to attach to nouns and roots to form adjectives.

This suggests that the definition of morpheme should be expanded somewhat to suit its actual behavior in the language: a morpheme is a minimal element that is either meaningful or that determines the function of a word.

SAME FUNCTION OR SAME MEANING?

As shown above, the 'meaning' of a morpheme sometimes simply provides a clue to the part of speech of the word bearing it. Consider the adjectival ending -*ous*. As with -*ary*, the only thing we can rely on in interpreting the suffix -*ous* is that it signals that the word bearing it is an adjective. Therefore, in *tetrapterous* 'having four wings' (like certain insects), -*ous* marks the word as an adjective. The roots here are *tetra* 'four' (compare *tetralogy* 'a literary work in four parts') and *pter* 'wing' (as in *helicopter*, literally 'helix-wing'). If we conclude from this example that -*ous* has an actual meaning ('having or possessing'), a look at other -*ous* words shows that this isn't true. The word *disastrous* does not mean 'having disaster' and *miraculous* does not mean 'having a miracle'. These examples push us back to a vaguer meaning such as 'characterized by'. But such a notion (common in dictionary definitions) is merely a kind of least common denominator, an attempt to capture what all of the different meanings of -*ous* share. It does not capture the different meanings themselves. One final problem with the use of 'characterized by' to express the meaning of -*ous* is that this notion is too general to distinguish the meaning of this suffix from that of other adjectival endings, like -*ic*, which could also be vaguely expressed as 'characterized by' in at least some words (e.g. *melodic, nostalgic*). We solve this problem by recognizing that the morpheme is a meaningful element without expecting it to have the same meaning in all of its occurrences. What actually unites the different occurrences of -*ous* is the fact that they all form adjectives. This common function is enough to make the different uses of -*ous* count as a single morpheme. We can infer the details of the meaning in any particular case from other facts, such as the sense of the sentence or context in which the word occurs. This is often the procedure we must follow in doing the morphological analysis or 'breaking down' of an unfamiliar word.

OTHER VARIATIONS IN THE MEANINGS OF MORPHEMES

Just as it is possible for different occurrences of a suffix to possess different meanings, meaning variation in prefixes and roots is also quite common. This is an inevitable consequence of the nature of language, which must constantly stretch to accommodate new situations in a changing world. A morpheme may start out with a particular meaning. Once it is used in different words, however, and those words themselves come to be used in a variety of situations slightly different from the ones for which they were initially coined, the morpheme may lose its original simple, unified meaning. The morpheme *ship* once meant 'ocean-going vessel' but in *airship* it simply means 'vessel'. Thus, although morphemes remain meaningful elements from word to word, we cannot expect their meaning to stay constant from word to word. Differences in the meaning of the same morpheme in different words become a little easier to deal with when we realize that there are often patterns to these variations in meaning. Two instances of a morpheme may not have exactly the same meaning, but the meanings may be related. For example, *pyr* sometimes means 'fire' (as in *pyrotechnics* 'fireworks') and sometimes 'fever' (as in *antipyretic* 'a medication that reduces fever'). The meanings are not the same, but they are related; in this case, the relationship has come about from the use of *pyr* 'fire' as a metaphor for the 'burning' of a fever's heat. (We will deal more with variation in meanings in chapter 7, where we discuss semantics.)

WORDS AS SYMBOLS

The word *apteryx* denotes the kiwi, a wingless bird of New Zealand. We can analyze or parse this word into its components: the prefix *a-*, which means 'without' or 'not', as in *atheist* 'without (belief in) God'; the root *pter* 'wing'; and the suffix *-yx* (a rather rare noun-forming suffix). If we assumed that the meaning of a word is completely determined by the meanings of its parts, *apteryx* would mean something like 'wingless thing'. But there is much more to a kiwi than mere winglessness. Such incompleteness in representation of meaning is the rule rather than the exception. The reason is that words are only symbols, not complete linguistic representations of the physical or conceptual world. Another example: *bibliophile* (from *bibl* 'book' and *phil* 'love') is a very general term for someone who loves books. Would it, by the same token, be reasonable to infer that a *pedophile* (*ped* 'child') is anyone who loves children? Not really. In *pedophile,* the 'love' is of a very specific kind, one involving sexual attraction, a sense hardly appropriate to *bibliophile*. Therefore, when we analyze the structure of an English word, even if we succeed in breaking it down into its individual morphemes, the task of figuring out the meaning of the word may not be over. We may get significant clues to the complete meaning, but the rest is left up to general knowledge or common sense or the idiosyncrasies of the word as a whole. The context in which a word appears can also provide important clues.

THE UTILITY OF MORPHOLOGICAL ANALYSIS

The analysis of words into morphemes not only provides clues to the meaning and function of words we have never seen before. It also deepens our knowledge of words we already know. For example, it can provide reliable spelling clues for less familiar words. If we realize that *elevator* contains the root *lev* (meaning 'light' or 'rise'), we will know that the second vowel, which is pronounced [ə], like the first vowel of *about,* is spelled with an ə rather than an *a* or some other vowel. Word analysis also provides constant reminders of the multitude of images on which our language is built. If you already know that *salient* means 'sticking out', you may not need to know that it is built on the root *sal,* which means 'jump'. But knowing that this word (and others containing the morpheme *sal,* such as *sally* and *salacious*) is built upon an 'image' of jumping may enhance its expressive power for you. Skill in word analysis will also help in recalling words that are not yet thoroughly familiar. Even though many characteristics of the kiwi are not expressed by any particular part of the word *apteryx,* we will have an easier time recalling its relationship to the notable 'wingless thing' because of its very common key elements: *pter,* which appears in many words having to do with wings or flying, and *a-* 'not, without'.

HOW WE MAKE WORDS

The kind of morphology outlined so far is limited to one type of word formation, in which morphemes are strung together into words. This is sometimes referred to as **concatenative morphology** (from the Latin word *catena* 'chain'). But this does not come close to exhausting the richness of the devices we use.

Compounds

Words can be **compounded** to form new words. This really is just another type of concatenation. Sometimes the resulting new word is written as one word:

> *workbook*
> *blackboard*
> *mailman*

But many expressions similar to these are ordinarily written as two words:

> *exercise book*
> *bulletin board*
> *mail carrier*

There are two "rules" (if we dare to call them that) that we are aware of for spacing in compounds. First, if at least one element is more than one syllable long, the words of the compound will tend to be written separately. That is the case with the last three examples.

Second, if the compound has been in the language for a while, or if it is used very commonly, then it will tend to be written as a single word. So even though the first element of

checkerboard

is two syllables long, there is no space in the compound.

Complicating this discussion is the problem-ridden hyphen. It tends to be used when the compound in question modifies a noun:

floating-point calculation
two-year-old cheese

The rules for punctuating compounds are obscure enough to warrant lots of variation in practice. So we find that the space is optional in the following examples:

hair spray
hairspray
and
bold face
boldface

English has compounds corresponding to many of the different parts of speech. Compound nouns abound, as illustrated by most of the examples in the previous paragraph. But verbs and adjectives with compound structure are also frequent: *update, stir fry, window shop, jet black, easy-going, able-bodied.* Expressions like *as much as, insofar as, in between, on account of,* among others, can be regarded as compound conjunctions and prepositions.

Zero Derivation

Now we move into some areas where word formation is not concatenative. **Zero derivation** gets its name from the fact that it involves deriving one word from another without the use of prefixes, suffixes, or similar items. When we form the verb *parent* from the noun *parent,* we don't add anything at all.

This process, which is more characteristic of English than of most of the other major languages of the world, leads to widespread pairs of verb/noun doublets:

table
water
control
ransom
release
express mail

and so forth. Sometimes the derivation of one form from another is marked by a stress difference. Compare the pronunciation of the verb and noun forms of the following words:

object
combat
addict
progress

Back Formation

Back formation is when a normal derivation process is reversed. From the verb *destroy* the noun *destruction* is formed, by suffixation of *-ion* and changes to the verb root. But how about the verb *self-destruct? Destruct* is not a word in English (though it had a brief life as a verb back in the seventeenth century), so *self-destruct,* which came into the language very recently, could not have come about by compounding *self* with *destruct.*

The answer is that *self-destruct* came into the language through back formation. The normal direction of derivation by the suffix *-ion* involves forming a noun from a verb by attaching the suffix *-ion* (as in *rebel/rebellion*). Here the process was reversed; *self-destruction* had its ending subtracted in order to form a verb that could have been its source: *self-destruct.*

Quite a few English words that are now regarded as totally normal had their humble beginnings in back formation. The word *pea* was *pease* in Middle English, where it was originally a singular noun. But the final *s* sound came to be taken as a plural ending, and so the ending was eventually subtracted to give a new singular form, *pea.*

Another famous example is the verb *peddle,* for which the OED gives a citation dating back to 1532. This verb came about through back formation from *peddler,* which goes back at least to 1377. Originally, the *-er* at the end had no relation to the ending *-er* that we find in *settler, beater,* and so on. But the resemblance in sound and meaning was so strong that it began to be regarded as an ending, and so it was subtracted to yield the new verb form *peddle.*

A more up-to-date example is *burgle,* which has been back formed from the noun *burglar.* This case is so recent that the verb may not feel totally acceptable as a replacement for the more conventional *burglarize.* On the other hand, another recent example that seems to have gained total acceptance is the verb *televise,* formed in reverse from the noun *television.*

The availability of a potential back formation by no means guarantees its acceptance, however. H. Marchand (in *The Categories and Types of Present-Day English Word Formation* [Munich: Beck, 1969]) lists a number of attempts that never caught on. Examples of missed opportunities include:

> *to auth*
> *to ush*
> *to buttle*

Folk Etymology

Similar in spirit to back formation is **folk etymology,** which involves analyzing strange words in a way that seems to make sense at the time, although it happens not to correspond to the actual derivation of the word. The *American Heritage Dictionary* (3rd ed.) lists the example *very close veins,* for *varicose veins,* apparently from the fact that this condition makes the blood vessels look very close to the surface of the skin. A New England school child once wrote about the affliction *dire rear,* when *diarrhea* was intended.

Though examples like these may sound quaint and decidedly nonstandard, many have taken over our collective linguistic consciousness without leaving a trace of inappropriateness. We take

> *uproar*

to designate a kind of roar, even though it can probably be traced to Middle Low German *rōr,* which meant 'motion' and had no relation to the word 'roar'.

> *Sockeye salmon*

feels like it designates a distinctive type of eye in this fish, but really it comes into English by folk etymology from the name of this fish in Halkomelem, a

Central Coast Salish language. In that language, the fish is termed *sthəqəy,* and that was too difficult for English speakers to deal with.

Use of the expression

Mary Jane

to refer to marijuana is a folk etymology. The only connection between

Jerusalem artichokes

and the city of Jerusalem is the similarity in sound (to English speakers) of the name of this city with the Italian term *girasole,* which means 'sunflower'; the Jerusalem artichoke is in fact a kind of North American sunflower.

Similarly, the Jordan almond has no real connection to Jordan. In Middle English, the borrowed French word *jardin* (which meant 'garden') was shifted by folk etymology to the more comfortable *Jordan.*

Folk etymologies should not leave us shamefaced, for even the term *shamefaced* is a folk etymology, coming from Middle English *shamefast,* 'bound by shame'.

Analogy

Not unlike these are cases of words that are formed by **analogy** to other words. It is conceivable that you have encountered the coined verb

caninify

which has not made it into most dictionaries. It appears to have been formed on the basis of

personify

substituting *canine* ('pertaining to dogs', used as a noun to mean 'dog') for *person.*

Sometimes the substitution process is a translation from another language. Thus

new wave

was arrived at by directly translating the French

nouvelle vague

Sometimes joking translations take common English words and convert them into learned sounding terms. A crossword puzzle buff may be termed a *cruciverbalist*. Prince Philip of Edinburgh has been credited with the coining *dontopedologist*, 'one who tends to put one's foot in one's mouth (or, literally, teeth)'.

The processes of back formation, folk etymology, and analogy all attempt to respect the shapes of morphemes and words that are part of the standard word formation devices of morpheme concatenation and word compounding. But there are other word formation processes at work that play tricks with existing morphemes and words.

Clipping

An example is **clipping,** the process of devising chunks of words that stand for the whole. Recent clippings like

> *high tech*
> *hyper*
> *info*

and very recent colloquial usages like

> *zza* (for *pizza*)
> *'rents* (for *parents*)
> *'hood* (for *neighborhood*)

join a host of earlier clippings that seem very ordinary:

> *ad lib*
> *auto*
> *blitz*
> *bus*
> *flu*
> *graph*
> *intercom*
> *lab*
> *pep*
> *radio*

tend

tuxedo

van

Another new example of clipping is the verb *morph,* meaning to convert one image into another digitally. This new verb is probably a clipped form of *metamorphosis.*

Blends

Our vocabularly is enhanced as well by **blends** formed from parts of two or more words. The standard example is

smog

a blend of *smoke* and *fog.* But English has many others, including the following entries from the *American Heritage Dictionary:*

sexploitation (*sex* and *exploitation*)

billion (*bi-* and *million*)

blotch (blot and *botch*)

motel (*motor* and *hotel*)

squiggle (*squirm* and *wiggle*)

Our guesstimate is that you will easily find many more examples like these. A recent source of blends is computer network exchanges, which, according to a *New York Times* article, include the *emoticon* (which describes a sideways "happy face" constructed of punctuation marks, along with other figures) and the concept of *netiquette,* or network manners.

Blending and Clipping

Blending and clipping work together in words like *aldehyde* (from *alcohol dehydrogenatum*) and *aflatoxin* (*afla* is a clipped form of *Aspergillus flavus*).

Acronyms

Another means of coining new words is the **acronym** (*acer* 'tip', *onym* 'name'). These are named for the fact that they are formed out of the first (figuratively, tip) letters in an expression. A frequently cited example is *radar*, which stands for 'radio detecting and ranging'. Others, from P. Dickson's *Words: A Connoisseur's Collection of Old and New, Weird and Wonderful, Useful and Outlandish Words* (New York: Delacorte, 1985), are:

> *scuba* ('self-contained underwater breathing apparatus')
> *Qantas* ('Queensland and Northern Territories Air Service')
> *Zip Code* ('Zone Improvement Program').

Cute acronyms are often sought by single-issue citizens' groups. Dickson gives the following examples:

> *CROC* ('Committee for the Recognition of Obnoxious Commercials')
> *SSSH!* ('Society for Silent Snowmobiles Here!').

High technology has introduced some commonly used acronyms, whose origin may be obscure to newcomers. An example is *SIMM*, a single in-line memory module, which incidentally is used for holding *RAM*, or random access memory.

Some acronyms undergo a further stage of development, in which they are converted into pronounceable words by changing some of their letters into syllables. Two good examples are:

> *veep* (from *VP*, for Vice-President)
> *jeep* (from *GP*, for general purpose vehicle).

It would be OK for you to look for others.

Sound Symbolism

Sound symbolism sometimes plays a role in word formation. According to most linguists, the normal situation with words is for sound and meaning to be totally divorced from one another (e.g. in *cat*, there is nothing inherent in the individual sounds or sound combinations that suggests the meaning 'cat'). But occasionally the sounds do suggest meanings.

For example, the sequence *fl* at the beginning of the words

> *flit*
> *flicker*
> *flutter*

suggest a wavering motion, and the vowels represented by *i* and *u* in these words (which are made with the jaw in a relatively closed position; see chapter 5 on phonetics) help to suggest that the motion is of a relatively light object.

Compare

> *flap*
> *flab*
> *flop*

which retain the idea of a fluttering motion, but, thanks to the vowel sounds represented by *a* and *o*, which are produced with the jaw in an open position, describe actions by a larger object.

Sound symbolism is real enough to be used by poets, and the above examples show that even outside of poetry sounds can sometimes be used to convey meanings. It would perhaps be a distortion of the normal notion of **morpheme** to call *fl* a morpheme, but sound symbolism does play a role in the shared meaning of some words beginning in *fl*, and we can find similar examples employing other sounds.

Sl indicates a certain slipperiness in

> *slip*
> *slick*
> *slither*
> *slide*

at least, and perhaps figuratively in *sly* as well. Also, research has shown that speakers of a variety of languages presented with the two totally made up words

> *takeete*
> *uloomu*

will overwhelmingly choose the first as the name of an angular object and the second as the name of a round one. Thus, awareness of the possible effects of sound symbolism may provide clues to the meanings of some words.

SUMMARY

Morphology is the study of the elements and structure of words. Morphemes are elementary meaningful units. Every word contains at least one root, which provides the core meaning element of the word; prefixes and suffixes may accompany the root. Prefixes modify root or word meaning; suffixes sometimes add to the meaning and usually mark the part of speech.

The meanings of a morpheme may vary from word to word. Some suffixes, like *-ary*, are primarily a way of marking the function of a word. The meanings of a morpheme in a specific word can often be derived from general knowledge, context, or an understanding of the systematic ways in which meanings vary.

EXERCISES

1. Using each of the following suffixes, give four examples of words to illustrate what part of speech they form. In general, what is the part of speech of the stem that each suffix is added to? Is there a general pattern to the meaning of the suffix besides the part of speech which it forms? (E.g. *-like* in *childlike, lifelike, dreamlike,* and *doglike* forms adjectives from nouns. These adjectives all mean 'similar to or resembling [the noun] in some respect'.)

    a. -ish   b. -ity   c. -ize

2. Each entry in the following list actually represents *two or more* distinct suffixes that happen to have the same spelling (and in some cases, the same pronunciation). For each one, determine the different suffixes it represents by naming the different type of word (e.g. noun, verb, adjective) that each is used to form. Give examples and explain the differences in meaning the suffix gives a word. (E.g. $-y^1$ is attached to a noun and forms an adjective meaning 'having or associated with [the meaning of the noun]' in the word *dirt-y* ; $-y^2$ attaches to a proper noun (a person's name) to make another (proper) noun with a diminutive or affectionate sense in the names *Bill-y, Joe-y,* etc.)

    a. -er   b. -ly   c. -ate   d. -al

3. Using a dictionary and/or the glossary in Appendix I, parse and gloss the word *antidisestablishmentarianism*. (Follow the model of *contemporary* = *con-* 'together, with' + *tempor* 'time' + *-ary* [adjective].) *Establish* should not be broken down further. How many prefixes does the word have? How many suffixes? Using the discussion of the word *apteryx* in this chapter as a model, indicate what portion of the meaning of the word given by the dictionary

definition comes directly from the glosses of the individual morphemes. What portion of the word's definition is not contained in the morphemes themselves but inferred from general knowledge or the actual use of the word? (Note that *disestablishment* is defined as "The withdrawal of especial State patronage and control from a church")

4. After studying the morpheme list for the preceding chapters, test your knowledge of the morphemes presented so far by parsing and glossing the following words. When parsing, use slashes to separate morphemes and put parentheses around any vowels which seem not to belong to a particular morpheme. (E.g. astrology would be parsed astr / (o) / log / y). With the aid of a dictionary, give a brief definition which partly or fully reflects the meaning of the individual morphemes.

a.   e n d o g a m y

GLOSS   prefix: _____ root: _____ suffix: _____

DEFINITION   _____

b.   i a t r o l o g i c

GLOSS   root: _____ root: _____ suffix: _____

DEFINITION   _____

c.   a m o r p h o u s

GLOSS   prefix: _____ root: _____ suffix: _____

DEFINITION   _____

d.   o m n i s c i e n t

GLOSS   prefix: _____ root: _____ suffix: _____

DEFINITION   _____

e.   c o n d u c i v e

GLOSS   prefix: _____ root: _____ suffix: _____

DEFINITION   _____

f.   p e r i n a t a l

GLOSS   prefix: _____ root: _____ suffix: _____

DEFINITION   _____

g.   c a c o l o g y

GLOSS   prefix: _____ root: _____ suffix: _____

DEFINITION   _____

4
Allomorphy

In the last chapter, we noted that morphemes, though meaningful, do not necessarily hold their meaning constant from word to word. Now we will learn to deal with another characteristic that also serves to make the morpheme a more elusive entity than we might like, namely that it changes its form from word to word. This creates a lot of problems, but each individual problem is quite small, and we will see that sometimes there are even advantages to **allomorphy,** the change in the form of a morpheme depending on its immediate surroundings. The word allomorphy contains the Greek elements *allo* 'other' and *morph* 'form'.

We can divide allomorphy into two types. In the first type a whole class of morphemes undergo the same set of changes. In the second, a change is restricted to a small number of morphemes.

An example of the first type is the changes in the prefix *con-* 'with, together'. The final n̲ changes to m̲ before a morpheme beginning with p̲, b̲, or m̲; e.g. *compose* = *con-* + *pose* 'put together'; *combine* = *con-* + *bine* 'two together'; *commute* = *con-* + *mute* 'change together'. The n̲ disappears entirely and is replaced in spelling by a copy of the consonant that follows it when that consonant is l̲ or r̲ as in *colloquy* = *con-* + *loqu* + *y* 'speaking together'; *corrupt* = *con-* + *rupt* 'break together'. These changes are not peculiar to the prefix *con-*. The same thing happens to the prefix *in-* meaning 'not' (cf. *imprecise* = *in-* + *pre* + *cise*) and to the prefix *in-* meaning 'into' (cf. *impel* = *in-* + *pel*). Using the word element lists, mnemonics, and other example words for this and later chapters, see if you can find words which show these changes in the two morphemes of the form *in-* when followed by the consonants in question, such as p̲, b̲, m̲, r̲, and l̲. Look for other prefixes ending in n̲. Do these prefixes undergo the same changes? Do any prefixes ending in n̲ not undergo these changes?

The second category of allomorphy applies to only a handful of morphemes. The 'privative' prefix *a-* 'not', for example, has the allomorph *an-* before vowels and h̲. (Compare this to the behavior of the unrelated English article *a*, which becomes *an* before a vowel.) Thus we get *a-* in *apnea, atheist, asymmetry*, but *an-* in *anesthetic, anhydrous*.

It helps to be as systematic and exhaustive as possible in our attempts to recognize allomorphy. For example, if we didn't know that the prefix *re-* had the allomorph *red-* before some roots beginning with a vowel, we would likely strike out in attempts to parse words like *redolent*. We might be tempted to analyze it as *re- dol -ent*, but this turns out to be wrong; there is no root *dol* in this word. The correct parse is *red- ol -ent*, where the root *ol* means 'smell', as it does in *olfactory*. The word *redolent* means 'fragrant'; by metaphorical extension, it means 'reminiscent'.

Knowing about allomorphy also helps us to recognize morphemes when meaning doesn't give a sufficient clue to their identity. Take the morpheme *mit*, derived from the Latin verb root meaning 'send'. The etymological meaning is preserved in *transmit* (meaning 'send across') and *emit* (meaning 'send out'), but *commit* does not mean 'send with', nor does *admit* mean 'send to' or 'send toward'. If we tried on the basis of meaning alone to establish whether there was a single root *mit* in all of these cases, we would be in trouble; our notion of shared meaning is not specific enough to be of much help here.

Fortunately, **shared allomorphy** provides the needed clue in cases like these. Notice what happens to the *mit* of *transmit* when the suffix *-ion* or *-ive* is attached; we get *transmission* and *transmissive*. This behavior is not common to all roots ending in t̲; from *abort* and *combat*, for example, we get *abortion* and *combative*. Rather, the change of *mit* to the allomorph *miss* seems to be peculiar to the morpheme *mit*. Thus, along with *transmission* and *transmissive*, we get *emission* and *emissive*. For the cases like *commit* and *remit*, where shared meaning didn't suffice to establish the identity of the morpheme, shared allomorphy provides the answer. The fact that we get *commission* and *remission* is evidence that we are dealing with a single morpheme *mit* in all of these cases.

To pursue this question one step further, let's consider another verb ending in the sequence of letters *m, i*, and *t*, namely *vomit*. Is this an instance of the morpheme *mit*? Recall that shared meaning may not provide a very useful criterion. Actually, meaning can even be misleading in this case, insofar as the meaning of the word *vomit* could be construed as involving a 'sending' of sorts! But if we search for shared allomorphy, we find no words such as **vomission* or **vomissive* (the * indicates a form that does not occur), and this helps to reinforce the answer that we may have suspected to be correct all along, namely that the last three letters in *vomit* do not constitute the morpheme *mit.*

IDIOSYNCRATIC ALLOMORPHY

Much of the allomorphy you will encounter in this book is restricted to just a few morphemes. We term this **idiosyncratic allomorphy.**

Fillers

The most common type of idiosyncratic allomorphy is marked by a meaning-less **filler** element at the right, like the second *or* of *corporate.* These fillers are relics of older patterns in the parent languages. A number of them used to be meaningful, signaling changes in tense, part of speech, and other things. Today, they have lost their last traces of meaning but persist because there has been no pressing reason for time to alter them.

One may get the impression that fillers help the words they are in to sound better, and indeed this is sometimes the case. For example, *bathyscope* probably does sound better to the English speaker's ear than *bathscope* would. But our language has dozens of words that are at least as awkward sounding as *bath-scope*—an example is *landscape.* The substitution of allomorph *bathy* for *bath* in *bathyscope* is simply a relic from earlier times.

In Morpheme set 6, we will encounter numerous examples of fillers. Here are a few examples from Morpheme sets 3 and 4. The root *noc* 'harm, death' has the allomorphs *nec* and *necr.* In the Greek root *necr*, which meant 'corpse', *r* was part of a suffix, and this *r* appears in most of the English words whose origin goes back to the Greek version of the root, as in *necrology* 'a list of people who have died' and *necrophilia* 'attraction to corpses'. One Greek-derived ex-ample of *nec* without suffixal *r* is *nectar*, the drink of the gods which was viewed as overcoming death (*tar* means 'overcoming'). In Latin, the same root *nec* meant 'kill' or 'death' in a word that has come into English as *internecine* 'mutually fatal or seriously harmful'). This root was changed in Latin into the allomorphs *nic* and *noc.* We see *nic* in *pernicious* 'harmful'. (Because this is the only example of this allomorph that we have found in English, it is not in-cluded in our formal listing of this morpheme.) *Noc* appears in *innocent* (which literally means 'not causing harm'); with the filler s̲ this allomorph also occurs in *noxious* (where x̲ results from collapsing c̲ and s̲). This information is sum-marized in the following example:

necr	**nec**
'corpse'	'kill, death'
originally Greek	originally Latin
Examples:	*Examples:*
necrology	internecine
necrophilia	pernicious
nectar (non-suffixed root **nec**)	innocent
	noxious

The root *ten* 'stretch, thin' (which appears in words like *tenuous* and *extenuating*) acquires the filler <u>d</u> in *tender* and *extend*). The allomorph *tend* in turn is the source of yet another allomorph, *tens,* which appears in the words *tensile* and *intense.* The change of *d* to *s* comes about as a result of another rule of allomorphy that will be introduced in a later chapter.

Incidentally, note the similarity of *ten* meaning 'stretch' to *ten* (in Morpheme set 3) meaning 'hold' or 'contain'. Both roots originated from the same early Latin root, whose initial meaning 'stretch' was extended to mean 'hold on to' and then to 'to hold'. For Present-Day English, we consider the two roots to be separate morphemes, because their meanings are quite different, and they do have separate sets of allomorphs.

As we have just seen, fillers include vowels like the final vowel sound of the allomorph *bathy* and consonants like the final *r* of *necr* or the final *d* of *tend.* Fillers also include vowel consonant sequences. An example already mentioned is the *or* of *corporal.*

There is one category of filler that is really not a filler at all. Because it is somewhat meaningful, it is an actual morpheme, even though it may resemble fillers or other meaningless elements. The *ul* that occurs in *corpulent, virulent, truculent, fraudulent, opulent, purulent* has the meaning "abounding in", which it inherits from the Latin source of these examples. For example, *corpulent* parses as *corp* 'body', the semi-morpheme *ul,* and the adjective ending -*ent.* Thus, it means something like 'having a sizable body'. Similarly, *virulent* is analyzed into root *vir* 'virus, poison' (not the same as the root *vir* 'man'), the element *ul,* and the adjective ending -*ent,* giving the literal meaning "extremely poisonous." This way of modifying the meaning of a root before an ending is quite rare, but its meaning is actually quite consistent from example to example, and so we point it up here to avoid confusion with fillers. (By the way, this *ul* is not to be confused with the *ul* in such words as *circular, tabular,* and *oracular.* That pattern results from inserting *u* before *l,* as described in chapter 6.) The morpheme *ul* has the allomorph *ol* in *somnolent* and the allomorph *il* in *pestilent.*

Vowel Changes: Ablaut and Weakening

There are two main idiosyncratic patterns in English vowel alternations. **Ablaut** usually involves an alternation between *o, e* (sometimes *a*), and no vowel at all. This alternation was inherited from the Indo-European mother tongue, the prehistoric ancestor of Latin, Greek, and other languages, as described in chapter 10. The other major pattern of alternations, involving changing the vowel *a* to *e* and changing the vowel *e* to *i*, was inherited from Latin. We will illustrate these two patterns in turn.

Several roots in Morpheme set 3 have a basic *o* which changes to *e* in some allomorphs and is lost entirely in others. These are what are known as ablaut forms. Examples are

> *gon/gen/gn* 'birth, source, origin' (e.g. *cosmogony; genetic; pregnant*);
> *pond/pend* 'hang, weigh, pay, consider' (e.g. *ponderous, dependent*);
> *tom/tm* 'cut' (e.g. *atom, tmesis*);
> *bol/bl* 'throw' (e.g. *symbol, parable*);
> *men/mn* 'think, mind' (e.g. *mental; amnesia*).

All three possibilities, known as "grades" (the *o* -grade, the *e* -grade, and the zero grade), are present in the first example, *gon/gen/gn;* only two grades are present in the others.

A second and even more common set of alternations replace a basic vowel *a* with *e* and replace *e* (or on rare occasion another vowel) with *i*. These changes reflect a process dating from classical Latin called **weakening.** In noninitial syllables, basic *a* is often modified to *e;* the allomorph in *e* often takes a final *t* as well. For example, *fac* 'do, make', which appears with an *a* in *factor*, becomes *fect* in *defect, infect; cap* 'take' changes its *a* in *capture* to *e* in *receptive*.

Furthermore, if this change does not add a final *t* to the allomorph, then most likely the *e* will undergo one more change and become *i*. Thus, *fac* not only becomes *fect* in *defect,* it also becomes *fic,* e.g. in *deficient*. And *cap* not only becomes *cept* in *receptive,* it also becomes *cip,* e.g. in *recipient*.

As in the case of ablaut, the three *a/e/i* variants are not all attested for all roots. Sometimes the alternant in *i* is missing, as in *apt,* which changes to *ept* in *inept* and *adept*. There is no allomorph *ipt*; words like **iniptitude* are not found. Sometimes the alternants in *e* and *i* are found but the basic form in *a* is lacking. This is the case with *spec* 'look, see', as in *respect*. This changes to *spic* in *conspicuous* and *despicable*. But there is no allomorph **spac*.

Here is a list of other roots in Morpheme set 3 exhibiting *a/e/i* alternations. Some combine this allomorphy with other kinds of allomorphy that we discuss elsewhere. Each set of allomorphs is followed by a set of examples: *apec/apic* (apex/apical); *frag/fring* (fragment, infringe); *sacer/secr* (sacrifice, desecrate); *se-men/semin* (semen, disseminate); *spec/spic* (spectator, conspicuous); *stat/stet/stit* (status, obstetric, constitute); *tag/teg/tig* (contagious, integer, contiguous); *ten/tin* (tenant, continent). (The rare alternation of *u* and *i* in *caput/capit* 'head' also fits under the category of weakening.)

There are other vowel changes that are too sporadic to list as separate patterns. Examples from Morpheme set 3 are *al/ol* (aliment, adolescent) and *erg/org/urg* (energy, organ, urgent).

Nasal Insertion

In **nasal insertion,** a nasal consonant (i.e. an *n* or *m*) is placed immediately after the vowel in the root, as in *cub/cumb* (incubate, incumbent); *tag/tang* (contagion, tangent); *frag/frang* (fragile, frangible); *vic/vinc* (victor, convince). The nasal consonant is the relic of a very ancient morpheme in a distant ancestor language, and is related to the alternation seen in English *stand* and *stood*. In English the *n* is not a morpheme—it has no meaning of its own.

Metathesis

In **metathesis** (from *meta-* 'beyond' and *the* 'put'), one sound or letter changes place with another, as in the roots *spec/scep* (spectacle, sceptic—also spelled *skeptic*); *cer/cre* (discern, secrete); *men/mne* (mental, amnesia). Some scholars think that the change in position was caused or encouraged by the desire to make words easier to pronounce. Like the other instances of allomorphy we are considering, there is no detectable meaning difference between the allomorph pairs.

Doublets

A number of instances of allomorphy can be traced to the fact that Latin and Greek had closely related variants of a morpheme that they both inherited from Indo-European, and that subsequently underwent different changes in each language. By adopting both variants or doublets, English acquired new instances of allomorphy.

Three of the number terms in Morpheme set 5 have variants that differ only in that the first letter of one is an *h* while the first letter of the other is *s*. These are *hemi/semi* 'half', *hex/sex* 'six', and *hept/sept* 'seven'. The allomorphs in *h* are from Greek, and those in *s* are from Latin. An example of the same alternation in a non-numeral is the root for 'creep' or 'reptile', which is *herp* in Greek and *serp* in Latin.

A different set of variants distinguishes Latinate *nomen* from Greek *onom*, the two basic allomorphs for the morpheme meaning 'name'. The Latin root *nomen* has the allomorph *nomin* (as in *nominal, nominate*). This is an example of the *a/e/i* alternations discussed above. The Greek root *onom* has the allomorphs *onomat* (as in *onomatology* 'the study of the origins of names') and *onym* (as in *synonym* and *antonym*).

Another doublet pair is *dent/odon* 'tooth'. We use Latinate *dent* for the more familiar *dentist*, and we use Greek *odon*, which has the allomorph *odont*, for the more scholarly *odontologist* 'one who studies teeth'. The pattern of using Latin roots for more common things and Greek roots for more specialized purposes is quite strong in English. Latin *vin* appears in *vine* and *vineyard*. Greek doublet *oen* appears in *oenophile* 'wine lover'. In the pair *mamm/mast* 'breast', *mamm* from Latin is used in *mammal* and *mammary* while Greek *mast* appears in the more clinical *mastectomy* and *mastoid*. The Greek-based allomorph also appears in *mastodon*, literally 'breast tooth', referring to the nipple-shaped structures on the teeth of this prehistoric creature.

OTHER ALLOMORPHY

Due to the complex history of English and of the languages we drew our vocabulary from, there will be cases of allomorphy too idiosyncratic to put into separate categories. Examples from future lessons are *dei/div* 'god', *auto/tauto* 'same', and *lith/lite* 'stone'. These will simply have to be learned individually. But the bright side of the picture is that most alternations in the form of English morphemes are more regular than those covered in this chapter. Their regularity is largely a result of the fact that they are, or used to be, governed by phonetic principles. We will turn to them after learning some terminology and concepts of phonetics in the next chapter.

See appendix II for Morpheme set 3.

EXERCISES

1. Define allomorphy. Illustrate your answer with three examples. What is the relevance of allomorphy to the goals of this course?

2. Write and give the gloss (i.e. the thumbnail definition) of the root in each of the following words. (You may want to confirm your answer in an etymological dictionary.) Give the variant forms (i.e. allomorphs) of the root that are listed in the glossary of the book. Make note of the dictionary's definition(s) of each full word as well.

a. *contiguous*

root: _____; gloss: _____; other allomorphs of the root: _____

b. *pertinacious*

root: _____; gloss: _____; other allomorphs of the root: _____

c. *pregnancy*

root: _____; gloss: _____; other allomorphs of the root: _____

3. After studying the morpheme list for this chapter, test your knowledge of the morphemes presented so far by parsing, glossing, and giving allomorphs for the following words. With the aid of a dictionary, give a brief definition which partly or fully reflects the meaning of the individual morphemes.

a.   conspicuous

GLOSS   prefix: _____ root: _____ suffix: _____

ALLOMORPHS   prefix: _____ root: _____

DEFINITION   _____

b.   deification

GLOSS   root: _____ root: _____ suffix: _____

ALLOMORPHS   root: _____ root: _____

DEFINITION   _____

c.   ectochromic

GLOSS   prefix: _____ root: _____ suffix: <u>ADJECTIVE</u>

DEFINITION   _____

d.   energy

GLOSS   prefix: _____ root: _____ suffix: <u>NOUN</u>

ALLOMORPHS   prefix: _____ root: _____

DEFINITION   _____

e.   incipient

GLOSS   prefix: _____ root: _____ suffix: <u>ADJECTIVE</u>

ALLOMORPHS   prefix: _____ root: _____

DEFINITION   _____

f.   seminal

GLOSS   prefix: _____ root: _____ suffix: <u>ADJECTIVE</u>

ALLOMORPHS   prefix: _____ root: _____

DEFINITION   _____

g.   deliberative

GLOSS   prefix: _____ root: _____ suffix: <u>ADJECTIVE</u>

DEFINITION   _____

5
Phonetics

INTRODUCTION

Phonetics studies the different sounds of language. Seeing how the sounds of English are pronounced will put us in a better position to describe and even to understand some of the allomorphy we encounter in English morphemes.*

Many changes in the pronunciation of morphemes are due to **assimilation** of one sound to another. Adjacent sounds that are already partially similar to one another often become even more similar, in fact sometimes identical. Thus, the *in-* of *inelegant* becomes *il-* in *illegal* and *ir-* in *irrelevant.* We will learn that [n], [l], and [r] all share a certain phonetic property and that this has something to do with why [n] changes to [l] and [r] in these cases. Before sounds like [t] and [d], the [n] of prefix in- does not assimilate, and so we get the forms *intolerant* and *indecisive*, not **ittolerant* or **iddecisive*. The prefix *con-* undergoes the same set of changes: *correct* (= *con-* + *rect*), *collect* (= *con-* + *lect*). Compare *contain,* which does not become **cottain,* and *condemn,* which does not become **coddemn.*

Phonetic principles also help to make sense of certain changes that don't involve assimilation. For example, the [m] at the end of *presume* and *redeem* is followed by a [p] when [t] is added, as in *presumptive* and *redemptive*. The [p] is inserted because it is more or less on the path that the speech organs (i.e. tongue, lips, teeth, etc.) follow as they move from [m] to [t]. The process of

---

*You may want to refer to the pronunciation guide for the sounds of symbols written in square brackets, such as [çš], in this chapter.

inserting a sound in between others is called **epenthesis,** from *epi-* 'on, over'; *en-* 'in'; *the* 'put'; *-sis* 'N'.

Phonetics also helps us to sort out the differences between pronunciation and spelling. As illogical and difficult as we may sometimes find the spelling system of English to be, it certainly seems to become ingrained in our consciousness, shaping (and sometimes distorting) our perceptions of the sounds that letters represent. It may come as a surprise to many readers that the words *cats* and *dogs* generally do <u>not</u> end in exactly the same sound: the sound at the end of *cats* is essentially the one we hear at the end of *hiss,* while the sound at the end of *dogs* is what we hear at the end of *buzz.* One reason that we miss the difference between the two sounds [s] and [z] is the single spelling of the plural morpheme as *s* of the plural ending. Just to clarify the point here, we do not mean to be attacking the spelling system of English for being phonetically inaccurate. In fact, our much maligned spelling system would be even harder to deal with if it faithfully recorded differences like this one, so that the plural of *cat* was *cats* while the plural of *dog* was *dogz.* We are better off with a single plural marker, *-s,* for the two phonetically similar allomorphs [s] and [z]. Our point is that when we focus on phonetics, we must be careful not to be misled by spelling, which is often a poor indicator of how a word is actually pronounced.

REASONS FOR STUDYING PHONETICS

Each sound in language can be broken down into a set of properties. We can understand the relation between one sound and another by comparing their characteristic properties. For example, even though we noted above that [s] and [z] are not identical, they are indeed very similar, differing only in whether the vocal cords are vibrating or not.

Many assimilatory changes become understandable when we compare properties of the sounds involved. As noted earlier, the [n] of *in-* assimilates totally to the initial [l] of *legal* and to the initial [r] of *relevant,* but not to other sounds. This makes some sense, because [n], [l], and [r] have, in common, the degree of openness of the vocal tract and the place in the mouth where they are made **(place of articulation).** This pair of characteristic properties occurs together only in these three sounds. The assimilatory change involves the loss of the distinctive trait of [n] that differentiates it from [l] and [r], namely the fact that it is made with a resonating nasal tract **(nasality).**

The fact that each sound is broken down into a set of characteristic properties makes learning new sounds an easier and less intimidating chore. If we understand the basic mechanism for producing a fricative sound (basically, positioning the speech organs so that air passes noisily), and if we understand how we produce a sound like English [k] or [g], this puts us in a fair position to produce a fricative like [x] (as in Scottish *loch,* Hebrew *Chanukah,* or German *Bach*), even though this consonant sound may seem unfamiliar to many English speakers.

One last benefit of a knowledge of phonetics is that the ability to describe sounds objectively in terms of how they are actually produced can help to dispel the emotional, value-laden notions we may have about the articulation of speech. It is not uncommon to hear disparaging remarks about a language which is pronounced in the back of the mouth, or complaints that a language sounds too "guttural". Worse yet, pronunciations that deviate from Standard English are sometimes taken as signs of laziness, ignorance, and even physical or mental handicaps. But how we judge a language's sounds or how we judge a particular individual's speech depends on the standards that we apply. English sounds just as peculiar to a speaker of Arabic as Arabic does to our ears. And, because our educational system trains most of us to value Standard English as the "correct" form, we are tempted to frown upon deviations from the standard—whether these deviations fall from our lips or from the lips of others. In fact, however, variations in pronunciation are a normal part of language. They come about for a variety of reasons and they stay on when they acquire a value for the speech community that adopts them. Later chapters will look at some far-reaching effects of changes in pronunciation and other aspects of language structure.

BASICS OF SOUND PRODUCTION

Figure 5.1 should be consulted for reference during the following discussion of the different places of articulation.

The Air Stream

Any speech sound involves an **airstream** whose flow is modified in some way by the speech organs. All of the sounds of English involve the passage of air from the lungs through the **vocal tract** and out the mouth or nose or both. As the air passes along, its flow can be arrested, slowed down, or diverted by the movement of various speech organs or **articulators.** The nature of these effects, and the location of the articulators that produce them, is what differentiates sounds in speech.

1 = *lips* (labial region),
2 = *teeth* (dental region),
3 = *alveolar ridge*,
4 = *hard palate* (palate),
5 = *soft palate* (velum),
6 = *uvula*,
7 = *tip of tongue* (apex),
8 = *blade of tongue* (lamina),
9 = *back of tongue* (dorsum),
10 = *vocal cords*,
in the larynx
(the glottis is the space
between the vocal cords),
11 = *nasal passages*.

THE ARTICULATORY APPARATUS: CONSONANTS

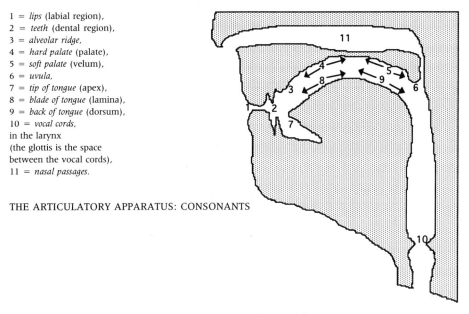

Figure 5.1. Idealized Cross-section of the Vocal Tract (alternative names in parentheses)

Manner of Articulation

Let us first consider **oral** sounds, that is, sounds whose articulation involves the flow of air through the mouth. Suppose that we send a stream of air from the lungs through the mouth. There are various places along the way at which we can stop the air from flowing. Stopping it at the lips will produce a **labial** sound, like [p]. If we stop it in the area just behind the upper teeth, the alveolar ridge, we produce an **alveolar** sound, like [t]. If we stop the airflow further back in the mouth, around where the bony structure of the roof of the mouth ends, we will hear a **velar** sound, like [k], named after the velum, the soft region just behind the hard palate.

Airflow can be stopped by bringing two articulators, usually an upper and a lower articulator, fully together. In the case of labial sounds, the upper and lower articulators are the two lips. For alveolar sounds, the upper articulator is the alveolum, and the lower articulator is the blade or the very tip of the tongue. For velar sounds, the upper articulator is the velum and the lower articulator is the back of the tongue. Sounds that are produced by stopping the airflow are called **stops.** A stop ends when it is released, causing a short burst of air from the mouth.

Slowly read the first sentence of the preceding paragraph aloud, seeing if you can determine which sounds involve temporary but total blockage of airflow.*

Most of the sounds of English do not involve complete stoppage of air. Some consonants are produced by bringing the upper and lower articulators close together but leaving enough of an opening so that air can pass through continuously. The narrowness of the opening causes the air to be emitted under some pressure, which results in a rushing noise that gives **fricatives** (with the root *fric* 'rub', as in *friction*) their name. The word *fricatives* itself has three different fricative sounds in it. You should be able to identify them.

The sounds known as **affricates** involve a transition from a stop closure to a fricative opening without much of a change in position of the articulators. The fricative sound at the beginning of the word *shore* contrasts with the corresponding affricate at the beginning of *chore*. Pronounce these words. Notice that the stop at the beginning of *chore* is produced in almost exactly the same place in the mouth as the fricative which immediately follows. The stop sound is considered a variety of [t], an alveolar stop, but its position is adjusted in *chore* to match up with the fricative part of the affricate. You can probably feel the difference by comparing the initial sounds of *tore* and *chore*. If you pronounce these two words as we do, you should feel that in *tore* it is the tip of your tongue that makes contact with the upper articulator, and it is pointed more upward than in *chore*. For *chore* a greater portion of the tongue makes contact, and contact extends to what is known as the **alveopalatal** region (i.e. between the back of the alveolar ridge and the front of the hard palate). The tip of the tongue is pointed more forward than it is for *tore*. Some speakers do this differently. Pronounce *tore* and *chore,* and see if you make the initial consonant closure in the same position for both.

Another affricate of English, [ǰ], occurs as both the initial and the final consonant of *judge.* Many English speakers produce the same sound at the end of *garage,* while others follow the original French more closely by producing a fricative, [ž]. Which sounds more natural to you?

All consonants involve some slowing down of the flow of air through the mouth, but the degree of oral constriction is not always so great as to create a rushing sound. The more open the oral cavity is, the less noisy the sound will be. Consonants produced with a relatively wide opening between the oral articulators are called **approximants.** They include the sounds [w] and [y] in *woo* and *you* and the sounds [l] and [r] in *row* and *low.*

Earlier we mentioned that [l] and [r] shared many properties with [n], in-

*In the first sentence they include (in order): [k], [b], [t], [p], [t], [b], [b], [t], [t], etc.

cluding the feature of permitting relatively unrestricted flow of air. Is [n], then, an approximant? No. In fact, when you pronounce the sound [n], you can feel a complete closure in the mouth. The air that is totally blocked from exiting the mouth, however, is permitted to pass freely through the nose. You can confirm this by reversing the flow of air. Try pronouncing an [n] while inhaling. Air will be flowing in, but you won't feel any air rushing in past your tongue. The inhaled air stream will be entering through your nose. The closure takes place in the alveolar region, in the same place as for the stops [t] and [d]. The sound [n]'s characteristic airflow through the nose is why it is called a **nasal** sound. The same goes for the labial nasal [m]. The general term for sounds that permit the relatively unrestricted flow of air is **sonorant.** Approximants are sonorants because air travels through the mouth unimpeded enough that frication is not produced. Nasal consonants are sonorants because even though air is blocked in the mouth, it passes unimpeded through the nasal cavity.

Place of Articulation

We have already looked at the places of articulation of a number of sounds. For the stops, we saw three different places of articulation: labial, alveolar, and velar. These places also relate to the production of nasal consonants. As you will recall, nasals involve a total obstruction of airflow in the mouth. In English this obstruction occurs at the same places that we have noted for stop consonants. This similarity in the articulation of nasals and stops has led some phoneticians to describe nasal consonants as 'nasal stops' (in contrast with non-nasal or oral stops).

To feel the similarities and differences between oral stops and nasal consonants, take three English words that differ only in that one has the labial stop [p], another has the labial stop [b] and a third has the labial nasal [m] (e.g. *pat, bat, mat; cup, cub, come*). Pronounce these words, and see if you can precisely identify the difference between the two stops on the one hand and the nasal on the other. Do the same with the alveolar stops [t] and [d] and the nasal consonant [n].

Or try producing sequences consisting of a nasal sound followed by an oral stop that is **homorganic,** i.e. that is produced by the *homo-* 'same' *organs,* and therefore at the same place of articulation. (Examples are *ambush* and *ending.*) What you may feel in the transition from the nasal to the oral consonant is a sort of tightening up in the area at the very back of the oral cavity. The velum (i.e. soft palate), which has been lowered in order to permit the free passage of air for the nasal consonant, is drawn to the back of the pharynx for the oral stop, creating a complete closure so that air that is blocked orally cannot escape through the nasal passage either.

Next, consider the velar stops [k] and [g]. Is there a nasal consonant that is homorganic to them? Your answer will depend on where you look. If you look for words beginning in a velar nasal consonant, parallel to the velar stops in *kill* and *gill*, you won't find any—not in English, though velar nasals do appear initially in other languages. But if you look in final position, you will find some examples.

Most speakers will also find examples in **medial** position (i.e. between two vowels). [k], [g], and the velar nasal consonant [ŋ] contrast in *backer, bagger,* and *banger.* Speakers of English will differ in whether they pronounce the last word [bæŋər] or [bæŋgər]. Try the two pronunciations [bæŋər] and [bæŋgər] and decide which feels and sounds the most natural for you. The velar nasal turns up in many cases where a nasal consonant is called for before a velar stop, for example in *anger* and *tanker.* To test your understanding of the relation between the terms velar, nasal, and stop, transcribe the word *ping* using the symbols in the pronunciation guide. Does it have three or four **segments** (i.e. distinct vowel and consonant sounds)? Check your answer by looking up the pronunciation in a dictionary.

Among stops and nasals, we have already found three places of articulation represented in English. If we add one more position, the palatal, midway between the alveolar and velar positions, we will also account for the difference in place of articulation of the approximants [w] and [y].

If you pronounce the [w] of *wood* and *weed,* you will probably first notice that the lips are rounded. This points to the fact that [w] is a labial sound, but there is more to its articulation than this labial gesture. Notice where the back of your tongue is for [w] in the word *way.* Say the word very slowly—try to make the [w] into a whole syllable—and feel what is happening. The lips are moving from a relatively rounded posture to a relatively spread one. But note also the movement of your tongue. At the beginning of the word, for the consonant [w], you should feel that the back of the tongue is raised toward the velum; as you move to the vowel of *way,* this changes so that the back of the tongue is no longer raised at all. This shows that, along with being a labial sound, [w] is also a velar sound. Many refer to this sound as a labial–velar or **labiovelar.**

Where [w] slows down the airstream at the labial and velar places of articulation, i.e. at either end of the oral cavity, the approximant [y] does just the opposite. For [y], the front and back regions of the mouth are relatively open, and the narrowing that takes place is in the middle. This is done by raising the body of the tongue toward the hard palate. Say the word *I.* You will probably feel your tongue and your jaw moving upward.

The approximants [r] and [l] are articulated in the alveolar region. [r] is the most variable sound in English, and so describing its position involves describing a number of the most common variants found in English dialects. For most American speakers, the tip and blade of the tongue are raised in the direction of the top and back of the upper teeth. The center line of the tongue from back to front is depressed, creating a round, tubular channel for air to pass through. For other speakers, the tip of the tongue is not only raised but also curled backward. Try this and see if the sound that comes out resembles your normal [r] or some other [r] that you have heard from speakers of American English. The [r] with tongue curled back is often used to stereotype or caricature American English speakers, even though a majority of speakers probably do not use this gesture to any great extent.

The approximant [l] involves contact with the back of the incisors or with the alveolar ridge. This raises an interesting question. If there is contact between the tongue and the back of the teeth or alveolar ridge, how can this sound be an approximant rather than a stop? That is to say, how can the air flow past this area? To answer this question, pronounce an [l]. The answer will be more apparent if you inhale while pronouncing the [l]. You should feel cool air where it is going past a constriction. As you probably have discovered, air escapes past one or both sides of the tongue, and it is this aspect of the mechanism for producing an [l] that has led to its being termed a **lateral** sound.

This leaves the fricative and affricate sounds. Imagine what it would take to make a labial sound that qualifies as a fricative. Try bringing your lips close enough together to produce noise when air passes through, without blocking the air entirely. You have probably produced a bilabial fricative, which English lacks but which many languages have. The closest that English comes to having a labial fricative is the labiodental fricatives [f] and [v], which are made by bringing the lower lip in partial contact with the upper teeth. Try this and see if it produces something that sounds like a respectable English [f] and [v]. If not, try it again in front of a mirror.

What happens if instead you use your upper lip and lower teeth? This sound technically qualifies as a **labiodental** fricative, but no known language has this sound.

Another kind of fricative involves touching the tip of the tongue to the edges of the front upper and lower teeth. This produces what are called **interdental** fricatives, written [θ] and [ð]. These occur in *thin* and *then*, respectively.

Next, if the tip and blade of the tongue move to the area around the alveolar region, the sounds [s] and [z] will be produced. If they are moved slightly further back, to the alveopalatal region, you should hear the sounds [š] and [ž], the medial consonant sounds of *dasher* and *measure*.

Try making the following sounds in sequence, and feel what your articulators are doing: [θ], [s], [š] (as in *thin, sin, shin*). You will feel your tongue retracting as you go through this sequence, and you may also feel that a progressively larger area of your tongue is getting involved as well. The same should happen for the sequence [ð], [z], [ž] (as in *heather, buzzer, treasure*). The alveopalatal region, where the sounds [š] and [ž] are made, is also the place of articulation for the affricates [č] and [ǰ] described above.

Voiced and Voiceless Articulation

There is one key aspect of the manner of articulation of consonants left to be described. The air stream, which originates in the lungs, must pass through the **glottis** (the opening between the vocal cords, located in the larynx) on its way to the articulators above the larynx. If the vocal cords are open, the air will pass freely, as it does for the sound [h] (referred to as a **glottal fricative**). But it is also possible to position the vocal cords so that an air stream passing through them will cause the vocal cords to vibrate. Essentially, this is done by bringing the vocal cords together yet leaving them slack enough that the pressure of air below them will briefly force them apart. They then close and, again, are forced open by the airstream. Each opening and closing constitutes one cycle of regular vibration that may take place a hundred or even several hundred times per second. It is this vibration that is known as voice or **voicing.** When you make a voiced sound, such as [v], it is possible to feel the vibration with your fingers. Place your fingers on your throat, at the sides of the bulge formed by the larynx (or Adam's apple), and pronounce a [v]; now compare the voiceless sound [f]. Or if you use your index fingers to cover the openings of your ears as you produce a good [v], you will feel your whole head vibrate; again compare [f]. Using these cues, decide which of the sounds in this sentence are voiced and which are voiceless.*

Voicing is heard as the buzzing sound that occurs with the sound [z] of *buzz*. This contrasts with the voiceless, hissing sound that occurs with the [s] at the end of the word *hiss*. Recall that [s] and [z] were described as alveolar fricatives. They differ only in that one is voiced and the other is not. Make one sound and then the other; see if you can hear the difference as well as feel it.

---

*Here is phonetic transcription of the sentence (pronounced in a very careful style): [yuzɪŋ ðiz kyuz dɪsaid hwich əv ðə saundz ɪn ðɪs sɛntɛns *ar* voist ænd hwlč *ar* voisləs]. (Note: Many people pronounce *which* as [wɪč].)

Table 5.1 Places and Manners of Articulation of English Consonants
(Fill in the blanks)

	labial	labio-dental	interdental	alveolar	alveopalatal	palatal	velar	glottal
stop	—,—			—,—			—,—	
fricative		—,—	—,—	—,—	—,—			—,—ᵃ
affricate					—,—			
nasal (vcd)	—,—			—,—			—,—	
approx. (vcd)	—,—ᵇ			—,—		—,—		
"" (lateral)				—,—				

ᵃ There is no distinctive voiced glottal fricative in English.
ᵇ This sound is simultaneously labial and velar.

Vowels

The understanding of the vocal apparatus that we have gained from our survey of consonants will help us to understand the production of vowels as well. Unlike consonants, vowels are made with a relatively open vocal tract. Like the consonant approximants [r], [l], [w], and [y], all vowels are sonorants. The vowels of English are also ordinarily voiced, as you can see, by applying the voicing tests you learned for consonants to the vowels in the words *I, we,* etc. In some circumstances, however, particularly when an unstressed vowel is surrounded by voiceless stops, the vowel becomes voiceless. Pay attention to the first vowel of *potato* and see whether you pronounce it as a voiced or voiceless sound. Does the speed with which you say it have any effect on it?

Vowel sounds vary much more from dialect to dialect than consonant sounds do. Consider regional American dialects or the English of the United Kingdom or Australia. Whether you are familiar with one of these variants of English or simply have been exposed to stereotyped imitations, chances are good that it will be the vowel differences rather than consonant differences that stand out. It is difficult to characterize English vowels in general terms in a way that does justice to them in all their diversity. Our descriptions are to be taken as a starting point. Our basic goal is to introduce the parameters that distinguish the vowel sounds, and to illustrate them with real English examples. These descriptions are not intended to prescribe how the different vowels *ought* to be pronounced—indeed we feel that no one is in a position to do this. If your pronunciations differ significantly from the ones presented here, we hope to provide you with vocabulary and concepts to help you describe your versions.

One of the basic features of the production of vowels is the differing location of the body of the tongue. For the sound [i] of *heed*, the body of the tongue is raised toward the palate; for the sound [æ] of *had*, the body of the tongue is lowered. The jaw is normally raised or lowered with the tongue. Starting with your tongue in the high position for [i], gradually lower it until you reach the position for the sound [æ]. The result may sound strange and animal-like, but if you listen carefully you may encounter some other English vowels in the course of going from the highest tongue position to the lowest.

The vowels [i] and [æ] and all of the vowels that fall between them are characterized as **front** vowels, because the body of the tongue is in a relatively forward part of the mouth for them. Other vowels are articulated with the back of the tongue; this is the case for the vowels [u] of *who* and [a] of the exclamation *Ha!* The vowel [u] is also pronounced with the lips **rounded.** Of the two back vowels, [u] and [a], which seems high and which low, in terms of tongue height?

Now try moving your articulators gradually from [u] to [a]. What you hear may once again sound distressingly inhuman on the whole, but you may encounter another English vowel or two along the way, particularly if you keep your lips rounded. (Note that the [ʊ] of *look* and the [o] of *coat* are, like [u], rounded vowels.)

Vowel sounds can be positioned corresponding roughly to where in the mouth they are articulated. Table 5.2 provides the basic vowel symbols, with illustrations from standard English words to give an idea of how these vowel symbols are pronounced. Note that the vowels [i u e o] are **long** and **tense** by comparison to their counterparts [I ɛ ʊ ɔ] which are considered **short** and **lax** vowels. The symbols ə and ʌ are used for two vowels whose articulatory positions can be very similar in American dialects. [ə] represents a stressless vowel whose place of articulation varies quite a bit (compare the mid central articulation of the stressless first vowel of *upon* with the higher, more front articulation of the stressless vowel of the final syllable of *kindness*), while [ʌ] represents a stressed vowel whose mid central place of articulation is relatively fixed.

Table 5.2 English Vowels (Monophthongs)

	front	**central**	**back**
<u>high</u>	i *(heed)*		u *(loot)*
	I *(hid)*		ʊ *(look)*
<u>mid</u>	e *(wade)*	ə *(upon)*	o *(coat)*
	ɛ *(wed)*	ʌ *(cut)*	ɔ *(caught* or *court)*
<u>low</u>	æ *(cat)*	a (the first half of *eye*)	a *(father* or *rod)*

For many of the vowels of English, the vowel itself involves a movement from one position to another. For the sound [ai] of words like *I* and *might,* our articulators start out somewhere around the position for [a] and move toward the position for [i]; for the sound [au] of words like *how* and *now,* we begin in the same position and move toward the position of [u]. Vowels that involve significant movements like these are called **diphthongs** (from Greek *di* 'two', *phthong* 'sound'). In addition to [ai] and [au], there is a diphthong [ɔi] in words like *boy* and *soil.*

We noted earlier that vowels are subject to a great deal of variation in English. Perhaps the largest source of this variation is the degree of diphthongization. Pronounce the vowels of the words *heed, wade, cat, loot,* and *coat* to see the extent to which they are diphthongs for you. Can you feel or see your tongue or jaw move during the vowel sound? To avoid the interfering effects of consonants, use consonants that are not made with the tongue, such as [h], [m], etc. In Standard English the amount of diphthongization on the high and low vowels is slight. Considerably more diphthongization occurs on the vowels of *raid* and *rode,* which start with a mid vowel and move toward a high vowel. In fact, these are often transcribed [ɛi] and [ɔu], respectively, but in the present text we will keep to the simpler representations [e] and [o].

ASSIMILATION

Assimilation is the single most important aspect of phonetics for the study of morphology. Several kinds of assimilation will be encountered by the student of English morphology.

The first is known as **voicing assimilation.** When the morpheme *reg* (as in *regular*) takes the form *rec* (as in *erect*), two things have happened: a [t] has been added to the end of the root to form an allomorph; and the [g] (a voiced velar stop) has been assimilated in voicing to the [t] (which is a voiceless alveolar stop), yielding voiceless [k]. (Note that [k] is spelled c in Latinate words). Voicing assimilation usually results from the presence of a [t] at the end of one of the allomorphs of a morpheme.

The second major type of assimilation is **place of articulation assimilation.** In the word *impossible,* the prefix is actually *in-.* In this case, the [n] (an alveolar nasal) has been assimilated to the initial [p] (a bilabial stop) of the following morpheme with respect to its place of articulation to become an [m], a bilabial nasal. Does the same thing happen to [n] before the bilabial consonant [m]? How about before the labiodental consonants [f] and [v]?

Both voicing assimilation and place of articulation assimilation are kinds of

partial assimilation. In both cases, the adjacent sounds become more alike, but still remain distinct.

In the end, we return to the kind of assimilation that began our discussion, **total assimilation,** which creates (at least in the written forms of words if not always in actual pronunciation) sequences of identical sounds. When the [n] of the prefix *in-* is followed by a sonorant consonant (e.g. [l], [r]), it is completely assimilated to that consonant. Illustrations are the words *illegal* and *irreverent.*

We can use our knowledge of the kinds of assimilation to assist in identifying variants of morphemes we encounter in the study of vocabulary. For example, the word *affect* has an allomorph of the familiar root *fac* which has had its vowel a weakened to e in *fec* and a [t] ending added. The presence of two fs is a strong clue that we are in the presence of a total assimilation. Checking our list of morphemes, we find one likely candidate for the first morpheme of the word, the prefix *ad-*. We may conclude that the [d] of *ad-* has been completely assimilated to the [f] of *fect*. Note that this does not happen to the occurrences of *ad-* in *admit, adapt, adhere* and *advocate,* but we won't find words like **adsume, *adsimilate, *adrive, *adnotate, *adleviate, *adproach, *adtract.* Instead we find *assume, assimilate, arrive, annotate, alleviate, approach,* and *attract.* Examining the phonetic characteristics of these sounds leads us to the generalization that the [d] of *ad-* will assimilate totally to a voiceless fricative, a stop, or a sonorant, but not to any other consonant. It also remains unchanged before a vowel. You may discover a few exceptions to this statement. But the exceptions will not be so numerous as to invalidate the general rule.

EASE OF ARTICULATION

We need to end this chapter with a note of caution about the role of phonetics in explaining assimilation. The kinds of changes that we have just seen make sense from a phonetic point of view because they show how sounds influence one another when they come together. Some linguists hold that there is a general tendency in language to evolve toward greater ease of articulation. The examples just cited as assimilations seem to support that trend, but it is important to note that the trend is extremely limited. If languages were merely subject to considerations of ease of articulation, they might all evolve into a single undifferentiated grunt! While the popular media make occasional facetious references to such developments (the speech of teen-agers is a frequent target), language as a whole is not in danger of succumbing to this trend.

To appreciate the limits of the tendency toward ease of assimilation, compare the behavior of *ad-* to that of other prefixes ending in a voiced consonant.

We have seen that the [d] of *ad-* assimilates totally to the following stop (*ad- + tain* > *attain, ad- + pos + -ite* > *apposite*). But compare *ob-*. We get assimilation before labial stops (*ob- + pos + -ite* > *opposite, ob- + press* > *oppress*). But not before alveolar stops: *obtain* does not become **ottain, obdurate* does not become **oddurate*.

The conclusion is that each prefix has its own pattern of allomorphy. While ease of articulation may be behind some of the assimilatory patterns we observe, it is not always an accurate predictor of patterns that allomorphy will take.

SUMMARY

Consonants can differ from one another in manner and place of articulation and in voicing. The basic characteristics of vowels are the height and backness of the tongue, rounding of the lips, and length or tenseness. Knowing about common features of different sounds helps us to understand a number of types of allomorphy, because sounds that are phonetically similar will sometimes behave in similar ways. Knowing how particular sounds are made also often helps us to understand why they cause or undergo certain changes, especially assimilation.

See appendix II for Morpheme set 4.

EXERCISES

General instructions: Remember that the letters used in writing English do not always accurately represent the sounds pronounced. In the word *housing*, for example, the letter s is pronounced as a voiced alveolar fricative [z], not a voiceless [s]. Therefore, if asked to identify voiced sounds, you would include the written s of *housing*. In the word *sick*, however, written s is pronounced [s], which is voiceless, and would not be marked as a voiced sound.

1. Transcribe the following words using phonetic symbols. For example, for *mention* you would write [mɛnšən] or [mɛnšn]

a. wounds	f. drained
b. grounds	g. spine
c. psychologist	h. thought
d. photograph	i. rather
e. photography	j. doughy

2. Identify the letter(s) representing each oral stop in the following sentence, at the same time indicating if it is voiced by writing a small plus sign (+) above the letter(s), or if it is voiceless, a minus sign (−). The first two oral stops are marked for you.

+   −

BRIAN STOPPED IN AN INSTANT AND, SOBBING RAPIDLY,

ASKED KEN AGAIN TO WATCH THE SNAKE, WHO WAS JUST

SHEDDING ANOTHER SKIN.

3. Identify the letter(s) representing each fricative in the following sentence, at the same time indicating if it is voiced by writing a small plus sign (+) above the letter(s), or if it is voiceless, a minus sign (−). The first two are marked for you. (Be cautious: _th_, for example, represents one sound, not two, in _there_.)

−   +

SURELY, NO ONE THERE PRESUMPTUOUSLY THINKS THAT THE

NATION CAN WITHSTAND SUCH MEASURES, HE COUGHED, AS

THE SMOKE BATHED HIS HEAVY-LIDDED EYES.

4. Describe fully each of the sounds represented by the phonetic symbols following the example. For each vowel indicate whether it is

- high, mid, or low
- front, central, or back
- rounded or unrounded
- tense or lax (ignore this if it does not belong to a tense/lax pair).

For each consonant indicate whether it is

- voiced or voiceless (nasals and approximants are always voiced)
- labial, labiodental, interdental, alveolar, alveopalatal, palatal, velar, or glottal
- stop, fricative, affricate, nasal, or approximant (and if an alveopalatal approximant, indicate if lateral or nonlateral)

a. [ž] — voiced alveopalatal fric-
            ative
b. [ə] —
c. [j] —
d. [ð] —
e. [e] —
f. [ŋ] —
g. [I —
h. [ɔ] —
i. [æ] —
j. [r] —
k. [b] —
l. [ʋ] —
m. [h] —

5. Give the phonetic symbol represented by each of the following articulatory descriptions, as in the example.

a. voiceless alveolar fricative — [s]
b. high back tense rounded vowel —
c. voiceless interdental fricative —
d. voiced velar stop —
e. low front unrounded vowel —
f. alveolar nasal —
g. voiced labiodental fricative —
h. voiceless alveopalatal affricate —
i. mid central unrounded vowel —
j. voiceless alveopalatal fricative consonant —

6. **Parse** each of the following words, using a slash (/) to separate morphemes. (Put parentheses around fillers and/or other meaningless elements.) **Gloss** with all meanings you have learned for each morpheme. For each morpheme, **give allomorphs** (if any).

a.   p h o t o r e c e p t i v e

GLOSS(ES)   root: _____ prefix: _____ root: _____ suffix: __

ALLOMORPH(S) root: _____ prefix: _____ root: _____ suffix: __

b.   i n c i d e n c e [Note: prefix isn't 'not'; root isn't 'cut, kill'.]

GLOSS(ES)   prefix: _____ root: _____ suffix: _____

ALLOMORPH(S) prefix: _____ root: _____ suffix: _____

c.   m e s o m o r p h i c

GLOSS(ES)   prefix: _____ root: _____ suffix: _____

ALLOMORPH(S) prefix: _____ root: _____ suffix: _____

d.   e x t e n u a t e

GLOSS(ES)   prefix: _____ root: _____ suffix: _____

ALLOMORPH(S) prefix: _____ root: _____ suffix: _____

e.   p r o g r e s s i v e

GLOSS(ES)   prefix: _____ root: _____ suffix: _____

ALLOMORPH(S) prefix: _____ root: _____ suffix: _____

f.   a c c e p t a n c e

GLOSS(ES)   prefix: _____ root: _____ suffix: _____

ALLOMORPH(S) prefix: _____ root: _____ suffix: _____

g.   a d e q u a t e

GLOSS(ES)   prefix: _____ root: _____ suffix: _____

ALLOMORPH(S) prefix: _____ root: _____ suffix: _____

6

Regular Allomorphy; Numerals and Number Words

REGULAR ALLOMORPHY IN GENERAL

In chapter 4 we cataloged a variety of processes that exchanged one allomorph for another on a more or less idiosyncratic basis. An example was the prefix *a-*, 'not', which has the allomorph *an-* before vowels and *h*. Allomorphy can be totally idiosyncratic. The verb *flu* 'flow, river' has the two allomorphs *fluc* and *fluv*. This combination, in which *c* and *v* alternate with zero, is unique in English. But some allomorphy is regular—that is, generally predictable—because it is due to adjacent sounds and some simple phonetic principles. With the understanding of speech sound production gained from chapter 5, we can now look at such phonetically based allomorphy.

Partial Assimilation According to Place or Manner of Articulation

Sometimes a consonant assimilates to a neighboring one (generally to its right) in place of articulation. The most common example is the nasal consonant *n* which occurs at the end of prefixes *con-* and *in-* (including the morpheme meaning 'in, into' as well as the one meaning 'not'). Before a morpheme beginning with a labial consonant this *n* becomes *m:*

> ***Rule 1.*** **Nasal Assimilation**
> **n → m / __ p, b, m**

(This notation means that *n* changes to *m* when it occurs in the slot appearing just before *p, b,* or *m*. The slash mark "/" is shorthand for "when it occurs".)

According to this rule, the words in the left column below will yield the analysis on the right. The first set illustrates an allomorph of the prefix *con*. The second set illustrates an allomorph of the prefix *in-* meaning 'not', as in *inaccurate*. The third set illustrates an allomorph of the prefix *in-* meaning 'into', as in *inaugurate*.

compose	**con** + pose → **com**pose
combine	**con** + bine → **com**bine
commute	**con** + mute → **com**mute
impossible	**in** + possible → **im**possible
imbalance	**in** + balance → **im**balance
immutable	**in** + mutable → **im**mutable
impose	**in** + pose → **im**pose
imbibe	**in** + bibe → **im**bibe
immerse	**in** + merse → **im**merse

The assimilation in these examples is called **partial** because only the place of articulation of the nasal consonant changes. Its nasality remains.

Another example of partial assimilation occurs when one sound assimilates to another in voicing. In many cases, a voiced consonant like *b* will become voiceless (i.e. *p*) before a voiceless consonant (often *t*). The symbol C below stands for "consonant".

Rule 2. Voice Assimilation
voiced C → voiceless C / __ voiceless C
voiceless C → voiced C / __ voiced C

The root *scrib* becomes *scrip* before the filler *t*. That is why *prescribe* changes its *b* to *p* in *scripture* and *prescription* Here are a few more examples:

regent	**reg +** ent (no change)
	reg + t + or → **rect**or
fragile	**frag +** ile (no change)
fraction	**frag + t +** ion → **fract**ion

Usually, this sort of voicing assimilation winds up converting voiced consonants into voiceless ones. But one example in which a voiceless consonant assimilates to a voiced one is the root *doc* 'teach':

docent	**doc** + ent (no change)
dogma	**doc** + ma → **dog**ma

Total Assimilation

Some English prefixes exhibit **total assimilation** before the sounds *l* and *r*. For example, the *n* at the end of prefixes *con-* and *in-* illustrated above before stop consonants undergoes a different change before *l* or *r*. The *n* is replaced in spelling by a copy of the *l* or *r*. (In speech, we only pronounce one *l* or *r*, even though two appear in the spelling. Rule 3 is formulated to account for the facts of spelling. The facts of pronunciation would require a rule that simply deletes the final *n* of these prefixes before *n* or *r*.)

> ***Rule 3.* Total Assimilation**
> **con-, in- → col-, il- / __ l**
> **con-, in- → cor-, ir- / __ r**
> **inter- → intel- / __ l**

Here are some examples:

collude	**con** + lude → **col**lude
corrupt	**con** + rupt → **cor**rupt
illegal	**in** + leg + al → **il**legal
irrational	**in** + ration + al → **ir**rational
intelligent	**inter** + lig + ent — **intel**ligent

English owes many of its double letters to the process of total assimilation. If you are having difficulty parsing a word that contains a double letter, do not forget to consider the possibility that the first of the pair may have come from a totally different one through total assimilation. By far the most frequent cases of total assimilation involve the assimilation of the final consonant of a prefix to the first consonant of a root. What are the basic forms of the prefixes in the following words: *syllogism, irradiate?*

Deletion

There are two regular processes of vowel **deletion.** A vowel at the end of a morpheme is frequently deleted when followed by another vowel or *h*. To symbolize the break between morphemes, we will use a plus sign in the rule. Capital V stands for "vowel," and the symbol Ø stands for "zero."

Rule 4. Vowel Deletion
$$V \rightarrow \emptyset / \_\_ + V, h$$

This rule works on the final vowel of a fairly large number of prefixes. It also works on the final vowel of the root before a variety of suffixes:

antagonize	**anti** + agon + ize → **ant**agonize
anode	**ana** + hode → **an**ode*
cathode	**cata** + hode → **cat**hode
cellist	**cello** + ist → **cell**ist
American	**America** + an → **Americ**an

Rule 4 should be distinguished from the spelling rule learned in grammar school, which leaves off the silent vowel *e* when certain suffixes are attached: *nude/nudist,* and so on. Rule 4 deletes from morphemes vowels that are actually pronounced in some allomorphs. The final vowel of the prefix *ana-* is pronounced in the word *analyze*; the final vowel of *cello* is pronounced in this word.

By another rule, a morpheme ending with *er* typically loses the *e* when followed by a vowel-initial morpheme or by a vowel filler. If we use the plus sign to separate morphemes from fillers as well as from other morphemes, the rule will look like this:

Rule 5. Vowel Deletion
$$V \rightarrow \emptyset / r \_\_ + V$$

Here are some examples:

centrist	**center + ist**
acrid	**acer + id**
astrology	**aster + o + log + y**

Insertion

When two roots are combined, a filler vowel is often inserted between them, particularly when it serves to interrupt a consonant sequence. This filler vowel is most often *o* (especially in Greek compounds), sometimes *i* (especially in

---

*The root *hod* 'way' has an allomorph *od* when it follows *n.*

Latinate compounds), and sometimes one of the other vowels. Because the identity of the inserted vowel varies from example to example, we will leave it unspecified in the rule. The rule thus simply says that some vowel, V, is inserted (i.e. it replaces zero) between two morphemes.

> ### Rule 6. Vowel Insertion
> 0 → V / __ + [morpheme]

The following examples illustrate the variety of words in which Rule 6 applies:

pathology	**path** + __ + log + y → **patho**logy
psychopath	**psych** + __ + path → **psycho**path
Sino-Soviet	**Sin** + __ + Soviet → **Sino**-Soviet
paucifloral	**pauc** + __ + flor + al → **pauci**floral
agenda	**ag** + __ + nd + a → **age**nda*

There is another fairly common rule of vowel insertion. According to this rule, the vowel *u* is inserted between a consonant and final *l* in stems followed by a vowel-initial suffix.

> ### Rule 7. *u* Insertion
> 0 → u / __ l + V

Here are some examples:

circular	**circ_le** + ar → **circu**lar
tabulate	**tab_le** + ate → **tabu**late
title	**tit_le** + ar → **titu**lar

Note that Rule 7 does not make provision for the *e* at the end of the words in the right column since it is silent.

PRACTICE ON RULES 1–7

Analyze the following words using the preceding rules to guide your analysis:

correct
triangulate
illicit

---

*See chapter 9.

antagonize
sacrifice
intellect

REGULAR ALLOMORPHY RESTRICTED TO PARTICULAR MORPHEMES

Some allomorphy, although restricted to a few morphemes, is still reasonably orderly because it is predictable from the environment in which it appears. This happens because the original phonetic environment of the historical change that first introduced the allomorph has not been totally obliterated by the passage of time. One such case is **rhotacism** (i.e. the process of making something into an *r*), which changed *s* in a number of Latin morphemes to *r*. In Latin, the final *s* of the word *mūs* 'mouse' changed to *r* before vowels, a change that survives in the Latin-derived English word *murine* 'pertaining to rodents'. A variety of other cases come under the rubrics of **deletion** and **insertion.**

Rhotacism

Rhotacism was named for rho, the Greek letter *r*. Some morphemes with a final *s* change this to *r* if a vowel follows.

> **Rule 8. Rhotacism**
> **s → r / __ V**

Here are some examples:

rustic (rus + t + ic)	rural (**rur** + al)
justice (**jus** + t + ice)	jury (**jur** + y)
agnostic (a + **gnos** + t + ic)	ignorant (i + **gnor** + ant)*

Deletion

Several types of allomorphy involve the deletion of one or more sounds or letters in a morpheme. First of all, there is the loss of morpheme-initial *s* after *ex-*.

---

*The example *ignorant* is interesting but difficult. The prefix *i-* is an idiosyncratic allomorph of *in-* 'not'. The change for *s* to *r*, which requires a vowel according to Rule 8, appears in English even where no vowel remains, and in the word *ignore*, whose final *e* is silent. The reason for this is that the allomorph *gnor* was followed by an actual vowel in Latin.

Rule 9. Extra s Deletion
s → 0 / ex + __

The reason for this is the [s] sound at the end of the prefix *ex-*, which phonetically is [ɛks]. English avoids double consonants—in pronunciation, not in spelling—inside words as tightly joined together as these:

expire   ex + spire → ex**pire**
execrable   ex + **secr** + able → ex**ecr**able
executive   ex + **secu** + t + ive → ex**ecu**tive

Some morphemes lose sounds before certain endings. Before the noun-forming suffix *-sis*, the final alveolar consonant (e.g. *t* or *s*) of a root is often lost. If the root is accompanied by a filler, it is the final consonant of the filler that is lost.

Rule 10. C Deletion
C → 0 / __ + sis

Here are some examples:

crisis   crit + sis → **cri**sis
osmosis   osmot + sis → **osmo**sis
diagnosis   dia + **gnos** + sis → dia**gno**sis
kinesis   kin + **et** + sis → **kine**sis

Insertion

There are two main cases in which an allomorph is formed by adding a filler to a root. Many Latinate verb roots have a longer allomorph created by the addition of *t*.

Rule 11. t Insertion
0 → t / Root __

Here are some examples:

convention   con + **ven** + ion → con**vent**ion
mental   men + al → **men**tal

crypt	cryph → **cryph** + t → **crypt**＊
capture	cap + ure → **cap**ture
receptive	re + **cep** + ive → re**cept**ive

The same root, **cap,** is involved in the last two examples. We saw in chapter 4 that some roots have an alternation between *a, e,* and *i. Cap* is one: *captive, receptive, recipient.* In the last example above, the allomorph *cep* acquires the filler *t.* Thus we see that allomorphs can have allomorphs of their own!

Greek roots ending in the letters *-m, -ma,* and *-me* have an allomorph in *-mat* when a vowel follows in the word. Since the letters *-me* are pronounced the same as *-m* in English, we can reduce these two cases to one in the following rule:

> ### Rule 12 . Greek *mat* Formation
> **m, ma → mat / __ + V**

The following forms illustrate the rule:

traumatic	**trauma** + ic → **traumat**ic
dramaturge	**drama** + urge → **dramat**urge
symptomatology	**symptom** + o + log + y → **symptomat**ology
traumatic	**trauma** + ic → **traumat**ic
theme	**theme** + ic → **themat**ic
scheme	**scheme** + ic → **schemat**ic

In the second example, the morpheme *urge* is an allomorph of the root *erg/urg/ org* 'work'.

OTHER SOUND CHANGES

The sound *d* at the end of dozens of Latinate roots becomes *s* (in a few cases *ss*) before certain vowel-initial endings—usually *-ive, -ion,* and *-ible.*

> ### Rule 13. *d* to *s*
> **d → s / __ + ive, ion, ible**

＊Note that this root changes the fricative [f] to [p].

Here are some examples:

elude	e + **lud** + ive → e**lus**ive
comprehensible	com + pre + **hend** + ible → compre**hens**ible
concession	con + **ced** + ion → con**cess**ion
procession	pro + **ced** + ion → pro**cess**ion

The same root **ced** is involved in the last two examples, even though there is a spelling difference in the basic verb, *concede* vs. *proceed*.

A similar change is from root-final *t* to *s* or *ss*, which happens with two Latin-derived morphemes:

> **Rule 14. *t* to *s* and *ss***
> mit → miss / __ + ive, ion, ible
> sent→ sens / __ + ive, ual

Here are some examples:

emission	e + **mit** + ion → e**miss**ion
missive	**mit** + ive → **miss**ive
sensual	**sent** + ual → **sens**ual
sensitive	**sent** + ive → **sens**itive

In the last example, *sent* acquires the filler *it* before *-ive*. It is not clear in this case whether it is the ending *-ive* or the filler *it* that triggers the **sent→ sens** rule.

A handful of Latinate morphemes ending in *v* change the *v* to *u* before a *t* filler:

> **Rule 15. *v* to *u***
> nav → nau /
> cav → cau / __ t +
> solv → solu /
> etc.

Here are some examples:

nautical	**nav** + ical → **nau**tical
caution	**cav** + ion → **cau**tion
dissolute	dis + **solv** + te → dis**solu**te
salutary	**salv** + ary → **salut**ary

The basic form of the root *cav* in *caution* can be seen in *caveat,* and the basic form of the root *salv* is found in *salvation.*

The fillers *s* and *t* also trigger vowel changes in Latinate morphemes:

> **Rule 16. *el* and *ol* to *ul***
>
> **el, ol → ul / __ s,t +**

Here are some examples:

compulsive	com + **pel** + ive → com**pul**sive
cultivate	col + ive + ate → **cul**tivate

The basic form of the root *pel* in *compulsive* can be seen in *compel,* and the basic form *col* from *cultivate* and *culture* occurs in *colony.*

PREFIX ALLOMORPHY

Several changes apply to individual prefixes.

> **Rule 17. Prefix Allomorphy**
>
> **ab- → abs- / __ t, c**
>
> **an- → a- / __ C** (not **h**)
>
> **re- → red- / __ V** (in a few roots)
>
> **se- → sed- / __ V** (in a few roots)
>
> **syn- → sy- / __ s**

Here are some examples:

abstract	**ab** + trac + t → **abs**tract
abscess	**ab** + cess → **abs**cess
redundant	**re** + und + ant → **red**undant
sedition	**se** + it + ion → **sed**ition
system	**syn** + stem → **sys**tem
systolic	**syn** + stol + ic → **sys**tolic

Our final example of prefix allomorphy is more complicated, and so we will deal with it separately. The prefix *ex-/e-/ec-* originated from two separate (though ultimately related) sources. The Greek prefix meaning 'out, away' is *ec-* and does not change. The Latin prefix *ex-* becomes *e-* before *b, d, g, v, j, l, r, m,* and *n* (all of them voiced consonants).

> *Rule 18. ex- to e-*
>
> **ex- → e- / __ b, d, g, v, j, l, r, m, n** (i.e. voiced consonants)

Here are examples of *ex-*, *e-*, and *ec-* in English words:

extract	**ex** + trac + t → **ex**tract (no change)
exact	**ex** + act → **ex**act (no change)
evade	**ex** + vade → **e**vade
emit	**ex** + mit → **e**mit
ecstasy	**ec** + stas + y → **ec**stasy (no change)
eczema	**ec** + zem + a→ **ec**zema (no change)

PRACTICE ON RULES 8–18

Analyze the following words using the preceding rules to guide your analysis:

redemption
salutary
abrasive
evasion
emblematize
impulse

NUMERAL MORPHEMES; DISTINGUISHING BETWEEN LATIN AND GREEK MORPHEMES

The numeral morphemes of Latin and Greek are among the commonest found in English words. Most of them are already familiar to you. Their use illustrates the tendency to combine Latin morphemes with other Latin morphemes and Greek morphemes with other Greek morphemes. For example, with the root *gon* 'angle' which comes from Greek, we use the Greek numeral morpheme *penta* 'five' in *pentagon* 'a five-sided geometrical figure'. But with the root *lat* 'side' (also: 'wide, broad'), which comes from Latin, we use the Latin numeral morpheme *quadr* 'four' in *quadrilateral* 'a four-sided geometrical figure'. Morphemes often occur with others from the same source language simply because we have borrowed the entire word from that language. The word *pentagon*, for example, originated in Greek; it wasn't first coined in English from Greek roots. Words that are coined anew in English frequently violate the tendency for a word's morphemes to be monolingual in origin. The word *monolingual* itself is a violation, as it is composed of *mono* 'one' [Gk] and *lingua* 'tongue' [L]. Other examples of this kind of 'mixing' are *neonate* [L, Gk], *amoral* [Gk, L], *dysfunction* [Gk, L] and *posthypnotic* [L, Gk].

These 'violations' are perfectly valid words, but it is useful to be aware of the strong tendency for words with roots from a given language to contain other morphemes from that language. There are some signs that will tell you when a prefix or root morpheme is Greek rather than Latinate. The best clues are the presence in one of the roots you know or encounter of

- a y̲ as in *hyper-, hypo-, myc, crypt/cryph, myo, onym, pachy,* etc.
- a k̲ as in *kilo, kerat, deka* (often spelled *deca*), *kin,* etc.
- a z̲ as in *zyg, zym,* etc.
- the combinations r̲h̲, p̲h̲, t̲h̲, c̲h̲ and (pronounced [k], not [č]) as in *rh, rrh, rrhag, rhin; pher, phor, troph, taph; he, esth, sthen, path, arch, chrom, chrys,* etc.
- an initial cluster beginning with p̲, such as
  p̲s̲, ([ps] in Greek, z in English) as in *psych, psitt, pseudo,* etc.
  p̲t̲, as in *pter, pto, pty,* etc.
  p̲n̲ as in *pne, pneu,* etc.
- an initial x̲ ([ks] in Greek, [z] in English) as in *xyl, xen, xer,* etc.
- an initial h̲ as in *hex, hept, hydr, heli,* etc. (with a few common exceptions, including Latinate *hes/her, hom,* and *hum*).

Almost without exception, if a root has one of these characteristics it is Greek in origin and will typically (though by no means always) combine with other Greek morphemes. Latinate morphemes provide a few clues to their origin as well. Generally, a morpheme in complex scholarly or scientific vocabulary cannot be Greek (and hence is probably Latinate) if it contains

- an f̲ as in *fer, fa, ferr,* etc.
- a v̲ as in *voc, cav, ven, ov, vin, ver, vid,* etc. (*vok* is an English respelling Latinate *voc.*).
- a q̲u̲ as in *qual, quant, quart, quadr, squam, equ, iqu, loqu,* etc.

The numeral morphemes are widely used. They usually precede the root they modify (or 'count' or 'order') as for example in *universe* 'whole' (literally: 'turned [into] one') and *sesquipedalian* 'one and a half feet long' (used of very long words). They are not, strictly speaking, prefixes, since they can occur without another root, as for example in *dual* and *monad*, in which *-al* and *-ad* are suffixes.

Latin	Greek	Meaning
un, sim	hen, mono	one
primo	proto	first
di, du, bi, bis	dich, dy, do	two
second, secund	deuter	second
tri, tris, ter	tri, tris, trich	three
quater, quart, quadr	tetra, tessara	four
quint	pent(a)	five
sex	hex	six
sept, septen	hept	seven
octo, octav	octo, okto	eight
noven, non	ennea	nine
dec, decem, deca	deca, deka	ten
	dodeca	twelve
	tris <u>kai</u> deka	three <u>and</u> ten (13)
vig/viginti/vic		twenty, a score
cent	hecto, hekto, hecato, hekato	hundred
mille	kilo, chilio	thousand
	mega	million
	giga [in computerese]	billion (10^9)
	(from *giga* 'giant')	
	tera [in computerese]	trillion (10^{12})
	(from *tera* 'monster')	
plur, mult	poly, myri	many
tot	omni, pan	all
pauc		few
semi, demi	hemi, hapl [< ha + ple 'half fold']	half
sesqui		one and a half
	dipl [<di + ple 'two fold']	double
ambi	amphi	both
	-ad	made up of a quantity of something (e.g. *dyad* 'group of two', *chiliad* 'group of 1,000')

WORDS FOR VERY SMALL AND VERY LARGE SIZES AND QUANTITIES

The words for very large numerals generally consist of a Latin numeral morpheme for an integer and the suffix *-illion*. Their use requires one small note. As a result of the independent development of science in the United Kingdom and the United States over the last two hundred years, there has been a split in usage of terms for the higher order numerals. The break occurs after the one million mark, counting upwards. In Britain (which is like continental Europe in this regard) for the numeral 10^9 (U.S. *billion*), either the word *milliard* or the phrase *thousand million* is used.

-on, -illion	large unit
million	10^6
[milliard], thousand million	[UK: 10^9]
billion	10^9 [UK: 10^{12}]
trillion	10^{12} [UK: 10^{18}]
quadrillion	10^{15} [UK: 10^{24}]
quintillion	10^{18} ...etc...
sextillion	10^{21}
septillion	10^{24}
octillion	10^{27}
nonillion	10^{30}
decillion	10^{33}
undecillion	10^{36}
duodecillion	10^{39}

[The prefixed number signifies the number of sets of three zeros over 1,000; e.g. <u>tri</u>llion = 1,000,<u>000,000,000</u>; <u>sex</u>tillion = 1,000,<u>000,000,000,000,000,000</u>]

cent(i)	hundredth
milli [symbol: m]	thousandth, 10^{-3}
micro [symbol: μ]	millionth, 10^{-6}
nano	billionth, 10^{-9}
pico [symbol: p]	trillionth, 10^{-12}

See appendix II for Morpheme set 5.

EXERCISES

1.i. In all but two of the following words, the last letter of the prefix has been assimilated to the first sound of the root. What is the original (i.e. unassimilated) form of the prefix in each word? (Use a dictionary to check your answers.)

ii. For each word, indicate whether the final consonant of the prefix has been completely assimilated to the initial consonant of the next morpheme or only partially. In each case say what phonetic characteristics of the final consonant of the prefix have changed as a result of assimilation to the consonant that follows it.

a. impossible	d. corrupt	g. effect	j. infect	m. suffer
b. irrelevant	e. embed	h. immemorial	k. annotate	n. opposition
c. committ	f. illegible	i. occlude	l. assimilate	o. submit

2. Analyze the following words using the rules in this chapter to guide your analysis:

a. constabular
b. rectitude
c. genesis

d. explosion
e. expect
f. abscond

3. The following examples were used in this chapter to illustrate the loss of *s* after *ex-:*

ex + **spire** → ex**pire**
ex + **secr** + able → ex**ecr**able
ex + **secu** + t + ive → ex**ecu**tive

Give examples of words in which these roots appear with their initial *s*. What is the meaning of each root?

4. What are the meanings of the boldface morphemes in these words, which appeared as examples in this chapter? For each word, find another word in which this boldface morpheme occurs. The morpheme may or may not have a different allomorph.

a. red**und**ant
b. im**mut**able
c. col**lude**

f. dia**gnos**is
g. con**vent**ion
h. **crypt**

d. an**od**e   i. **naut**ical
e. **cris**is   j. **cult**ivate

5. For each of these words, change the boldface morpheme into one that will take a different allomorph for the prefix. For example, (a) could change by replacing **und** with **pent,** to give *repentant.*

   a. red**und**ant
   b. im**mut**able
   c. col**lude**
   d. an**od**e
   e. syl**log**ism
   f. ir**radi**ate
   g. con**vent**ion

6. What <u>series</u> of two or more individual changes (including assimilations or other changes in the place or manner of articulation) would account for the common pronunciation of the consonant sequences which we write c͟c͟ and g͟g͟ in the words *succeed* [səksid] (from *sub-* + *ceed*) and *suggest* [səgjɛst] (from *sub-* + *gest*)? (Hint: the morphemes *ceed* and *gest* originally had 'hard' c͟ and g͟ (i.e. [k] and [g]) sounds. Keep in mind that front vowels are produced by constriction of the tongue near the alveopalatal region of the mouth and that certain vowels may significantly change the pronunciation of nearby consonants.)

7. Coin adjectives for the following definitions using the numeral morphemes in this chapter and other roots you have learned up to this point. Some of the words you will create may be found in the dictionary, others may not. Don't try to capture every bit of the meaning of the definition in the actual morphemes of the term you coin; a prefix and a root or two should be sufficient. Try to restrict yourself to only Latin or only Greek morphemes within each word.

   a. Outside the priesthood.   _____al
   b. Having the head of a human.   _____ic
   c. Having a different origin.   _____ic
   d. Having six heads.   _____ic
   e. Occurring every 20 years.   _____ial
   f. Governed by a two-member group.   _____ic
   g. Having a hundred angles.   _____al

    h. Having three gods.   _____istic

    i. Having three letters.   _____al

    j. Having two feet.   _____al

8. The word *semester* contains two roots (a numeral and one other), both of which are heavily disguised, idiosyncratic allomorphs of the forms shown in the glossary. (Hint: It does not contain the numeral *semi*.) What are the forms and meanings of these roots as given in the glossary? Use the etymological notes in a dictionary entry for the word *semester* to provide the answer.

9. What do the numeral morphemes in the words *pentateuch, decalogue,* and *deuteronomy* 'count'? (E.g. in the word *tritium,* the *tri* 'three' counts isotopes; *tritium* is the third possible isotope of hydrogen.) Use the dictionary entry on the origins and definitions of these words for the answer.

10. Parse (using slashes and parentheses) and give all glosses and allomorphs you have learned. Primary (') and secondary (') stresses are marked to aid in pronunciation and recognition of the word.

a.   héctolìter

GLOSS   _____   _____'liter'_____

ALLOMORPHS   _____

b.   mèr(it)ócracy

GLOSS   _____'deserve'_____   _____

ALLOMORPHS   _____

c.   tètrálogy

GLOSS   _____

ALLOMORPHS   _____

d.   prìmogén(it)ure

GLOSS   _____NOUN

ALLOMORPHS   _____   _____

e.   inflátionàry [note: <u>in-</u> isn't 'not']

GLOSS   _____

ALLOMORPHS   _____

f.   perámbulàte [note: <u>per-</u> isn't <u>peri-</u>]

GLOSS   _____

ALLOMORPHS   _____

11. The following words from the fields of literature and rhetoric contain several morphemes you may not yet have encountered in the course. With the help of an unabridged dictionary (like *Webster's Third New International Dictionary,* which includes almost 500,000 entries), and/or a specialized dictionary of literary or rhetorical terms,* and using a glossary or dictionary of roots, give a brief definition for and parse and gloss each term. (Note: No glossary contains all the roots used in English words, so you might have to look in more than one place.) For example:

  catacosmesis: Opposite of *climax.* A downward ordering or arrangement of words in a list (e.g. in the motto *for god, country and Yale*).

cata	cosm	(e)	sis
'down'	'order'		N [action or result]

a. synaeresis   b. metanoia   c. informatio   d. cacozelia
e. stichomythia   f. aposiopesis   g. variatio   h. paronomasia

---

*One of several useful books for this purpose is *A Handbook of Rhetorical Terms: A Guide for Students of English Literature,* by Richard A. Lanham (Berkeley: University of California Press, 1968).

7
Polysemy and Semantic Change

MULTIPLE MEANINGS AND SHIFTS IN MEANING

So far we have been mostly concerned with various kinds of allomorphy, that is, with changes in the <u>forms</u> of the morphemes we encounter in English words. Now we will consider some additional aspects of <u>meaning</u> in the elements of English vocabulary. Mastering both allomorphy (variation in form) and **polysemy** (multiplicity of meanings) will make you much better able to <u>recognize the components</u> and <u>interpret the meaning</u> of unfamiliar words.

We have already seen many cases of polysemy, as when we had to deal with the multiplicity of meanings for morphemes like *macro* -'long, large' and *path* 'feel, suffer, illness'. It is important to understand the difference between polysemy and **homonymy.** In both, the same word form is said to have two (or more) different meanings, but in homonymy those meanings are not related except by accident. The words *ring* 'jewelry worn around the finger' and *ring* 'to make a bell sound' are completely unconnected except by the accident of sharing a single form. (Incidentally, there was a time in their history when the sources of these two words were distinct in both sound and meaning.) Similarly, you have encountered pairs of homonymous morphemes in the case of *in-* (one of two allomorphs) 'in, into' and *in-* 'not'. There are even triplets of homonymous morphemes in English, such as those with the form *liber*, which has the distinct meanings 'weigh, consider' (as in *deliberate*), 'book' (as in *library*) and 'free' (as in *liberate*). In this book, homonyms are listed as separate items in the morpheme lists and glossary, while polysemy is indicated by giving more than one meaning beside a single form. The focus of this chapter is polysemy, which is much more common than homonymy and a greater challenge to the student of English vocabulary.

One group of morphemes whose variety of meanings we have more or less left our readers to unravel for themselves is the suffixes, which have a kind of rudimentary polysemy. We noted that some suffixes, like *-ous* and *-ary,* primarily dictate the part of speech of the word on which they occur. Some, however, contribute more to the meaning of a word. For example, *-oid* signifies not only that the word on which it occurs is an adjective or noun, but also that the thing described by the word *resembles* the thing described in the root. In this way, we understand that something (say a planet), is a *spheroid* because it is like, or resembles, a (geometric) sphere. (Astronomers say that many planets are spheroids rather than spheres; they are not perfectly round but actually somewhat pear-shaped.) Similarly, a *humanoid* (a creature familiar from science fiction which, while not biologically human, looks more or less like a human being) is 'something resembling a human'. So, we might say that the meaning of *-oid* is 'resembling N, thing resembling N' (i.e. it marks a word as either an adjective or a noun). The fact that *-oid* can be used to form both nouns like *spheroid* and adjectives such as *deltoid* 'shaped like the symbol Δ (the Greek letter delta)' can be considered a kind of polysemy as well. Many adjectives are extended to use as nouns. (Compare the occasional use of a word like *pretty* as a noun, as in *come here, my pretty*). In the case of *-oid,* the noun-marking function has now largely replaced the adjective-marking one.

Like *-oid,* most suffixes in English are polysemous. In fact, the suffix *-ous* itself is one of these. It can mean 'having ROOT N', as in *polysemous* ('having polysemy') and *glamorous,* 'characterized by', as in *gracious* ('characterized by grace') and *joyous,* 'practicing ROOT N' as in *exogamous* ('practicing exogamy, i.e. marriage outside a defined social group'). It can have other adjectival meanings as well. The adjective suffix *-ic/-tic* has a whole range of senses; 'causing ROOT N' *(analgesic);* 'consisting of ROOT N' *(runic);* 'like ROOT N' *(angelic);* 'characterized by ROOT N' *(panoramic).* (Other senses include 'with ROOT N', 'connected with ROOT N', 'characteristic of ROOT N', 'of ROOT N', 'belonging to ROOT N'.)

For most suffixes (which because of their commonness are generally quite familiar to anyone with a basic knowledge of English), it is not necessary to list the full range of possible meanings here. These can almost always be understood from the context in which the word occurs. Here is a test of your ability not only to gather the meaning but to determine variants of pronunciation of a suffix which is used to form adjectives, nouns, and verbs. What is the part of speech of the word with the *-ate* suffix in each of the following sentences? How is the suffix pronounced in each case?

a. I **advocate** the abolition of television. [*ad-* 'to, toward'; *voc* 'speak, call']
b. I am an **advocate** of equal rights for women.
c. He will **delegate** authority to his subordinates.
d. He was a **delegate** to the convention.
e. Joe was **desolate** when Pete left us.
f. They will **desolate** the city.

As you can see, adjectives and nouns in *-ate* are generally pronounced to rhyme with *cut*, while verbs in *-ate* usually rhyme with *mate*.

The morphemes *-ance/-ence*, *-ancy/-ency*, *-sis*, and *-ion* are examples of suffixes with relatively little polysemy. These all share something close to the single meaning 'action of ROOT V' as in the words *pre-sid-ency*, *ana-ly-sis*, and *bene-dict-ion*. (In some words, such as *penance* and *latency*, this may not be as readily apparent since English has not borrowed the Latin verbs (meaning 'to repent' and 'to lie') from which these nouns were derived.)

In prefixes and roots, polysemy is not usually quite so broad as in the case of suffixes like *-ous*, but it does involve some special *shifts in meaning* which are not quite so easy to determine from context without understanding a few basic rules. As with some kinds of allomorphy we have discussed, polysemy in roots and prefixes is often the result of historical processes of change. Just as we undo some of the effects of sound change or phonological rules when we identify *cand* (in *candle*) and *chand* (in *chandelier*) or *fac* (in *factor*) and *fec* (in *defect*) as pairs of allomorphs belonging to the same morpheme, we can undo the effects of **semantic shift** or **change** (i.e. shift or change in meaning) to get at the underlying relationship of the different meanings of a given morpheme in actual usage.

We have already seen cases of the polysemy which results from semantic change many times, as when we had to deal with the multiplicity of meanings for various roots. You don't need much imagination to see the relationships between the different meanings, in e.g.

macro-	'long', 'large'
path	'feel', 'suffer', 'illness'
extra-	'outside', 'additional'

But what about the morpheme *cosm*, which can mean 'universe' as in *cosmos*, 'world' and in *microcosm*, or 'ornament' as in *cosmetic*. Should we have separated this into two or even three separate morphemes, each with a separate meaning, and not worry that they have the same form? This is certainly necessary with the semantically distinct but formally identical prefixes *in-* 'in' and *in-* 'not'. We believe it more useful to treat *cosm* as a single polysemous morpheme, however, because we know that the student can roughly reconstruct the process by which this polysemy came about historically. The change in meaning in *cosm* arose in ancient Greek, where the word *kosmos* (Greek used no <u>c</u> in spelling) originally meant 'order', and then came to mean 'that which is ordered'—i.e. the universe or the world—a systematic and ordered whole, at least in the Greek world view. Finally, *cosm* occurred in words in which it meant '<u>well</u> ordered', '<u>properly</u> arranged'. From this we have English *cosmetic* 'giving a proper appearance (because of being properly arranged or put together)'. Another case of this type is *troch* which means 'run' in *trochaic* (an adjective used of a poetic meter based on a certain type of 'running' foot) and 'wheel' in *trochoid* 'revolving on an axis (like a wheel)'. Here, *troch* originally just meant 'run' but eventually came to be applied to the most essential component of a 'running' vehicle, its wheels.

In the gloss of the root *fac* (and its allomorphs *fec* and *fic*), we concentrate on the senses 'do' or 'make'. Of course not every occurrence of the sequence of letters that resembles a morpheme is an actual occurrence of that morpheme (cf. false parsings like that of *helicopter* as *heli* 'sun' – *copter* '??' instead of the correct parsing *helic(o)* 'spiral' – *pter* 'wing'/'flight'). Take the example of *efface*. Knowing that *efface* contains the prefix *ex-* (where the <u>x</u> assimilates to the first consonant of the root), and the familiar root *fac* 'face' found in *face, facial, deface,* and so on, it might seem improbable that we have one morpheme *fac* with as broad a range of meanings as 'do'/'make' and 'face'.

In **etymological** terms (i.e. in regard to the actual history of words), however, it is true. *Face* and *efface* are historically related to *fact* and *effect*. But what semantic connection is there between 'do'/'make' and 'face'? The answer is that it is an indirect connection which came about via one meaning of *fac*: the verbal meaning 'to <u>make</u> into a particular form' or 'to shape'. *Fac* in *face* therefore originally meant 'form'; the meaning 'external or <u>surface</u> form' is merely a more restricted sense of 'form'.

When we are not aware of such historical relationships we resort to the operating principle that the relationship of the various meanings of what is identified as a single morpheme should be fairly transparent. But what is transparent to one person may not be transparent to another. Being able to unravel polysemy may then become a matter of individual imagination or additional knowledge. We can sometimes economize on the number of separate morphemes we must learn by gathering as many keys to related meanings as possible from whatever sources are available. You should soon be able to create many mental 'lines of association' when learning new morphemes and the meaning they contribute to the words in which they occur. You will then be able to understand relationships which, although sometimes initially unclear, can make sense with some extra thought. In other words, etymology should be a guide when it is useful, but not a tyrant to which the language (or an effective understanding of it) must bend.

REASONS FOR SEMANTIC SHIFT

In order to understand the kind of semantic change which leads to polysemy, consider first why meaning should change at all.

Errors and Misinterpretation

In certain situations, a speaker may be unable to communicate his/her intention perfectly. A well-known example is involved in the history of the word *bead*. Originally, *bead* meant 'prayer'. Because, however, one counted the small spherical objects on a rosary as a way of keeping track of the number of times one said a particular prayer, one who was counting prayers could also be seen counting the objects on the rosary's string. Similarly, the word *since* originally meant 'after', but because effects are ordinarily seen to follow causes in time (as in *Since Jim came Mary left*), the word came to mean 'because' as well.

Creative Variation

In literature, folk speech, slang, and other realms of language use in which creativity and the avoidance of hackneyed phrases or cliché are at a premium, we seek to adapt words to new uses as a way of maintaining fresh and lively discourse and displaying our skill with language. Words like *cool, slick,* and *heavy,* for example, have been extended to cover not just physical attributes but also aspects of personality, mood, and esthetics.

Abbreviation

The need to express oneself quickly and efficiently often leads to a situation in which one word comes to carry the burden of a longer phrase of which it is a part. Ellipsis or 'dropping out' of the word *doma* from the longer Greek phrase *doma kuriakon* 'house of the Lord' leads to the source of the English words *kirk* (found in dialects of Scotland), and (after some more substantial sound changes) *church*. A similar process has occurred in the case of *daily* (paper).

Change in the Things Named

Sometimes meanings are extended or changed less for linguistic reasons than because the object that the word once described has itself changed. As we noted in chapter 3, a *ship* was once only a vessel for use on large bodies of water, but today can be a flying machine (or airship) or vessel for interplanetary travel (a spaceship). Likewise, the word *pen* (which originally meant 'feather' or 'quill pen') has a range of meanings because of such changes in writing technology since the eighteenth century as the invention of the steel nib and the fountain, ballpoint, and felt tip pen.

The Finite Word Stock

Ultimately, the most important single reason for extending and multiplying the meanings of words is that the number of vocabulary items we have to work with is relatively small, compared to the infinite variety of the things we need to say. We have to use an inherently limited body of terms to discuss things of almost unlimited complexity and bend them to accommodate a wealth of new ideas, events, and entities. We have three choices: make new words, use longer phrases, or extend the duties of existing words. The first option is not employed as often as the second; the second is often cumbersone. But people extend the meanings of words quite frequently. One such extension of meaning has appeared just in the last generation or so in the speech of younger Americans. This is the case of the word *guy*. Until quite recently, this word was applied only to males (e.g. in the title of the musical, *Guys and Dolls*) while today a young woman might well say to a group of her female friends *I really like you guys*. One could say in the case of *guy* either that the meaning has changed from 'male' to 'human' or that to the meaning 'male' has been added a second one 'female'. (Interestingly, before it was used to mean 'male person', *guy* was just a man's proper name, *Guy*.)

Cases where extending a word's meaning either leads to polysemy or disguises the original, basic meaning are the most problematic. For example, some developments of meaning for the word *horse* over roughly a thousand years are shown in table 7.1.

Table 7.1 Stages in the History of the Word *Horse*

time period	meaning
9th cent. (earliest record in OE)–present	'the animal species *equus caballus* or a member of that species'
16th cent.–present	'the constellation *Pegasus* (the Flying Horse of Greek mythology)'
16th cent.–present	'cavalry soldiers'
18th cent.–present	'four-legged structure on which something is supported (e.g. for sawing)'

In each case it seems that when the meaning was extended, the oldest meaning was still somehow involved, since each extension was derived from it. Therefore, we can think of the meaning of *horse* by the eighteenth century roughly as represented in figure 7.1, where both the range of current meanings and their paths of development are shown by the arrows from the oldest meaning to the later ones.

Sometimes, however, an original basic meaning is lost, leaving only extended meanings which are hard to trace to the original sense. This is the case with the word *commit*, which in Latin originally meant 'send together' (which shouldn't be surprising in light of the meanings of its component morphemes, *con-* and *mit.*) After time, however (in Latin and French and, after it was borrowed, in English), this word took on a broad range of other senses, many of which disguise the original one. These meanings include such wide-ranging notions as 'entrust' (as in *commit someone to a doctor's care*), 'perpetrate' (as in *commit a crime*) and, most recently, 'promise to involve (oneself)' (as in *commit (oneself) to a relationship*).

As figure 7.2 shows, the situation with *commit* is quite different from that of *horse. Commit* never meant 'send together' in English. The gap between this original Latin meaning and the others is quite wide and the relationships among these are vague. This may be because there were other, intermediate meanings that do not survive but that acted as bases for those that do. All in

Figure 7.1. Developments of the Meaning of *Horse*

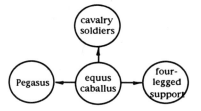

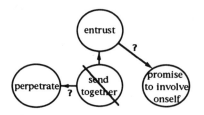

Figure 7.2. Developments of the Meaning of *Commit*

all, it is impossible to state a single basic meaning for the word *commit* today. In addition, it is also hard to contend that *con-* invariably means 'together' or 'with' or that *mit* always means 'send' or 'do'.

In a case like *commit*, knowledge of the original meaning of a word or its morphemes offers at best only slight assistance. But this is not as big a problem as it might at first seem. Most people are so familiar with words like *commit* that they don't need to analyze them. These are common words which in practice present little difficulty. It is also comforting to note that such vague relationships between the various senses of a word are not typical of specialized scholarly, technical, and scientific vocabulary, the bulk of which is of fairly recent vintage and has therefore had little time to undergo really radical transformations of meaning. Finally, even when we do have to deal with meaning shifts, we find that most of them can be understood fairly easily, and many are so obvious that they scarcely have to be mentioned. With a few basic rules, you can learn to reconstruct semantic changes fairly easily.

PATHS OF SEMANTIC SHIFT

Generally speaking, some kind of **association** is involved in every semantic shift. We accept the associations between the different meanings of the morphemes *macro-* ('long', 'large') or *path* ('feel', 'suffer', 'illness') with little or no difficulty. The precise nature of the association usually falls into one of two categories. The first is the extension of a word to something which somehow resembles the thing originally designated by that word in either its <u>form</u> or its <u>function</u>. This kind of change is based on **metaphor** (a notion probably familiar to you from literature or poetry), and is called **metaphoric shift.** The second category is reserved for cases of association based not on resemblance but on some other connection, often in physical space, time, or the relationship of cause and effect. This kind of change is based on **metonymy** and is called **metonymic shift.**

Metaphor

Metaphor often involves extension from one physical object to another which resembles it in some respect, as when we use the word *leaf* to refer to a page in a book. (We know that this use is later than *leaf* (of a plant) because books are more recent, and in some sense less basic than plants. This was even truer for the typical unlettered speaker of ancient Old English.) Metaphor is clearly involved in the extensions of meaning in at least some of the cases with the word *horse* (discussed previously) as well as in the polysemy of the word *foot*, whose first use in reference to the *foot* of a mountain or of a bed was the result of the application of a metaphor in which it is understood to mean 'the bottom or end of a long or tall object' rather than the more basic 'lowest extremity of an animal/human'. These changes are represented in figure 7.3.

Metaphor can also involve a shift from the concrete (i.e. physical) to the abstract (i.e. intangible, conceptual). A metaphoric shift is apparent if we take apart the word *understand*, which at first literally meant 'stand below'. The figurative usage involved the image of being 'covered' by an idea. (Compare the colloquial expression *to get behind* meaning 'to support or agree with'.) Likewise, the words *comprehend, apprehend,* and *grasp* are all extended metaphorically to express the 'seizing' of something intellectually. Similarly, when we speak of *shelving* an old idea, we are using the metaphor of putting aside some useless physical object (like an out-of-date book) in reference to an idea, an abstract thing.

The **spatial metaphor** is essential to extension of meaning in human language. Most of the prefixes taught in this course are spatial in their basic sense, but in most uses are metaphorically extended to express nonspatial meanings. Examples are provided in table 7.2. (The abbreviation *lit.* means 'literally'.)

Figure 7.3. Metaphoric Relationships for *Horse* and *Foot*

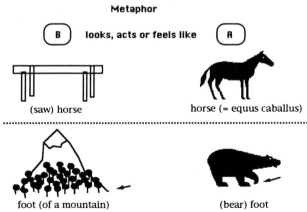

Table 7.2 Metaphoric Extensions of Meaning of Spatial Prefixes

Prefix	Spatial Sense	Use in Extended Sense
de-	down, away	negative—*despair:* lack hope [lit. hope away]
		intensive—*declare:* make totally clear [lit. clarify away]
	in reverse	undo an action—*de-emphasize:* reduce emphasis upon [lit. emphasize in reverse]
pre-	in front of, forth	earlier—*precocious:* matured early [lit. cooked in front of]
sub-	below, under	as part—*subsume:* take in as member of a larger unit [lit. take under]
		open or exposed to—*subject:* bring into sphere of influence [lit. thrown below]
per-	through	thorough, strong—*pertinacious:* believing thoroughly [lit. hold through]
ex-	out, away	open, visible—*expose:* render visible or open [lit. put out]
		not included—*except:* exclude or bar [lit. take out, take away]
ob-	towards, against, down	negative, destructive—*obloquy:* abusive language [lit. speak against]
extra-	outside	beyond, not—*extraordinary* unusual [lit. beyond (the) ordinary, not ordinary]

In each case here, the meaning has been extended in at least one way, but generally in a manner that still allows you to see the source meaning which lies behind the extended one.

Metaphor is the commonest kind of semantic shift. It is used so frequently that we often have to qualify what we are saying to indicate that we are <u>not</u> speaking metaphorically. When we say something like *His heart stopped with fright* we are expected to be speaking metaphorically, and we can only cancel out this expectation by adding the word *literally* if we wish to communicate that death was the actual result of the fright.

Metonymy

Metonymy is a shift in meaning from one thing to something connected with that thing, though it doesn't actually resemble it. For example, in nineteen forties slang one might call a woman a *skirt.* The use of the word *pulp* to refer to a certain kind of magazine (and the kind of literature found in such magazines) of the 1930s through 1950s was a metonymic shift of the word's use as the name for the material out of which such magazines were made to that of the magazines themselves. When we talk of the *throne,* meaning the person who sits on it (i.e. a queen or king), we use a metonymic shift. Wheat, as its sounds may vaguely suggest to you, took its name from one of its parts or, more properly, one of its characteristics—its lightness of color or <u>whiteness</u>. Other examples of metonymy include the use of a word like *youth* to refer to an individual or group of young people, calling a soldier who wears a red coat a *Redcoat,* or referring to a language as a *tongue.* As these examples show, the connection involved in a metonymic change can be of almost any kind other than resemblance, including such things as **source ↔ product** and **person/ thing ↔ characteristic/possession.**

Synecdoche is often considered a special kind of metonymy in which the name for an entire thing (or collection of things) comes to be used for a part (or individual in a collection), or vice versa. An example is the use of *hand* to mean 'workman'. When someone says 'the *cops* arrested John for hitchhiking' he may well have been picked up by only a single cop. Metonymy and synecdoche are often confusingly similar and some shifts are hard to place firmly in either group.

A kind of language-internal metonymy is **sound contamination,** which takes place when words that resemble each other in sound come to have common meanings. We have recently heard *heart rendering* used in place of an older *heart rending* (i.e. 'tearing'). This is not unreasonable if 'render' is taken to mean 'melt' (rather than an earlier meaning, 'change') as in *to render fat.* In this example semantic change results not from one word adopting a new meaning but rather from two different words coming to have the same or similar meaning and form.

OUTCOMES OR RESULTS OF SEMANTIC SHIFT

A frequent result of semantic change is **narrowing** (also called **specialization**). This involves the restriction of a word to a subset of the things it originally denoted. Thus, the word *deer* which now refers to a particular well-known type of animal has narrowed its meaning. As recently as the seventeenth century (i.e. Shakespeare's time) the word referred to an animal of any sort. Another example of narrowing is *adder,* which meant 'snake' in Old English and in Middle English but now refers only to a few varieties of snake.

The opposite result of change is also common. **Widening** (also called **generalization**) involves the extension of a word to a class of meanings which is in some sense a superset of its original meanings. The Old French ancestor of the word *arrive* comes from the Latin prefix *ad-* and the root *ripa > rive* 'shore'. (The symbol > means 'becomes'. Note that a river, in one sense, is 'the water between two close shores.') This original word, meaning 'to come ashore', was widened to refer to the reaching of any destination. The Old English word *brid* (the ancestor of Present-Day English *bird*) meant 'young bird' (or 'young animal'), the word *fowl* being reserved for avian adults. Only later did *bird* become the general term for a mature, flying, nonmammalian vertebrate. You may also think of adding new grammatical functions to a word as a kind of widening. For example, when *floor,* originally a noun, was first used as a verb in *That really floored* (i.e. *astonished*) *me* or *He floored it* (i.e. the gas pedal) *when he saw the police car in his rear view mirror,* it was a type of semantic (or grammatical) widening.

Sometimes semantic change results in neither widening nor narrowing. This is the case when one specific meaning ousts another. One example is the word *book,* which originally meant 'scroll' but is now chiefly used for printed or written works consisting of sheets of paper bound on one side.

Words often shift their meaning in relatively value-neutral ways, but we also find radical shifts from positive associations to negative associations and the reverse. An example of **amelioration** (shift from negative to positive) is seen in the word *nice.* Its Latin forebear was *nescius* 'ignorant' (*ne* 'not' + *sci* 'know, discern'). An entire chain of shifts shows how it 'improved its lot': 'ignorant' > 'simple' > 'foolishly particular' > 'particular' > 'proper' > 'pleasant'. (Some would say that its meaning is shifting back and is now almost neutral—i.e. 'not disagreeable'.) The opposite of amelioration, **degeneration** (or **pejoration**) is probably more common. This happens frequently with words that are used **euphemistically** (to cover taboo terms) for example (as in the case of *toilet* 'dressing room or table'). Degeneration has also applied to *notorious,* which originally simply meant 'widely known' but is coming to mean 'widely known for something scandalous'. These evaluative shifts often occur side by side with other shifts, like narrowing.

For the most part, it is whole words and not individual morphemes (which do not ordinarily occur on their own) that undergo semantic shifts. When we say, for example, that there has been a change (at least for a substantial number of speakers of American English) in the meaning of the word *reticent* from 'reluctant or hesitant to speak' to simply 'reluctant' or 'hesitant', the morpheme *tac/tec/tic* itself has not altered its meaning 'silent', and we do not see this morpheme ceasing to refer to speech in other words, such as *tacit.* Similarly, the word *pretend* originally meant 'stretch forth, assert' and only later came to mean 'falsely claim'. It would be misleading to suggest that the individual morphemes *pre-* and *tend* changed their meaning to include the sense 'false', for only in combination in the word *pretend* is any such sense associated with them.

APPLYING PRINCIPLES OF SEMANTIC SHIFT TO WORD ANALYSIS

Ultimately, semantic change can be difficult to precisely describe and explain because so many factors may be involved. It is hard to reconstruct any historical event, and this is especially true here since meaning is a matter of mind; events of semantic change are entirely mental, and hence not as easily recordable as sounds and morphemes.

To understand how the morpheme, in the creation and evolution of a particular word, may have lost its simple, original sense, and how the gloss you have learned for that morpheme relates to the current meaning of the word as a whole, you may need to use a certain amount of ingenuity. For example, one has to wonder at first about a verb like *insist,* whose parts mean 'in, into' and 'stand' but whose commonest meanings today are 'refuse to yield' and 'assert something'. Rather than simply take a surface interpretation—something like 'stand in'—at face value, we should be prepared to start thinking metaphorically right away, because metaphor is by far the commonest kind of semantic shift. Keep in mind that even the native English word *stand* has many different meanings beyond the basic, literal one. Examples in the kind of language you use every day may occur to you, such as those in the sentences *Kim won't stand for it* or *The mayor stands up for the little guy,* or *Pat had to take a stand.* In each of these examples, we can see subtler semantic shadings that include 'tolerate, support, be steadfast'. We may even want to compare such other words containing the root *sist* as *persist, resist, desist, subsist, persist,* and *exist.* They all have senses which partially overlap with these uses of *stand* and, for that matter, *insist.* In the end, while you certainly won't arrive at a precise etymological reconstruction of the semantic development of *insist,* you will not be surprised to learn that it actually followed a course of shift which can be roughly outlined as follows.

> 'stand upon' >
>   'continue on a course' >
>   'continually affirm or assert' >
>   'strongly affirm or assert'

Note that this shift (actually, set of shifts) involves several of the processes discussed in this chapter and observed throughout the book (e.g. in morpheme sets). First is the flexibility of spatial prefixes. (Here, *in-* doesn't literally mean 'in' but something similar: 'upon'). Second is the case where a concrete, physical phenomenon becomes increasingly abstract. One aspect of the action or state of standing, specifically, remaining (or continuing) in one place—comes (via metonymy or synecdoche) to be the primary meaning. By this point, we have arrived at the meaning 'refuse to yield' which can be seen simply as a matter of maintaining a course of action regardless of obstacles. The next development is a narrowing or specialization of meaning so that only a particular kind of course is continued: that of a belief or contention. (This is probably the outcome of some additional metaphoric or metonymic change which we can only guess at today.) Finally, we see a shift that appears to involve a metonymy between doing something continually and doing something strongly, possibly a matter of connection between cause and effect, since doing almost anything continually requires effort—in other words, doing it 'strongly'.

Now, this may all seem a bit too much, especially since you already know the word *insist* and are unlikely ever to have to analyze it to understand a sentence. But the same principles illustrated in this case will also apply to less familiar words, such as *perspicacity*, which would be glossed as 'through, bad' + 'look, see' + A, N + N. In a context like *Medicine is not a science of souls. Physicians lack the perspicacity to find the world-weary patient's real illness*, it would probably be unnecessary to do much more than take the two possible surface readings, roughly, 'bad seeing/looking-ness' or 'through seeing/looking-ness' and attempt to interpret them in some plausible and straightforward (but not simplistic) way. It is entirely likely then that you would arrive at a meaning for *perspicacity* like 'insight', 'vision', 'deeper wisdom', etc. rather than 'ugliness' (i.e. 'badlookingness') 'x-ray vision' (i.e. 'throughlookingness') or some not-very-serious alternative along these lines. And the accuracy of your interpretation would be supported by a dictionary which defines the word as 'acuteness of perception, discernment, or understanding', all good synonyms for your likeliest educated guesses.

EXERCISES

1. The following is a pair of cognate morphemes in which both the formal resemblance and the relation of meaning is problematic, at least without some special knowledge: *graph* 'write' as in *calligraphy/crab* 'crab' as in *fiddler crab*. Should *graph* and *crab* be considered allomorphs of the same morpheme if we can state a rule of allomorphy which relates the g and p̲h̲ of *graph* and the c̲ and b̲ of *crab*? Where would you draw the line, and why?

2. Which of the two meanings given for each of the words below is earlier? What knowledge about semantic shift or other factors leads you to this conclusion? (Use an etymological dictionary like the *Oxford English Dictionary* to check your answer.)

    a. **text** 'weave' as in *textile* or **text** 'compose' as in *textual*
    b. **ex-**[1] as in *expose, extend* or **ex-**[2] as in *ex-wife, ex-doctor*
    c. **divine** 'godly' or **divine** 'wonderful'

3. Following the example of *insist* from the last section of this chapter, detail the major developments along the paths (e.g. metaphor, metonymy) and outcomes (e.g. narrowing, widening) of semantic shift involved in the history of the word *inaugurate* from its beginnings in ancient Rome to the present. Be sure to propose plausible metaphoric or metonymic factors for every step you can.

    'take omens from the flight of birds' >
         'begin officially' >
                'open with ceremony' >
                      'install in office'

4. Each of the following words has undergone either a metaphoric or metonymic shift in meaning. Identify the type of shift from the earlier meaning (on the left of the arrow) to the current meaning (on the right) that you feel is most plausible. (You may use a dictionary as an aid if you like.) Explain your answer in a sentence or two. (Note: While many kinds of meaning shift can be categorized under one of the above headings, some cannot be confirmed by the historical record or cannot be attributed to a single type of shift. If you believe that there is more than one plausible answer in a particular case, give and explain both.)

    a. *vermicelli*
         'small or thin worms' > 'a kind of thin macaroni not unlike spaghetti'
    b. *redbreast*
         'the red breast of the robin (a bird)' > 'the robin'
    c. *seminary*
         'a place where seeds are sprouted and nurtured' > 'school of religion'
    d. *convince*
         'to physically overcome' > 'to intellectually persuade'
    e. *urbane*
         'pertaining to cities; urban' > 'sophisticated'
    f. *muscle*
         'a little mouse' > 'an organ or tissue used for movement'

g. *sandwich*

'name of the inventor of the food consisting of two slices of bread and a filling' > 'food consisting of two slices of bread and a filling'

5. English possesses numerous words with Latin spatial prefixes. Table 7.3 indicates (by means of an 'x') most of the more common combinations of spatial prefixes and the roots *duc/duct* 'lead, draw, pull', *pos* 'place, put', *port* 'carry', *jac/jec* 'lay, lie', *sist* 'stand, *mot* 'move', *cap/cep/cip/cup* 'take, contain'.

Among the words involving these combinations of morphemes are:

abducent 'drawing apart, said of a muscle when it moves a limb away from the center axis of the body (lit. 'pulling away')';
abduct to carry off by force (lit. 'pull away');
adduce to present or bring forward a point for consideration in a discussion or analysis (lit. 'draw toward')
adductor a muscle that pulls a body part in the direction of the center axis of the body (lit. 'draw toward')
apport the moving or producing of a physical object by a spiritualist medium (e.g. at a seance) without any apparent physical activity, or any object produced in this way (lit. 'carry toward' or 'bring', etc.)

Others include *circumduction, conducive, conduct, comportment, deduce,* and *deduction.*

Choose five interesting and/or unfamiliar combinations from this list that form words which seem to have undergone a semantic shift of some kind from the meaning suggested by a simple, literal reading of their morphemic glosses. Use an unabridged dictionary like *Webster's Third New International Dictionary* and/or a sophisticated etymological dictionary like the *Oxford English Dictionary* (possibly in conjunction with the *Oxford Latin Dictionary*) to investigate a sampling of the range of meanings the words have had over time. So, for example, if you do not know words combining *sub-* and *sist* or *tra-* and *ject* very well, look them up and determine some of their major meanings at various points and attempt to account for their changes by semantic shifts of the type you have studied. (Don't forget that allomorphy, especially partial or total assimilation, may disguise some morphemes in certain combinations.)

Table 7.3

root	duc	duct	pos	port	jac(t)/ jec(t)	sist	cap/cep/ cip/cup
(suffixes)	(-ate, -ive, etc.)	(-ive, -ion, etc.)	(-ition, etc.)	(-ive, -ion, etc.)	(-ion, -ive, etc.)	(-ant, -ive, etc.)	(-ion, -ive, etc.)
prefix(es)							
ab-/abs-	X	X			X		
ad-	X	X	X	X	X	X	X
circum-		X	X				
con-/co-	X	X	X	X	X	X	X
de-	X	X	X	X	X	X	X
dis-/di-			X	X	X		
ex-/e-	X	X	X	X	X	X	X
in-	X	X	X	X	X	X	X
inter-					X		X
intro-	X	X					
ob-			X		X		X
per-						X	X
pre-			X				X
pro-	X	X	X		X		X
re(d)-	X	X	X	X	X	X	X
se(d)-	X	X					
tra-	X	X			X		
trans-	X	X	X	X		X	
sub-		X	X	X	X	X	X

6. English possesses numerous words with Greek roots and spatial prefixes. Table 7.4 indicates (by means of an 'x') most of the more common combinations of spatial prefixes and the roots *log* 'study, speak', *phor/pher* 'carry', *the* 'put', *leg* 'pick, read', *tom/tm* 'cut', *bol/bl* 'extend, throw', *stat/stas* 'stand, condition'.

Among the words involving these combinations of morphemes are:

anaphoric (grammatical term) 'referring to a preceding word or phrase' (lit. 'carrying back');
analogy 'similarity of properties, ratios, etc.' (lit. '(the act of) studying back').
anathema 'something banned or cursed' (lit. 'thing put back');

Others include *diathesis, epitome, epilog, anabolic, prosthetic,* and *synthesis.*

Choose five interesting and/or unfamiliar combinations from this list that form words which seem to have undergone a semantic shift from the simple, literal meaning of their morphemic glosses. Use an unabridged dictionary like *Webster's Third New International Dictionary,* and/or a sophisticated etymological dictionary like the *Oxford English Dictionary* to investigate the range of meanings the words have had over time. So, for example, if you do not know words combining *hypo-* and *stat/stas* or *syn-* and *log* very well, look them up and determine some of their major meanings at various points and attempt to account for their changes by semantic shifts of the type you have studied. (Don't forget that allomorphy, especially partial or total assimilation, may disguise morphemes.)

Table 7.4

root	log	phor/ pher	the	leg	tom/tm	bol/bl	stat/ stas
(suffix(es))	(-**y**, etc.)	(-**ic**, etc.)	(-**is**, etc.)	(-**tic**, -**sis**, etc.)	(-**ic**, etc.)	(-**ic**, etc.)	(-**y**, -**ic**, -**is**, etc.)
prefix(es)							
ana-	X	X	X	X	X	X	
apo-	X						X
anti-			X				
cata-	X	X	X	X		X	X
dia-	X	X	X	X	X	X	X
ec-	X			X	X		X
en-					X		
epi-	X				X		X
hyper-						X	
hypo-			X				X
meso-				X			
meta-		X	X			X	X
para-					X	X	
peri-		X					
pro-	X		X			X	X
pros-			X				
syn-	X		X			X	

8

Usage and Variation

MANY ENGLISHES

Up to now, we have been considering English to be a language. That seems eminently reasonable, yet in a sense it is inaccurate. What goes by the single name 'English' is not a single language. Instead, it is a broad range of **varieties** that manage to pass for English in different parts of the globe, in different social situations, and on different occasions.

Earlier chapters have touched briefly on variation in style (for example, in words with formal as opposed to informal connotations). We have also dealt indirectly with variation in professional or technical usage. Doctors, farmers, social workers, bakers, biologists, carpenters, philosophers, exterminators, psychologists, actors, educators, lawyers, gardeners, and physicists all either work with a set of special terms or use more general terms in special ways. Of course, a major goal of this book is to provide access to such specialized vocabularies and, in particular, to the words associated with more formal and scholarly styles.

In this chapter we consider the notion of whether formal styles have some sort of privileged status over other styles. We also look at attitudes toward usage that arise from social groups other than the most prestigious and from communities located in different parts of our country or the world. Variation of this kind may involve not only vocabulary but also pronunciation, spelling, and other aspects of language.

ROOTS OF VARIATION AND CHANGE

In chapter 2 we saw how **external** forces, including war, invasion, geography, migration, commerce, and both social and technological change may have profound affects on a language. (Special attention has been paid to the impact these influences have had on English vocabulary.) Likewise, **internal** factors, including phonetics and semantic change as described in chapters 5, 6, and 7, may lead to both minor and major differences in pronunciation, meaning, word formation, and language use. Together, internal and external forces combine to differentiate a single language into separate varieties. Ultimately they may, in time, create different languages which, though historically related, are largely incomprehensible to each other's speakers.

SEEDS OF DIALECTAL DIVISION

Those who set themselves up as linguistic authorities are not known for their tolerance to dialect variation. As the Latin used in ancient Rome developed into the different Romance languages, the trend met with frequent resistance. In the eighth century, Charlemagne actually tried to get his subjects to go back to using Latin rather than French. Additional 'degenerate' varieties of Latin came to be spoken by Roman troops and colonial subjects in other parts of the Roman Empire and met with similar resistance by linguistic authorities. Yet each regional variant flourished and developed into modern-day French, Spanish, Italian, Portuguese, Romanian, and other distinct languages.

An equally interesting but different set of developments mark the history of English. Since the invasion of the British Isles by speakers of different varieties of West Germanic, England has never been truly unified by a single spoken variety. To this day there are northern and southwestern rural English folk whose speech is nearly incomprehensible to Americans and often even quite difficult for those from other parts of England to understand. Elsewhere in Britain, too, distinct types of English survive (and in some cases thrive) among the modern Scots, Irish, and Welsh descendants of earlier Celtic populations. Beyond the British Isles, new varieties of English have sprung up in Australia, New Zealand, the United States, and South Africa.

Still further from the heart of the world settled by English speakers, even more linguistic differentiation has occurred. In the former British colonies of India, Sri Lanka, Nigeria, Singapore, Malaysia, and many others, contact with local languages and other factors have created what have been referred to as "New Englishes". The English used in these countries has official status and is taught in schools at various grade levels. It serves as an important language of mass communication and business, functioning in these nations as a **lingua franca,** a common language for groups who share no other language. Originally, such local English was modeled on the speech and writing of educated, upper-class Britons, but today the population at large in these countries often speaks a rather un-British kind of English. In Indian and African varieties, for example, because national ties with Britain have weakened considerably since independence, the model for English is increasingly a local one. The result of this is that these national varieties are moving ever further from their historical roots in England; in time, they may come to differ as much from our English as its cousins, Dutch and German, do today. In a sense, then, the very status of English as a "world language" contains the seeds for its eventual diversification and division.

WHERE DO STANDARDS COME FROM?

A **standard language** is a set of linguistic norms established by some generally accepted political or social authority. In the extreme case, a standard may be shaped by the practice of a single respected speaker or writer or group of speakers or writers. This is not too far from the situation in England, where the Queen's or King's English has always been standard. In the United States, a case could be made for saying that the standard is set by the broadcast media. But they probably follow the standard that has been set by the educated northern establishment.

Sometimes the model for a standard is a variety used in religious scripture, such as the variety of Arabic in which the prophet Mohammed composed the Quran, or the language of the King James Version of the Bible adopted by the Puritans. On occasion the authority is a description of a language written by a grammarian, or the compilation of vocabulary by a **lexicographer** like Samuel Johnson (whose dictionary of English was the first to seek to exhaustively enumerate the words and meanings of the language of the well educated), or Noah Webster (who sought to promote national unity and independence by recording the vocabulary of the new American variety of English). Using the language established by an authority typically lends the user some of the symbolic or actual social status of that authority; standards are quite often based on the language of those in a society who are judged most powerful.

The development of printing also prompted attempts to **standardize.** This was the case with the earliest Standard English used by a book manufacturing industry which had to cross lines of regional variation in speech and writing throughout Britain.

Speaking Versus Writing

We distinguish between spoken and written standards, for these are not the same. All of us normally acquire the spoken language of our community before receiving any formal education. If our community is considered to speak the standard, then, our actual schooling in language (a process which actually takes many years and much practice) is devoted to reading and writing a literary standard which differs from standard speech in a variety of ways.

Spoken varieties continue to change even when a written language or accepted literary form remains fairly immobile. Writing is generally conservative—as it is, for example, in the retention of letters no longer pronounced in a word like *knight*. Still, in time, writing usually comes into line with speech. Some languages—for example Norwegian and Russian—have reformed their spelling to eliminate inconsistencies. English has also undergone such reforms, though with limited success. The sequence *ough* is pronounced differently in each of the following words: *rough, bough, through, thought, trough, though,* and *hiccough*. The sound [š] can be spelled as in *fish, motion, passion, sugar,* and *facial*. Such inconsistencies are often bemoaned, but at the same time there is resistance to such modest innovations as *lite* and *thru* for *light* and *through*.

Changing Standards

We need only compare the literary usages of Shakespeare's time with our own to see that standards themselves can and must change. This flexibility is worth fostering in a standard language. To the extent that the standard has vitality and wide usage, it may serve to unite a nation, facilitate communication, and therefore serve the common good. But this is not to say that the only valid language is a standard one, even though some "experts" behave as if that is the case. Let us explore some cases where the standard language is actually inappropriate.

Where the Standard Fails

A standard serves many purposes, but it is by no means the appropriate medium for all communication. After Latin had evolved into the distinct Romance languages, it remained the written and spoken standard for members of the European priestly and scholarly community. Yet they, like their associates and neighbors, spoke local Old French, Old Spanish, and Old Italian varieties in many nonofficial contexts. Today, although government, business, and other authorities support the use of a single written standard, large numbers of people in France, Italy, and Germany grow up speaking a distinct regional variety of their languages. Regional dialects are often sources of great pride, often bolstered by rich oral traditions and sometimes a written literature. Although the level of literacy in the standard is very high in these countries and all students study it in school, regional varieties are still often preferred for talk between relatives and friends, folk traditions, and a range of other activities.

You may even find yourself in a situation where using Standard American English of the type taught in school or used in literature is clearly not the best way to communicate. In the streets of Brooklyn, where one of the authors of this book grew up, insisting on speaking an educated standard (for example, a typical college professor's pronunciation, word choice and syntax) could have resulted in being shunned by associates and mistrusted by strangers. This is not so much because speaking Standard English would have hampered his ability to communicate as because it may have been socially inappropriate. Brooklyn is of course hardly unique in this respect.

Most of us generally speak like the people we grew up with unless we have been careful to modify our language for particular purposes, like Texas-born newscaster Dan Rather or Georgia-born actor Kim Basinger had to do for their respective careers. Would they have made an effort to "standardize" their speech if they had not chosen careers in media and entertainment?

CAN OUR TUNG BE CLEANE AND PURE?

Some experts can be quite tolerant of regional dialects yet very protective of the standard language that they command. Since the time of the earliest English standard, there have been those who have seen fit to criticize certain differences in usage as 'corruptions', 'barbarisms', and marks of intellectual, even moral, 'decline'. We can trace such **prescriptive** approaches to language at least as far as Rome in the first century A.D., where the rhetorician Quintilian prescribed a variety of Latin which took what he considered the best authors and the speech of the social elite as its model. In England in the seventeenth century Sir John Cheke, a 'language purist' responded to those who used words borrowed from French, Latin, and other foreign sources by writing, "I am of the opinione that our own tung sholde be written cleane and pure, unmixt and unmangled with borrowing of other tungs." Perhaps he should have reconsidered his own choice of words before writing, since the words *opinion, mix, mangle,* and *pure* are themselves borrowed. (We wonder how Cheke would feel about our modern 'corruptions' of the spellings he seems to have preferred.)

Gripes about innovative usages have come from many quarters, ranging from some of our most distinguished authors to national governments. Jonathan Swift despised the use of *rep* for *reputation* that was common in his day and condemned the practice of clipping words in this way. An author writing in 1872 labeled the word *belittle* "incurably vulgar." Fowler and Fowler, in *The King's English,* take the position that Americanisms should be treated as "foreign words" in British English. Straining to give American English its due, these authors conclude, "The English and the American language and literature are both good things; but they are better apart than mixed." French law still imposes fines on using outlawed foreign words in the media when a French equivalent exists.

What unites these attempts to control linguistic change is their failure. No language has ever really been frozen and there is no good reason to expect that any ever will; few prescriptivists seem to understand this fact, and many of them seem unaware that they virtually always lose their linguistic battles in time. A striking change occurring at the moment is the "positive *anymore*" construction in American English, heard in *You see a lot of Chevy vans around here anymore.* (Note that the word *don't* is <u>not</u> missing from the preceding sentence.) For many speakers, *anymore,* once found only in a negative context and meaning roughly "no longer," has come to be synonymous with "nowadays." This usage (which seems to have originated in a variety of British English transplanted to America) has been spreading from a central East Coast point of origin for several decades and is being used with increasing frequency at many points farther west. The change is moving so quickly that it appears to have a fairly good chance of surviving in spite the fact that prescriptivists have condemned it.

A common justification used by purists is their desire to uphold clarity and precision in language. This is no doubt sometimes well founded, but often it is just a flimsy, pseudoscholarly excuse for preferring the old to the new.

Logic is another type of justification offered for resisting language change. Samuel Taylor Coleridge equated rules of grammar with rules of logic. But this couldn't be right. Experts want us to say, *It is I* rather than *It is me,* allegedly because the word *is* (due to its equational meaning) logically takes the predicate nominative rather than objective case. But this is not logic; it was merely a rule of Latin. In French, it is the opposite. It is totally ungrammatical to say *C'est je* ('It is I'). The correct thing to say is *C'est moi* ('It is me'). What is correct does not always coincide with what is logical.

There are those who frown upon the use of *hopefully* as a sentence adverbial in *Hopefully, it will rain soon.* The most common complaint against this usage is a logical one. According to our experts, *hopefully* means 'in a hopeful manner'. Since it is illogical to say *In a hopeful manner, it will rain soon,* it follows that it is illogical to say *Hopefully, it will rain soon*. Yet we are permitted to put adverbs like *largely* and *especially* before adjectives, as in *largely irrelevant* or *especially important*, even though it is peculiar to say *irrelevant in a large manner* or *important in an especial manner*. Hopefully, the experts will be able to explain their apparent inconsistency. Until they do, we can rest comfortably in the fact that the meaning of *Hopefully, it will rain soon* is clear to all, even if the expression upsets some people.

We do not mean to imply that purists are totally unjustified in their attempts to preserve the language. Many of them probably are sincere in their belief that without their continuing efforts, the language will disintegrate over time. But the history of language change offers many reassurances that they are wrong on this count. We must also recognize that some of the prescriptivists' points are well taken. In our view, the following prescriptive principles seem entirely reasonable.

- There are often good reasons to conform to accepted usage.
- If one is to violate rules and ignore standards, one will do a more effective job if one understands the rules being violated and the standards being ignored.
- Certainly some of the things that get uttered are dreadful, ignorant, totally unclear, and so on.

There is much to be said for knowing the rules and when to apply them. Shakespeare's plays are full of odd usages. His characters violated then current canons of correctness with expressions like "between you and I" and "There's two of you." He originated slang expressions like "done me wrong" and "beat it." He got away with his linguistic tricks partly because he understood what he was doing and partly because he came to be so respected that anyone opposing his verbal inventiveness would look stupid.

CORRECTNESS IS RELATIVE

The real problem with prescriptivism arises when it is put forth as an absolute. Some experts act as if there is only one standard—theirs. This is so far from the truth that it is silly. The varieties of English that they habitually ignore (regional dialects, ethnic dialects, local variants) are just as valid, useful, and appropriate in their contexts as standard formal English is in its contexts. Consider this analogy. We all go by different names at different times. Our friends know us by a first name or by a nickname. Our family may know us by a different nickname. In other settings, our first name may not be appropriate, and our last name will be used. There is nothing wrong with this. The same goes for language use in general.

Language serves a multitude of needs determined both by our nature and our environment. As long as it remains flexible it remains vital. If the primary purpose of speech and writing is the expression and communication of thought, we can evaluate any particular language or variety of language on the basis of its usefulness for these purposes. This is what we are really asking when we question whether it is 'right' to use *lite* or *light, irregardless* or *regardless, hopefully* or *I hope that, ask* or *aks,* or *contact* used as a verb or as an entire phrase like *make contact with.* Since no choice in these pairs is inherently superior to its partner, the question must be "Which is more effective for communication on a particular occasion?"

When we find ourselves in a new community of any kind we should be sensitive to the norms of that community and learn at least some of its language if we want to understand and be understood without difficulty. In a sense, we must all become adept in multiple varieties of language just as an international traveler may have to learn different languages to function effectively in different lands.

But surely it is possible to learn and apply the rules of standard formal English without imposing them on other dialects. And surely it is possible to master the rules of Standard English without concluding that there is anything wrong with nonstandard dialects. Some experts want to bring a homogeneity to the language that simply is not there, and that would rob the language of some of its expressive resources, while robbing some of its speakers of the pride that they take in their speech. This to us is the real danger in prescriptivism.

WORD CHOICE AND CLARITY OF COMMUNICATION

Since this book is concerned with expanding vocabulary, we ought to address some of the deeper purposes for word study. Gaining access to the vocabulary of a scholarly or specialist group gives us some of the power of that group. Becoming familiar with a group's specialized language is one step toward membership in that group. While not all scholars and specialists intend to exclude the rest of us, we can all probably remember times when specialized vocabulary was used not to communicate effectively but to mystify and bedazzle us, perhaps to make us feel like outsiders. English legal language, for example, has caused centuries of confusion and consternation to the average citizen. In recent years, legislators in many locales have found it necessary to pass laws that require legal documents to be written in "plain English." Now nonlawyers can take a more active role in matters that may significantly affect the quality of their lives.

Control over advanced vocabulary includes recognizing the danger that it can be used to obfuscate or disguise rather than clarify meaning. An enhanced vocabulary brings the ability to decode the sometimes vague or unnecessarily altiloquent, arcane words of the initiated. We are probably better off with this knowledge than without it. For example, to learn from your physician that you are suffering from *otitis externa* may appear more significant, perhaps even more upsetting than hearing that you have a simple inflammation of the outer ear. Similarly, we don't want to be too impressed, put off, or confused by the use of a phrase like *longitudinal extent* for the more straightforward *height*. Other kinds of examples include the empty phrases that have come to be known as bureaucratese (e.g.*We explored a comprehensive set of options before the finalization process*) and well-meaning, 'politically correct' euphemisms (e.g. *vertically challenged* to describe a person of less than average height)

This is not to belittle the technical use of language but only the pretentious use of it. In fact, technical terminology serves a very important function in every discipline as a means of communicating both precisely and unambiguously. And multiple stylistic levels of vocabulary may in fact allow even the nonspecialist to manipulate not merely different connotations (such as degrees of formality) but also fine distinctions in denotational meaning that often accompany different word choices. In both cases, the clear transmission of ideas may require a choice of specific terms that one might not use in in ordinary conversation.

The use of a special vocabulary in writing is also necessary at times. Written style differs from spoken style (among other ways) in that it suffers certain disadvantages as compared to speech. For example, it lacks the devices of intonation, pause, and other subtle aspects which spoken language allows, not to mention the expressiveness that face and body movement provide in face-to-face interaction. Compared to speech, written language has limited ways of expressing emphasis, emotion, and other important aspects of meaning. So choosing the right word can be more critical to writing than to speech.

Ultimately, an enhanced and enlarged vocabulary, like any part of the complex phenomenon called language, is a multipurpose tool. Like a hammer it can be used either to drive nails into beams and planks to build or wielded as a weapon to injure. The individual is responsible for the use to which it is put.

EXERCISES

1. In chapter 5 attention was drawn to the two possible pronunciations of the word *which*. Some people pronounce this word as [hwĭč] and others as [wĭč]. Determine which of these two pronunciations you use. (A good test for this is

to pronounce the words *witch* and *which* and see if there is any difference. If there is none, you may assume that *which* is pronounced [wɪč].) Then, survey eight to ten people from different parts of the United States or elsewhere in the English speaking world to see how they pronounce these words. Paying attention to the geographical backgrounds of the individuals as far as you can ascertain them, can you make any generalization about who pronounces *which* [hwɪč] and who pronounces it [wɪč]? Besides the speaker's geographical background, is there any other factor that seems to play a role in the pronunciation of this word?

2. Look up the dictionary* entries for the following words, paying attention to any variation in spelling and pronunciation given as well as to notes on etymology or word history and standard versus nonstandard usage. Describe, explain, and evaluate the indications of variation and any usage arguments made in light of the discussion found in this and earlier chapters as well as your own knowledge of variation in their pronunciation, spelling, and your sense of usage. (In the case of spelling, you may have to consult multiple dictionaries or, perhaps, compare the entries in British and American dictionaries.)

a. hopefully	b. irregardless	c. either	d. ask	e. which
f. nuclear	g. shall; will	h. ain't	i. anxious	j. hectic
k. prodigious	l. process	m. fair	n. host	o. disinterested
p. every	q. cohort	r. convince	s. balding	t. contact [verb]

2. Deobfuscate—that is, render into plain, effective English—the following paragraphs, paying particular attention to the often sesquipedalian words in **boldface,** wherever possible. You may have to rewrite the words in plain type if you are to make sense. (Some words are 'real'; others, created for this exercise, may be interpreted in any reasonable fashion in light of the meanings of their component words or morphemes. Use an unabridged dictionary to investigate the meaning of the word and its morphemes.)

a. The **plenipotentiary, recumbent** in the **solarium, desolate** and **suffused** with the **analgesic fructifications** of **viticulture** was no **oenologist.** He had been **negligent** of the **maxim: miscation** of **liquors** is **maleficent.**

* *The American Heritage Dictionary of the English Language* (3rd ed.) is recommended for this exercise.

b. The **preeminent** scientist's **sesquipedalian soliloquy**: '**Pentadactylic genera** are **evidently arboricolous** as a **sequela** of their **prehensile capacity, whereas adactylic** (even **apodal**) **geozoans** are **inherently nonascensive.**'

c. While **reconnoitering** a **nocturnal sanctuary accompanied** by an **assemblage** of **adept martial spelunkers, I encountered** an **ursine behemoth** of such **amplitude** that I found myself **dispatched** into **spasms** of **trepidation** and **recognized** with **unqualified** and **thoroughgoing certitude** that **demise** was **imminent.**

d. The **obliteration** of **paleographic, archeophonic** and **epigraphic** evidence has for **millennia** caused **superagitation** among **philologists implicated** in **glottogonic speculations.**

3. The following words from the field of medicine contain several morphemes you have not yet encountered. With the help of an unabridged dictionary and/or a large dictionary of medical terms as well as a glossary or dictionary of roots,* briefly define, parse, and gloss each term. For example:

nephrolithotomy: 'Removal of kidney stones'

nephr	(o)	lith	(o)	tom	y
'kidney'		'stone'		'cut'	N

a. leukocytotaxia   b. achromotrichia   c. brachymetacarpia
d. aphonogelia   e. retrocalcaneobursitis   f. antixerophthalmic
g. endosteoma   h. lithotroph   i. paraplegia
j. hemostasis   k. chromaffinoblastoma   l. paronychia

Dorland's Illustrated Medical Dictionary is one of several good larger medical dictionaries generally available. If you cannot find a particular term in the dictionary you use, you may still find portions of it or similar words which will allow you to make an educated guess at the meaning of your word. (E.g. with *antixerophthalmic*, you might only find *xerophthalmic* or *xerophthalmia*, which should suggest that *antixerophthalmic* means 'against *xerophthalmia*.)

9

Latin and Greek Morphology

Colleges and high schools used to place a greater emphasis on Latin and Greek than they do now. In Europe, some universities used to require that doctoral dissertations be written in Latin. Times have changed, and the special status once accorded to classical languages is now given to other subjects, including modern languages. But the classical languages remain our most important source of new words, as shown by additions like *polygraph, computer, cyclotron.*

One of the aims of this book is to present those aspects of Latin and Greek that are still the most useful to an English-speaking student. One important component is the morpheme sets. Another, which we introduce in this chapter, is the basics of the **inflectional** and **derivational** systems of those languages. This will help to reduce some of the mystery surrounding the types of allomorphy that Latin- and Greek-derived words exhibit in English.

In English the inflectional morphology of a word may indicate such things as

- its role in a sentence (e.g. whether a noun is acting as a subject—as in *He is swimming*—or object—as in *Sandy kissed him*),
- number (e.g. singular *table* versus plural *tables*),
- tense (e.g. verbs indicating action in the past—as in *Lee smiled*—versus present—as in *Lee smiles*).

Inflections perform similar functions in Latin and Greek, as we will see. As for derivation, this is the process of creating a full word from either an incomplete stem or from another word. Chapter 3 listed a variety of ways in which words were derived in English. In Latin and Greek, derivation is mostly limited to

121

adding morphemes that alter the meaning or function of a basic form. This will make the study of derivational morphology considerably simpler for the classical languages than for English.

INFLECTION IN ENGLISH NATIVE FORMS AND BORROWINGS

Most English nouns take the ending *-s* (or, if the stem ends in an alveolar or alveopalatal fricative or affricate, *-es*) to form a plural:

> *dogs, things, houses, riches,* etc.

There are a few native words which are exceptions to this general tendency. Examples include:

> *man/men, mouse/mice, goose/geese, sheep/sheep*

Now look at borrowed words. They frequently take the endings that they took in their source language. In the examples that follow, the plurals are in fact much more commonly used than the singulars.

Singular	Plural	Origin
graffito	**graffiti**	Italian, 'a little scratching'
cognoscente	**cognoscenti**	Italian, 'one in the know'
datum	**data**	Latin, 'fact'
hasid	**hasidim**	Hebrew, 'member of a certain Jewish sect'

This chapter will provide an extensive set of plural endings from Latin and Greek that are commonly used in borrowings from these languages.

INFLECTIONAL DIFFERENCES BETWEEN ENGLISH AND THE CLASSICAL LANGUAGES

The forms of Greek and Latin nouns and adjectives involve a few special principles. The most important notion is that of **grammatical gender.** (This phenomenon will not be new to you if you have ever studied a language like French, Spanish, German, Russian, or even Old English.) In Latin and Greek, grammatical gender requires that each noun (or adjective applied to a noun) be assigned to one of three groups, each of which corresponds in a rough sense to the gender or sex of the thing it refers to. This idea is illustrated by three

Greek words: *adelphos* 'brother', *gyne* 'woman', and the abstract noun *kriterion* 'standard'. In these words, the endings -*os*, -*e* and -*on* indicate that the nouns they are attached to are masculine, feminine, and neuter, respectively. Like Greek, Latin indicated gender by word endings: e.g. masculine -*us* (as in *filius* 'son'), feminine -*a* (as in *filia* 'daughter'), and neuter -*um* (as in *donum* 'gift'). But not all nouns in Greek and Latin represent things that have an obvious natural or biological gender (like the words for 'man', 'son', 'woman', and 'daughter'). Still, all nouns in Greek and Latin had to have a grammatical gender, and the words for many things that speakers of English would probably consider genderless might take a masculine, feminine, or neuter ending. Thus, the Latin word for 'running' (a meaning which an English speaker would have to work a bit to associate with any sex or natural gender in particular) is *cursus*. This word is masculine and takes the Latin masculine ending -*us*.

Both Latin and Greek had a variety of inflectional endings for each grammatical gender. The singular form of each word would be assigned one of the endings appropriate for its gender. Table 9.1 gives a general idea of the range of Latin and Greek singular endings and their corresponding plural forms.

Here are some common English words that use the Latin endings:

-us/-i
hippopotamus/hippopotami
radius/radii
sarcophagus/sarcophagi
syllabus/syllabi
terminus/termini

Table 9.1 Latin and Greek Singular and Plural Suffixes

Latin	masculine	feminine	neuter
	us/-i	-a/-ae	-um/-a
	alumnus/alumni	*alumna/alumnae*	*datum/data*
		-s/-es	∅* /-ia
		index/indices	*animal/animalia*
			-us/-era
			opus/opera
Greek	masculine	feminine	neuter
	-s/es	-is/-es	-on/-a
	larynx/larynges	*crisis/crises*	*criterion/criteria*
			-ma/-mata
			schema/schemata

Note: Some endings occur with more than one gender or number.

* ∅ indicates the absence of any ending.

-a/-ae
antenna/antennae
alumna/alumnae
larva/larvae

-um/-a
cranium/crania
crematorium/crematoria
memorandum/memoranda
millennium/millennia
symposium/symposia

-x(=ks)/-ces,-ges
appendix/appendices
index/indices
vertex/vertices
matrix/matrices
coccyx/coccyges

The only commonly encountered singular and plural Greek endings are:

-on/-a:
phenomenon/phenomena
philodendron/philodendra
polyhedron/polyhedra

Note that words like *octagon, pentagon, paragon, marathon,* and *comparison* do not belong in this list since in these words the sequence of letters *on* is not a separate morpheme. (The final morpheme in *pentagon* is *gon* 'angle'.) Words like *garrison* and *galleon* also do not belong here and are best regarded as **monomorphemic** (i.e. not analyzable into more than one component morpheme). There are other words that look like they might but really don't belong in this list. One is *octopus,* from Greek *octo* 'eight' and *pous* 'foot' (an allomorph of *pod*), which does not really have a separate *us* ending. When Latin borrowed the word from Greek by changing it from *octopous* to *octopus,* it kept the Greek plural *octo-pod-es.* (Some English language dictionaries list this Greek plural, with stress on the second syllable, among the plurals of *octopus.*) A number of dictionaries also include *octopuses* and *octopi. Platypus* [from Greek *platy* 'flat' + *pous* 'foot'] is similar, but this word seems only to take the plural *platypuses* in English. Words that for various reasons do not belong in the *-ges/ -ces* plural category are *crucifix, prefix, six, annex,* and *complex.* They always have the regular English *-es* plural forms.

We don't always <u>have</u> to use the Latin and Greek plural endings. Many of the words we got from Latin and Greek have been **nativized** and take the usual English plural marker *-s* or *-es*. *Polyhedrons* is just as respectable a plural form as *polyhedra*. The plural of *colon* (either the punctuation mark or the body part) is *colons,* rarely *cola*. Latin borrowings in *-um* tend to take either the English or the Latin plural ending:

> *aquariums* or *aquaria*
> *atriums* or *atria*
> *fulcrums* or *fulcra*
> *maximums* or *maxima*
> *minimums* or *minima*
> *referendums* or *referenda*
> *spectrums* or *spectra*

The word *medium* is interesting in the way it treats the plural form. If the word is taken to refer to a means of mass communication (e.g. television), the plural is *media* (and this in turn is coming to be interpreted as a singular). If the word is taken to mean any other kind of medium, such as a psychic, the plural is *mediums*.

As English changes and the distance between the modern language and classical culture continues to increase, we may expect that fewer words will occur with Latin and Greek plurals.

LATIN VERB MORPHOLOGY

The Latin verb stem is the source of more than its share of morphemes in this book. It was usually composed of a root (often one syllable long) and, sometimes, one or two additional vowels (indicated in parentheses in *ag(e)* 'act, do, drive' and *sap(ie)* 'taste, perceive'). The verb stem was highly expandable. It could serve as the basis for several kinds of derivation, and it was inflected in a variety of ways. Typically, derivation would modify the function of the verb, changing it into nouns and adjectives, as illustrated in the next section.

The verb received a set of inflections. Latin grammars list four **principal parts** for a verb, from which the different forms of the verb can normally be predicted. The four principal parts of the verb *ago* 'I do' are:

present tense, 1st person sing.	infinitive	past tense, 1st person sing.	past passive participle
ago	**agere**	**egi**	**actus**
'I do'	'to do'	'I did'	'done'

The important parts for our purposes are the second and the fourth, since these give the building blocks for the most common borrowings into English. First, we will deal with words that derive from the infinitive.

Forms That Derive from the Infinitive

The Latin **infinitive** has the following structure:

root	theme vowel	infinitive ending
ag	**-e**	**-re**

The **theme vowel** appears in some forms derived from the root. This is why the English word *agent*, for example, has an *e* in the second syllable. The theme vowel differs for different verbs. There were three main possible theme vowels in Latin:

Latin root	theme vowel	English example
err	a	errant
doc, ag	e	docent, agent
sent	i	sentient

The English examples on the right all come directly from the **present active participle** of the Latin verb. The present active participle was formed from the verb root by adding the theme vowel and the participial suffix *nt*. If the theme vowel was *i*, this vowel was changed to *ie*. The English examples above correspond exactly to Latin participial forms meaning, from top to bottom, 'wandering', 'teaching', 'doing', and 'feeling'. These forms functioned as adjectives (as in '**wandering** minstrel'). The actual Latin forms required an inflectional ending to indicate the gender, number, and case of the the adjective. These endings are introduced in chapter 11.

The Latin present active participle is the source of essentially all the English nouns and adjectives that end in **-ent** and **-ant**, including *present, president, constant,* and *attendant.* Closely related to these endings are the endings *-ence/-ance* and *-ency/-ancy* in *essence, avoidance, residency,* and *constancy.*

Another similar form of the Latin verb is the **future passive participle,** which describes an action to be performed in the future. It is derived from the verb root by adding the theme vowel and the suffix *-nd.* In two of the English examples below, you will find the Latin inflectional suffixes *-um* and *-a.*

Latin root	theme vowel	English example
err 'wander' **a**		errand
ag, leg	**e**	agenda, legend
de + fin	**ie**	definiendum

(The verb form *defin* is not actually a root . The root *fin* 'finish' has the prefix *de-* attached, giving it the meaning 'define'.)

Forms That Derive From the Past Passive Participle

We have said that the two key principal parts of the verb for our purposes were the infinitive and the past passive participle. We have just illustrated forms that derive from the Latin infinitive. Now let us turn to the **past passive participle** (p.p.p.), which expresses an action that has been completed. The forms of the past passive participle differ quite a bit from root to root. The simplest form adds either *t* or a vowel plus *t* to the root. The voiceless *t* causes a preceding stop or fricative to become voiceless. For example, *ag* becomes *ac* before *t*. This is the source of the *t* that triggers the rule of voicing assimilation discussed in chapter 6. Once again, in the English examples, you will sometimes see the Latin inflectional endings at the end.

Latin root	p.p.p. allomorph	English example
err 'wander'	**at**	errata
ag	**t**	act
fac	**t**	fact
d 'give'	**at**	data
cred	**it**	credit

In another large set of forms, the past passive participle morpheme does not contain a *t*. Instead, the Latin root has its last consonant modified. These changes are the source of a few of the rules of allomorphy studied in chapter 6.

Latin root	modified root	English example
vid	**vis**	supervise
ced	**cess**	success
trah	**trac**	tract

Special Uses of the Past Passive Participle Stem

The past passive participle (p.p.p.) stem is the source of many derived words whose meaning has nothing to do with past, passive, or participial meanings. All of the endings listed here are modifications of Latin endings that were attached to the past passive participle form of the verb.

Eng./Lat. -or

Latin root	p.p.p.	suffixed example
ag	**act**	act**or**
ced	**cess**	success**or**
trah	**tract**	tract**or**

Eng. -ure, Lat. -ur

Latin root	p.p.p.	suffixed example
leg	**lect**	lect**ure**
find	**fiss**	fiss**ure**
cap	**capt**	capt**ure**
ping	**pict**	pict**ure**
n 'birth', etc.	**nat**	Eng. nat**ure,** Lat. nat**ur**a 'nature, character, tendency'

Eng. -ion, Lat. -io

Latin root	p.p.p.	suffixed example
leg	**lect**	elect**ion**
find	**fiss**	fiss**ion**
cap	**capt**	capt**ion**
il+lumin	**illuminat**	Eng. illuminat**ion,** Lat. illuminat**io** 'light'

Eng. -ive, Lat. -iv

Latin root	p.p.p.	suffixed example
leg	**lect**	elect**ive**
mit	**miss**	miss**ive**
cap	**capt**	capt**ive**
ping	**pict**	depict**ive**
con+jung	**conjunct**	Eng. conjunct**ive,** Lat. conjunct**iv**a 'connective membrane (of the eye)'

Several other affixes also attach to the p.p.p. form of verbs.

LATIN NOUN MORPHOLOGY

We have already seen that some Latin nouns take inflectional endings. Latin had a number of derivational morphemes that could be attached before these endings to alter the basic meanings of the roots. These morphemes correspond to English suffixes that normally appear without reflexes of the Latin inflectional endings, although a few examples below take the inflectional endings -um and -a. For each of these examples, determine how the basic meaning of the noun is modified by the suffix.

Diminutive: -ule
granule
molecule
capsule

Place: -ary
library
sanctuary
dispensary
aviary
aquarium
columbarium

Action or abstraction: -ment
torment
momentum
complement
compliment
detriment

Action or abstraction: -mony
matrimony
patrimony
acrimony
alimony
hegemony

Action or abstraction: -ty, -ity, -ety
loyalty
fidelity
sobriety

ADJECTIVE-FORMING SUFFIXES

Nouns and verbs in Latin took other derivational endings to form adjectives. In Latin these endings were followed by inflections that have been dropped in English.

Capable of or similar to: -ile
facile
fragile
puerile

Fullness: -ous, -ose
magnanimous
verbose
bellicose

Able: -ble, -bil-
capable, capability
tangible
affable

GREEK

Greek inflectional and derivational morphology was quite similar to that of Latin. But the variety of words that English has inherited from Greek is far less that what has entered from Latin; and so there is quite a bit less to say about Greek morphology.
Here are the Greek suffixes that are most commonly found in English words:

Agent: -tor
mentor
chiropractor

Action: -sis
praxis (< prag + -sis)

analysis
homeostasis

Object: *-ma, -m, -me*
schema
scheme
theme
gram (as in *epigram*)

See appendix II for Morpheme set 6.

EXERCISES

1. Based on what you've learned in this chapter and the meanings of the roots (some of which you can find in the glossary and others in a dictionary), parse the following Latin and Greek expressions. Then give a short definition that reflects, at least in part, the meanings of the individual morphemes. (In the following examples, 'Ending' means 'inflectional suffix'.)

Latin
Past passive participle: Stem + (V)t + suffix **cap + t + us** captured
                                                appar + at + us prepared

desideratum   _____ + ___ + _____ _____
                    Root   Ending   Meaning in English

(terra) incognita _____ + ___ + _____ _____
                    Root   Ending   Meaning in English

errata   _____ + ___ + _____ _____
                    Root   Ending   Meaning in English

succubus   _____ + ___ + _____ _____
                    Root   Ending   Meaning in English

invicta   _____ + ___ + _____ _____
                    Root   Ending   Meaning in English

vista (Italian)   _____ + ___ + _____ _____
                    Root   Ending   Meaning in English

sonata (Italian) _____ + ___ + _____ _____
                    Root   Ending   Meaning in English

**Present active
participle:**
         Stem + V**nt** + suffix   **par + ent + s > parens** parent
                                   aud + ient + s > audiens hearing

multiplicans _____ + ___ + _____ _____
                    Root   Ending   Meaning in English

parent (English) _____ + ___ + __Ø__ _____
                    Root   Ending   Meaning in English

errant (English) _____ + ___ + __Ø__ _____
                    Root   Ending   Meaning in English

**Future passive
participle:**
         Stem + V**nd** + suffix   **add + end + um** thing to be added

explicandum _____ + ___ + _____ _____
                    Root   Ending   Meaning in English

memorandum _____ + ___ + _____ _____
                    Root   Ending   Meaning in English

corrigendum _____ + ___ + _____ _____
                    Root   Ending   Meaning in English

referendum _____ + ___ + _____ _____
                    Root   Ending   Meaning in English

agenda _____ + ___ + _____ _____
                    Root   Ending   Meaning in English

pudenda _____ + ___ + _____ _____
                    Root   Ending   Meaning in English

disputandum _____ + ___ + _____ _____
                    Root   Ending   Meaning in English

explicanda _____ + ___ + _____ _____
                    Root   Ending   Meaning in English

Greek

suffix -ma:

schema _____ + _____ _____
Root Ending Meaning in English

schemata _____ + _____ _____
Root Ending Meaning in English

stoma _____ + _____ _____
Root Ending Meaning in English

stigmata _____ + _____ _____
Root Ending Meaning in English

2. The following terms from the field of botany contain several morphemes you have not yet encountered.* (Note that some consist of two words: the first for the genus and the second for the species. Most botanical terms have endings taken from Latin.) With the help of a large dictionary and/or a specialized dictionary of botanical terms and a glossary or dictionary of roots, briefly define, parse, and gloss each term. For example:

calochortus pulchellus: 'yellow globe-tulip, a plant with delicate yellow flowers. Its bulbs are considered a delicacy in India.'

cal	(o)	chort	us	pulch	ell	us
'beautiful'		'feeding place, garden'	N [Lat masc sg]	'beautiful'	[diminutive]	A [Lat masc sg]

(Note that the adjective *pulchellus* has the same number and gender as the noun it modifies, *calochortus*. You can see from this example that the connection between the meaning of the morphemes and the characteristics of the thing being described can be quite a distant or tenuous one.)

a. rhizocorm   b. filiformis   c. procumbens   d. oryza angustifolia
e. caulocarpous   f. leucospermus   g. involutus   h. pleniflorus

*The use of Latin in botany is described in considerable detail by William T. Stearn in *Botanical Latin* (London: Nelson, 1966). This book also has a useful glossary.

3. The following words from the fields of biology and medicine contain several morphemes you have not yet encountered. With the help of an unabridged dictionary and/or specialized dictionaries of biological and medical terms and using a glossary or dictionary of roots,* briefly <u>define, parse, and gloss</u> each term.

a. tectospondylic b. endolymphangial c. pithecanthropus d. insessorial

4. Parse, gloss, and give allomorphs for the following words.

a.   v i v í p a r o u s

GLOSSE(S)   _____

ALLOMORPH(S)   _____

b.   o c c á s i o n

GLOSSE(S)   _____

ALLOMORPH(S)   _____

c.   s ú p p l i c a n t

GLOSSE(S)   _____

ALLOMORPH(S)   _____

d.   d ò l o r í f i c

GLOSSE(S)   _____

ALLOMORPH(S)   _____

* A *Dictionary of Word Roots and Combining Forms* by Donald J. Borror is recommended.

e. ecléctic ìs m   [<u>Note: root isn't 'law, charge'</u>]

GLOSSE(S) _____

ALLOMORPH(S) _____

f. ás sonance

GLOSSE(S) _____

ALLOMORPH(S) _____

10

Prehistory of English and the Other Indo-European Languages

THE DISCOVERY OF THE DEEPER LINGUISTIC PAST OF ENGLISH AND RELATED LANGUAGES

The origins of language and of the different languages of the world have preoccupied human beings throughout history. The story of the Tower of Babel in the Hebrew Bible and myths in other cultures about the divine origin of language and linguistic diversity are tokens of the central role of language in human belief systems.

Medieval European theologians took Hebrew to be the original language (i.e. the language of Adam). Since the Middle Ages, however, new knowledge about diverse languages and other aspects of culture has been gained through intensive investigation. Together with the figurative shrinking of the earth's vastness thanks to improvements in transportation and communication this has brought about radical changes in Western perspectives on language.

The current tradition of scientific inquiry into linguistic classification (i.e. defining families of languages sharing a common ancestor) began in the eighteenth century, when scholars proposed that Hungarian and Finnish, until then considered quite separate languages, were in fact related through descent from a single hypothetical ancestor. In a 1786 address, the British jurist Sir William Jones stated the hypothesis that the major languages of Europe and the ancient Indian language Sanskrit were part of such a 'family'. Jones, who served in India during the British colonial period, was one of the first Europeans ever to intensively study Sanskrit, which functions as the ecclesiastical language of Hinduism, much as Latin did in Roman Catholicism. He proposed that Sanskrit, Latin, and Greek might have 'sprung from some common source', which itself might no longer be spoken.

Table 10.1 Cognate Words in Latin, Greek, and Sanskrit

meaning	Latin	Greek	Sanskrit
'ten'	decem	deka	daša
'three'	tres	treis	trayas
'family'	genus	genea	janas
'he/she/it crawls'	serpet	herpei	sarpati

The evidence for this hypothesis is observable in some striking similarities among words with similar or identical meanings in the three languages.

Jones's address kicked off a boom of historical linguistic scholarship in the nineteenth century. These investigations clearly established the existence of the family of languages that came to be identified as 'Indo-European', so called because speakers of the languages identified as belonging to it occupied, at the dawn of the Western historical period, much of the Eurasian land mass stretching from the Indian subcontinent to the western boundaries of Europe.

THE INDO-EUROPEAN LANGUAGES

Divergent dialects arose as the Indo-Europeans migrated to far flung areas of Europe and Asia and became isolated from each other. These dialects gave rise to the individual sub-groups of the Indo-European family. There are thirteen branches of Indo-European, eight of which have living descendants; some of these are listed below.

Germanic—with its descendants: English, German, Dutch, Yiddish, Norwegian, Swedish, Danish, Icelandic, etc.

Italic—Latin, with its Romance descendants: French, Italian, Spanish, Portuguese, and Romanian, etc.

Hellenic—Ancient (i.e. Mycenean and Homeric), Classical (Attic), and Modern Greek

Celtic—including Scots Gaelic, Irish, Welsh, and Breton (spoken in France)

Balto-Slavic

Baltic—including Lithuanian and Latvian

Slavic—including Russian, Ukrainian, Czech, Polish, Serbo-Croatian, Bulgarian, etc.

Indo-Iranian

Indic—Sanskrit and its descendants spoken in or near India: including Hindi, Bengali, Urdu, Romany ('Gypsy'), Punjabi, Gujarati, etc.

1–Balto-Slavic   6–Albanian
2–Germanic   7–Anatolian
3–Celtic   8–Armenian   PIE?=likely general
4–Italic   9–Indo-Iranian   location of PIE homeland
5–Hellenic   10–Tocharian

Figure 10.1. Geographical Extent of Indo-European Languages (to the first millennium B.C.E)

Iranian—including Farsi (Persian or Iranian), Pashto (of Afghanistan), etc.

Armenian

Albanian

The branches of the Indo-European family that are known from written records but have no living descendant languages include Tocharian, Anatolian (including Hittite), Phrygian, Illyrian, and Thracian. Most of the groups represented by living languages once also contained additional languages which have since died out (e.g. Gothic, from the Germanic branch). Figure 10.1 indicates roughly where the major known living and extinct branches were probably situated at or near the beginning of recorded history.

FROM INDO-EUROPEAN TO GERMANIC

One of the most important discoveries about the relationship of the Indo-European languages (and an important factor in the establishment of linguistics as a scientific study governed by regular principles) was the elucidation of the sound correspondence usually called 'Grimm's Law', named for Jakob Grimm (one of the two brothers who collected the popular stories known as Grimm's fairy tales). The reconstruction of regular and systematic relationships between Germanic and other Indo-European languages hinged on the discovery of the relationship of certain consonants in the descendants of Indo-European words in Germanic to stops in the Indo-European parent language. These relationships are seen in the groups of cognates in table 10.2, where English is used to

Table 10.2 English, Latin, Greek, Sanskrit Sound Correspondences and Reconstructed PIE

English	Latin	Greek	Sanskrit	English	Latin	Greek	Sanskrit	PIE
father	pater	pater	pita	f	p	p	p	*p
three	tres	treis	trayas	θ	t	t	t	*t
heart	cors	kardia	—	h*	k	k	k	*k
apple	Abella	—	—	p	b	b	b	*b
ten	decem	deka	das/a	t	d	d	d	*d
kin	genus	genea	janas	k	g	g	g	*g
be	fuit	pʰuei	bʰavati	b	f	pʰ	bʰ	*bʰ
do	facit	ti-tʰesi	da-dʰati	d	f	tʰ	dʰ	*dʰ
goose	hanser	kʰen	hansa	g	h/ø	kʰ	h	*gʰ

*Present-Day English *h* was pronounced as the voiceless velar fricative [ç] in prehistoric Old English. This sound is preserved in certain kinds of Scots English—for example, in the word *light*, pronounced [lIxt].

represent the Germanic languages. (Note especially the initial consonants of these words.) The asterisk (*) shown before the sounds and forms indicates that the form is a **reconstruction,** based on inference, and not actually recorded in written form. **Proto-Indo-European (PIE)** is the ancestral language that linguists have reconstructed on the basis of surviving evidence in Indo-European languages.

Notice that in most cases, the Sanskrit sound is the same as the reconstructed PIE sound, while the Latin and Greek sounds are almost as frequently identical to PIE. The sound [b] was very rare in proto-Indo-European, especially in word-initial position, so it is illustrated word-internally in table 10.2.

These correspondences can be most easily understood as the result of a sound shift in proto-Germanic that regularly affected the <u>manner</u> of articulation of the stop consonants without substantially changing their <u>place</u> of articulation. Thus, we can see a shift in which

1. the <u>voiceless</u> stops

   *p   *t   *k

   changed their manner of articulation from that of stops to that of the similar <u>fricatives</u>

   f   th   x (as in *Bach,* and later, h as in *have*);
2. the <u>voiced</u> stops

   *b   *d   *g

   lost their voicing to become the <u>voiceless</u> stops

   p   t   k
3. the <u>voiced</u> stops which were originally <u>aspirated</u> (i.e. accompanied by a puff of air)

   *bʰ   *dʰ   *gʰ

   lost their aspiration to become the simple (unaspirated) voiced stops

   b   d   g

This may leave one with the following question: if voiced aspirates lost aspiration and plain voiced stops became devoiced and voiceless stops became fricatives, why didn't <u>all</u> these sounds eventually fall together into the voiceless fricative class? The answer is that one part of the shift must have been completed before the next could begin, so that first voiceless stops became fricatives, then voiced stops became voiceless stops, then voiced aspirates became non-aspirates. This makes Grimm's Law a **chain shift** of sounds, not unlike the Great Vowel Shift, which was discussed in Chapter 2.

THE INDO-EUROPEAN WORLD

Indo-European was the first large language family with which Western scientists were able to practice true 'linguistic archaeology'. Vocabulary shared by disparate branches of the Indo-European diaspora show them once to have shared a substantial lexical and cultural base and tells us more about the Indo-Europeans than ordinary archaeology has yet been able to.

By comparing words in the descendant languages and extrapolating from the regular correspondences observed in words like those noted above, linguists have been able to infer a great deal about the Indo-European language and the Indo-Europeans themselves as they lived five or six thousand years ago. The following aspects of the physical and conceptual universe are just a few of those represented by the Indo-European morphemes which have been reconstructed. (Stops with a raised <u>w</u> to their right (e.g. k^w) were pronounced with simultaneous lip rounding.)

a. Religion, spiritual culture: *deiw 'shine, day, god' (preserved in the names *Zeus, Jupiter,* and *Tiw,* as in *Tuesday*); *egni (as in *ignite* and the name of the Hindu fire god *Agni*) and *pūr (cf. the root *pyr*), both meaning 'fire', are distinct in that the former was conceived of as an animate entity (i.e. living and invested with a spirit) or a god.

b. Politics: *g^{h}osti 'one with whom one has reciprocal duties of hospitality' (giving the Germanic word *guest* and the Latinate *host*), *reg 'rule' [meaning 'king' in the cognates *rex* and *raja*].

c. Agriculture: *grəno 'grain' (in Germanic *corn* and Latinate *grain, granule*) *sē 'sow' [in *seed, seminal*], *yeug 'yoke' [as in *conjugal*], *g^{w}ou 'cow' (in Germanic *cow*, Latinate *bovine* and Greek *bulimeia*), *k^{w}on 'dog' (in Germanic *hound*, Latinate *canine*, Greek *cynic*), *ek^{w}o 'horse' (in Latinate *equestrian*, Greek *hippopotamus*), *peku 'flock, medium of exchange' (in Germanic *fee*, Latinate *pecuniary*).

d. Material culture: *k^{w}el 'go around' (in Germanic *wheel*, Greek *cycle* and Latinate *collar*), *dhwer 'door' (in Germanic *door*, Greek *thyroid*, Latin *forum*), *wes 'to clothe' (in Germanic *wear*, Latinate *vestments*], *weg^h 'transport in a vehicle' (in Germanic *wagon*, Latinate *vehicle*).

e. Flora and fauna; climate and the heavens: *deru/dreu 'tree' [in Germanic *tar* and *true*, Latinate *durable*], *peisk 'fish' (Germanic *fish*, Latinate *Pisces*), *mus 'mouse' (in Germanic *mouse*, Latinate *muscle*), *b^{h}āgo 'beech tree', *b^{h}erəg 'birch tree', *mē 'moon' (in Germanic *month*, Latine *menses*), *sāwel 'sun' (in Latinate *solar*), *ster 'star' (in Greek *aster*), *nek^{w}t 'night' (in Latinate *nocturnal*), *(s)neig^{wh} 'snow' [whose initial [s] is lost in some Indo-European daughter languages] (in Latinate *nival, niveous,*), *neb^h 'sky, cloud' (in Latinate *nebular, nimbus*), *(s)tenə 'thunder' (as in Germanic *Thor*, Latinate *detonate, astonish*).

e. Human beings, body parts: *g^{w}en 'woman' (in Germanic *queen*, Greek *gyn*), *wīro 'man' (in Germanic *werewolf*, Latinate *virile*), *pəter 'father' (in Latinate *paternal*), *māter 'mother', *b^{h}rater 'brother' (in Latinate *fraternity*), *swesor 'sister' (in Latinate *sorority*), *dent 'tooth' (in Latinate *dental*, Greek *odontology*) *leb 'lip' (in Latinate *labial*), *ous 'ear' (in Latinate *aural*), *ped 'foot', *dnghū 'tongue'.

f. General terms: *es and *b^{h}euə 'be', *sed 'sit' (in Latinate *preside*, Greek *polyhedron*), *stā 'stand', *b^{h}er 'bear' (in Latinate *fertile*, Greek *phosphor*), *d^{h}e 'put, make' (in Germanic *do*, Latinate *factory*, Greek *thesis*), *ed 'eat' (in Latinate *edible*), *g^{w}ei 'live' (in Germanic *quick*, Latinate *vivid*, Greek *biology*), *genə 'give birth' (in Germanic *kin*, Latinate *genus*, Greek *gonad*), *newo 'new' (in Latinate *novel*, Greek *neologism*), *k^{w}o 'relative or interrogative pronoun' (in Germanic *what*, Latinate *quantity*), *nd^{h}er 'under' (in Latinate *infer-/infra-*). Words for highly fortified settlements included: *d^{h}ūno (in Germanic *dune*, Celto-Germanic *town*), *bhergh (in Germanic *borough, iceberg*, Latinate *fort*).

OTHER FEATURES OF THE PROTO-INDO-EUROPEAN LANGUAGE

In addition to the actual forms of words, it is possible to reconstruct a great deal else about proto-Indo-European, such as the fact that it had

a. heavily inflected nouns and verbs, like its descendants Latin, Greek, Germanic [incl. OE], Slavic, Indic, etc.

b. relatively flexible word order (made possible in part by the indication of relations of subject, direct object, indirect object, etc. by case marking morphemes)

c. a rich system of inflectional marking of tense, active versus passive voice, and grammatical 'mood' (such as the archaic English 'subjunctive mood' in the verb of the phrase *were I king.* . . .)

d. various kinds of 'relic' morphology we can still see traces of but which occurs only very irregularly and cannot now be completely understood (This is a frequent source of highly irregular allomorphy, and includes:

    α. Ablaut: gon/gen/gn; tom/tm; pher/phor;

    β. Nasal infix: tag/tang; frag/frang

IMPORTANT POST-INDO-EUROPEAN CHANGES IN LATIN AND GREEK

Following the dissolution of Indo-European the descendant languages underwent many independent changes, such as Grimm's Law in Germanic. Most
significant for our purposes are those that occurred in Latin and Greek. A few
of the most important of these are listed below. (The symbols ">" and "<"
here and elsewhere in the text are to be read as "becomes" and "comes
from", respectively.)

Greek
i.   Devoicing of voiced aspirates: $*b^h > p^h$ (later [f])
                                       $*d^h > t^h$ (later [θ])
                                       $*g^h > k^h$ (later [x]) (Cf. examples
                                       above.)
ii. Initial $*s > h$ (Cf. Lat *super, sub, sex* and Gk *hyper, hypo, hex*)
iii. $*w$ becomes h or disappears (cf. Eng *water* and Gk *hydro*)
iv. $* y$ becomes h or z (cf. the cognates Eng *yoke* and Gk *zeugma*; Eng
     year and Gk *horoscope*)
v. $*g^w > g$, b: ($*g^w$en 'woman' *gyne*); ($*g^w$ei 'live' *bio[-s]*); this and
     other labiovelars change differently depending on the sounds
     around them.

Latin
i.   Rhotacism: s sometimes becomes r: *rustic/rural, osculate/oral, justice/*
     jury; inquire/inquisitive
ii. $*dt$ (from a root final d̠ and fol-
     lowing past participial t̠) $> s$
     (*cad/cas, vad/vas*)
iii. Various kinds of assimilation in place and/or manner of articulation
     (Cf. the earlier chapter on phonetics.)
iv. $*g^w > g$, sometimes b, v ($*g^w$ou $> bos$), ($*g^w$em $> venire$; cf. Eng
     come)
v. $*w > v$ ($*wir > vir$)
vi. $*b^h, *d^h > f$ (Cf. examples in tables above)
vii. Weakening and other vowel changes

RELEVANCE TO THE STUDY OF ENGLISH WORDS

We have accounted for a kind of allomorphy (some of which has lasted for
five millennia) which can aid in associating Latin and Greek morphemes with

Table 10.3 Consonant Correspondences for PIE, Greek, Latin, and Native English Words

PIE	Greek	Latin	English
*p	pater	pater	father
*t	tris	tres	three
*k	kard	cord	heart
*b	kannabis	—	hemp
	—	Abella 'a town'	apple
*d	deka	decem	ten
*g	gonia 'angle'	genu	knee (in which k was originally pronounced)
*bh	pher, phor	fer	bear 'carry'
*dh	thumos 'spirit'	fumus 'smoke'	dust
*gh	charis 'grace'	hortari 'urge'	greed
*m	mesos	medium	middle
*n	nux	nox	night
*l	leukos	lux	light
*r	eruthros	rubeus	red
*w	histor 'wise'/ [w]ideia 'idea'	video 'I see'	wit
*y	zugon	jugum	yoke
*s	hals	sal	salt

each other and with native and other English words. To use this knowledge as a key to recognizing and learning a new Latin or Greek morpheme, you can guess at its possible English cognates by applying the expected sound correspondences. (This can be done even more easily using the *American Heritage Dictionary* (3rd ed.), which indicates PIE roots and their major English, Greek, and Latin descendants.)

The correspondences between cognates in table 10.3 are valid for most initial consonants and many medial and final consonants.

See appendix II for Morpheme set 7.

EXERCISES

Indo-European Stop Correspondences: Knowing Grimm's Law allows you to identify many cognates of English words in the classical languages. Greek and Latin usually preserve the original Indo-European stops which have undergone Grimm's Law in the Germanic languages (e.g. I[ndo]-E[uropean] *pəter, Greek **pat**er, Latin **pat**er, English **fath**er). However, as a result of independent sound changes in Latin and Greek, the Indo-European voiced aspirates **bh**, **dh**, and **gh** changed so as to create the following relationships:

PIE *$\mathbf{b^h}$ corresponds to Greek **ph** and Latin **f.**
PIE *$\mathbf{d^h}$ corresponds to Greek **th** and Latin **f.**
PIE *$\mathbf{g^h}$ corresponds to Greek **kh** (often transcribed **ch**) and Latin **h** or no consonant.

1. The members of each of the following pairs of words or underlined morphemes share a single proto-Indo-European source. In each pair one has been borrowed into English from Latin, French, or Greek while the other is an inherited, native Germanic word. On the basis of your knowledge of consonant correspondences, determine which word in each pair is borrowed by writing a B beside it. E.g. foot ___   pedal _B_

a. <u>s</u>ediment _____   <u>s</u>itter _____   f. <u>fl</u>oat   _____   <u>pl</u>uvial _____

b. <u>cr</u>am   _____   a<u>g</u>o<u>r</u>a _____   g. <u>f</u>antasy _____   <u>b</u>ea<u>c</u>on _____

c. <u>d</u>ike   _____   <u>f</u>igure _____   h. s<u>p</u>ume _____   <u>f</u>oam   _____

d. e<u>rod</u>e   _____   <u>r</u>at   _____   i. <u>far</u>ina   _____   <u>bar</u>n   _____

e. <u>eat</u>en   _____   <u>ed</u>ible _____   j. <u>v</u>ehicle _____   <u>w</u>agon _____

2. Fill in the blanks using your knowledge of Grimm's Law by providing the Greek and Latin root forms and their cognates in modern English. All IE roots given below are shown with a * before them, signifying that these are historically **reconstructed** and not actually recorded forms. The symbol √ means 'root'. In your answers give the correspondences to the IE consonants shown in **boldface** type. (Leave the slots marked ——— blank in the Latin and Greek columns in some rows.) Some meanings are intentionally left blank to avoid giving away the answer.

IE √	Greek √	Latin √	English word	IE √ MEANING
a. *$\mathbf{d^h}$eu	———	———	_ew	'flow'
b. *$\mathbf{b^h}$a	_a, _e	_a, _e	_an	'speak'
c. *$\mathbf{bend}$	———	———	_en	'protruding point'
d. *$\mathbf{b^h}$er	_er, _or	_er	_ear	'carry'
e. *$\mathbf{pet}$	_ _er	———	_ea_er	'fly'
f. *$\mathbf{ten}$	_on	_en(d)	_in	'stretch'

g. *kerd	__ard	__ord	__eart	
h. *bʰu	__yt	__u	__e	'plant, grow'
i. *ker	__ran	__orn	__orn	'head'
j. *aug	au	au__	e__e	'increase'
k. *gel	———	__el	__ool	
l. *pau	__ed	__auc	__ew	'little'
m. *ter	———	__rans	__rough	'cross over'
n. *kan	———	__an	__en	'sing'
o. *pa	———	__an 'bread'	__ood	
p. *swad	he__	sua__	swee__	'pleasant'
q. *gel	(gan)__l	__lob	__lue, __lump	'ball'
r. *gʰreib	———	———	__ri__	
s. *treud	———	__rud 'push'	__rea__	'squeeze'
t. *dʰe	__e	__ac 'make'	__o	'put, set'

3. With the help of dictionaries and a book of roots (e.g. Borror 1960), parse, gloss, and simply define the following electronics terms:

a. rheostat b. electrode   c. anhysteresis   d. florescent   e. resistance
f. impedance g. potentiometer h. superheterodyne i. commutator j. insulation

4. Parse, gloss, give allomorphs, and brief dictionary definitions for the following words:

a.   éffluent

GLOSS(ES)   _____

ALLOMORPH(S)   _____

DEFINITION   _____

b.   quìncenténnial

GLOSS(ES)   _____

ALLOMORPH(S)   _____

DEFINITION   _____

c.   ìnterlócutor

GLOSS(ES)   _____

ALLOMORPH(S)   _____

DEFINITION   _____

11

Latin Words, Phrases, and Abbreviations in English

In this chapter we apply what we have learned about Latin and Greek morphology to translating phrases and abbreviations from the classical languages. All of the expressions listed here occur in English, some of them in everyday uses and others in more specialized contexts. In chapter 9 we saw singular and plural endings for some Latin and Greek forms; now we will take a more comprehensive look at the inflectional endings for case, number, and gender of nouns and adjectives.

LATIN PHRASE AND SENTENCE SYNTAX

Latin nouns and adjectives appear in several declensions. Each declension has its own set of inflectional suffixes. The suffixes designate the number (singular or plural) and case (nominative, genitive, dative, accusative, or ablative) of the noun. The nominative, dative, and accusative cases are used for the subject, indirect object, and direct object, respectively. The genitive case indicates a possessor or the object of the preposition 'of'. Finally, the ablative case often serves the function of designating the object of the prepositions 'from', 'out of', 'by', etc.

The following chart illustrates these and other uses more fully using English examples:

Nominative   Independent noun or adjective; subject of a sentence: *girl*; *A girl hit the ball*

Accusative   direct object: *A girl hit the ball*

	with some prepositions: *Pat hit the ball toward <u>the wall</u>*
Genitive	possessor: <u>*the girl's*</u> *ball; the home* <u>*of the president*</u>
Dative	indirect object: *A girl gave <u>the boy</u> a ball*
	with some prepositions: *The ball is in <u>a hole;</u> John did it for <u>the poor</u>*
Ablative	= 'with', 'under the circumstances':
	[With] <u>the signal</u> [having been] <u>given</u>, the train advanced with prepositions, especially those meaning 'from'/'out of'/'by':
	The shelf is made out of <u>wood</u>; He was directed by <u>the police-man</u>

Table 11.1 illustrates the case endings for the three most common declensions of the Latin noun and adjectives. (Here, as throughout our discussion of actual Latin words, differences in vowel length are omitted, since these are not usually shown in the use of Latin expressions in an English context.) Where the endings differ within a category, the most common ones are included.

Study the following list of Latin expressions and their approximate English translations. Use your knowledge of borrowed words (like *initial* and *origin,* for the first two examples) and remember the morphemes you have learned thus far, including the Latin inflectional and derivational morphology discussed in chapter 9. You should find that you can arrive at a meaning very close to that of the translation without paying too much attention to the suffixes for

Table 11.1 Three Latin Declensions

	Decl. 1 (fem.)	Decl. 2 (masc./neut.)	Decl. 3 (masc./fem./neut.)
Singular			
Nominative	-a	-us, -um[a]	-s, -∅[b]
Genitive	-ae	-i	-is
Dative	-ae	-o	-i
Accusative	-am	-um	-em
Ablative	-a	-o	-e, -i
Plural			
Nominative	-ae	-i, -a[a]	-es, -a[b] -ia
Genitive	-arum	-orum	-ium
Dative	-is	-is	-ibus
Accusative	-as	-os, -a[a]	-es, -ia
Ablative	-is	-is	-ibus

[a] This form is used for the neuter gender only.
[b] Recall that ∅ is a symbol for no ending.

number, gender, and case. Note that most of the prepositions used below are nearly identical in form to the familiar prefixes whose meanings they largely share. (The abbreviation *lit.* below means 'literally'.)

INDIVIDUAL WORDS

> **collegium** a collection of people with similar pursuits, a grouping of colleagues *(con, leg, -um)*
> **interregnum** period between reigns *(inter, reg* [a rare allomorph with final n], *-um)*
> **infra** below [often meaning 'see below']
> **qua** as [used in English expressions like I'm speaking *qua* student, not *qua* average citizen.]
> **quasi** as if, seemingly [She took a *quasi* objective stance in her argument.]
> **quiditas** lit., a 'whatness' = an indefinite something, a 'je ne sais quoi'
> **sic** thus [used in quotations where a quoter indicates that, however doubtful in appearance, the quote is accurate, as in David wrote "There's *[sic]* times I think so and times I don't."]
> **supra** above [often meaning 'see above']

PREPOSITIONAL PHRASES = [PREPOSITION + NOUN]

In these phrases, the preposition, which corresponds closely in form to a prefix of the same or similar meaning, is followed by a noun or noun phrase. One can generally ignore the case of the noun in such a phrase in its English translation.

> **ab initio, ab ovo** from the beginning *(ab = ab-, ov/oö* 'egg')
> **ab origine** from the first
> **a fortiori** lit. 'from the stronger (reason)' = all the more *(a = ab, fort* 'strong', *-or* 'more)
> **a priori** lit. 'from the prior' = from cause to effect, inductively *(a = ab)*
> **a posteriori** lit. 'from the later' = from effect to cause, deductively *(a = ab)*
> **ad gustum** to taste *(ad = ad-, gust* 'taste')
> **ad absurdum** to (the point of) absurdity
> **ad hoc** for this (purpose) *(hoc* is a pronoun meaning 'this [neuter = 'thing']')

ad hominem against the man (used of an argument based on personal, not logical, factors)

ad infinitum to the unlimited, to infinity (*fin* 'end')

ad nauseam lit. 'to nausea' = until you get sick of it [Nausea originally meant 'seasickness']

ante bellum before the war (specifically, the American Civil War) *(ante-, bell)*

cum grano salis with a grain of salt (*cum* = *con-*, *gran* 'grain', *sal* 'salt')

cum laude with praise (*cum* = *con-*, *laud* 'praise' [as in *laudable, laudatory*])

   also: **magna cum laude** with great praise *(magn, cum, laud)*

   summa cum laude with highest praise (*sum* 'topmost' [as in *summit*])

de facto lit. 'from fact' = in reality *(de-, fac)*

de jure lit. 'from law' = as stated in the law or the rules *(de-, jud/jus/jur)*

de novo anew *(de, nov)*

ex cathedra lit.'from the chair' = with authority (originally Greek: *ex, cata* 'down', *hedr* 'seat, side')

ex post facto from what is done afterward = as a Monday morning quarterback *(ex, post, fac)*

(in) re in the matter = regarding (*re* 'thing, matter')

in medias res in the midst of things [said sometimes of a story that begins when the action is already underway] (*re, med* 'middle')

in situ in (its own or its natural) place (*situ* 'site, place' [as in *situation*])

inter alia among other things (*inter, al/all/allelo, -ia* '[Latin neuter plural]')

in vivo in life (i.e. an organism) *(viv)*

in vitro in glass (i.e. in the test tube) (*vitr* 'glass' [as in *vitrify*])

per annum per year *(per = per-, ann)*

per diem per day (cf. *carpe diem*, above)

per capita lit. 'per head' = per person *(caput)*

per se in or by itself; as such (*se/sui* 'self')

pro bono (publico) for the (public) good *(pro-, bene/bon)*

pro forma lit. 'for form' = as a formality *(pro-, form)*

sub rosa lit. under the rose = in secret *(sub-)*

NOUN PHRASES: NOUN + NOUN IN THE GENITIVE CASE

amicus curiae friend of the court (*am/em* 'love', *cur* 'court, council' [from *con-* + *vir* 'man'], *-ae* '[Latin feminine genitive singular]')

aqua vitae lit. 'water of life' = whiskey *(aqua, vit, -ae)*

Dies Irae day of wrath or judgment *(di* 'day', *ir* 'anger' [as in *ire, irate*])

curriculum vitae lit. 'course of life' = a résumé *(cur/curr* 'run', *-cule* '[N diminutive]', *vit, -ae* [Lat feminine genitive singular]

modus operandi way of working (the 'm. o.' of detective fiction) *(mod* 'mode, manner, measure, control', *op, -ndi* 'of VERBing')

modus vivendi way of living (i.e. getting along) *(mod, vit/viv* 'life', *-ndi* 'of VERBing')

NOUN PHRASES: NOUN + ADJECTIVE, ETCETERA

These phrases have at their core a noun which is modified by an adjective or other word or phrase.

alma mater nurturing mother *(al/ol* 'nurture, grow' [as in *alumnus*], *mater)*

animal bipes implume lit. 'a featherless biped (i.e. two-footed) animal' = a human being *(bi, ped/pod, in-, plum* 'feather')

(causa) sine qua non lit. 'cause without which not' = a necessary condition *(caus* 'cause', *sine* 'without', *qua* 'which', *non* 'not')

deus ex machina lit. 'god from machine' = unforseeable intervention in a plot *(ex = ex-)*

magnum opus great work = crowning acheivement *(magn, op* 'work' [as in *operate*])

ne plus ultra lit. 'not more beyond' = perfect *(ne* 'not', *plus, ultra = ultra-)*

quid pro quo lit. 'what for what' = something expected in return for something else

persona non grata an unacceptable person *(grat)*

prima facie lit. 'at first face' = at first sight (This adjective noun combination is in the ablative, which provides the meaning 'at') *(prim, fac* 'face')

rara avis rare bird

vox populi voice of the people *(voc, popul* 'people')

terra incognita an unknown land

sui generis of its (own) type = one of a kind *(se/sui* 'self, own', *gon/gen/gn)*

terminus a quo point from which, a starting point *(termin* 'point, end')

terminus ad quem point up to which, an ending point

ABLATIVE ABSOLUTE CONSTRUCTIONS

These phrases typically consist of [adjective + noun] or [noun + adjective], both in the ablative case, and are translatable as '(with) NOUN being ADJECTIVE'.

aequo animo with equanimity, in an even tempered spirit
bona fide in good faith (*bene/bon, fid* 'trust, bold')
ceteris paribus other (things) being equal (*ceter* 'other' [as in *etcetera* 'and other (things)'], *par* 'equal' [as in *parity, par*])
mutatis mutandis making the necessary changes (lit. with changes having to be changed) (*mut* 'change, exchange' [as in *mutate, immutable*], *-nd*)

ADJECTIVE PHRASE

non compos mentis not sound of mind *con-* + *pon/pos* 'place, put' = 'composed', *ment*)

SENTENCES IN WHICH THE VERB 'IS' OR 'ARE' IS UNDERSTOOD

amantes amentes lovers (are) lunatics (*am/em* 'love', -ant [see Ch.2], *a/an* 'not', *ment* 'think, mind')
ars gratia artis art (is, exists) for the sake of art (i.e. for its own sake and not necessarily functional) (*ar/art* 'art', *grat*)
ars longa, vita brevis art (is, that is, lasts) long, life (is) short (*ar/art, viv/vit, brev* 'short')
in vino veritas in wine (is) truth (*vin, ver*)
nil novi sub sole nothing (is) new under the sun

SENTENCES WITH AN EXPLICIT VERB

amor vincit omnia love conquers all *(am/em, vic/vinc, omni)*
caveat emptor buyer beware (*cav* 'caution', *am/em* 'take' [as in *exempt*])
de gustibus (non est disputandum) lit. 'concerning taste (there is nothing to be disputed) = there's no accounting for taste (*de* roughly = *de-*, *gust* 'taste, enjoy', *non* 'not', *est* 'is', *-nd, -um*)

de minimis non curat lex (or **praetor**) the law (or leader) is not concerned with trifles (*min* 'little', *cur* 'care', *leg, prae* = *pre-*)

de mortuis nihil nisi bonum lit. 'of the dead, nothing if not good' = do not speak ill of the dead ('speak' is understood) (*de-, mort, nihil, nisi* 'if not', *bene/bon*)

non sequitur (it) doesn't follow (*sequ/secu* 'follow')

(pecunia) non olet (money) doesn't stink (*pecu* 'wealth, property', *ol* 'smell')

primum non nocere (the first (thing is) not to harm (*prim, non* 'not', *noc*)

sic transit gloria mundi thus passes the glory of the world (*trans, mund* 'world' [as in *mundane*], *-i* '[Lat. masc./neut. sg. possessive]')

stet (Let it) stand (i.e. remain) *(sta)*

tempus fugit time flies

veni, vidi, vici I came, I saw, I conquered *(ven, vid, vic/vinc)*

IMPERATIVE SENTENCES

carpe diem Seize the day! (*carp* 'pluck, fruit' [as in *excerpt*], *di* 'day' [as in *diary, diurnal*])

cave canem Beware of dog! (*cav, can* 'dog' [as in *canine*])

vade mecum lit. 'Go with me' = a manual or other indispensible item one takes everywhere *(vad, cum)*

EXPRESSIONS USUALLY SEEN IN ABBREVIATED FORM

The following abbreviations are used in a variety of ways in different kinds of works, including dictionaries, listings of biographical information, and references to books contained in footnotes. Many of these abbreviations are not used by typical college students but they can easily be learned by understanding the Latin words or phrases they represent.

c. or **ca. circum, circa** about, approximately [often used with dates] (*circ* 'around')

cf. confer compare [used to refer to another relevant idea or publication] (*con-, fer* 'carry')

et al. et aliis and others [usually, other authors] (*et* 'and', *al*)

etc. etcetera and other things (*et* 'and', *ceter* 'other', *-a*)

e.g. exempli gratia lit. 'for sake of example' (*grat* 'sake, grace')

fl. floruit lit. 'he/she flourished' = was active or alive [used with dates] (*flor* 'flower')

id. idem same ['author, work, etc.' is understood] (*idem* 'same'[as in *iden-t-ity*])

ibid. ibidem same place (ibi 'place' [as in *al-ibi* 'other place'], *idem* 'same')

i.e. id est that is; in other words (*id* 'it'/'that', *est* 'is')

loc.cit. loco citato (in the) place cited ('previously' is understood) [used in footnote references to avoid repeating details already given] (*loc, cit* 'cite')

op.cit. opere citato (in the) work cited ('previously' is understood) [used in footnote references to avoid repeating details already given] (*op, cit* 'cite')

q.e.d. quod erat demonstrandum (that) which was to be demonstrated [used at the end of a proof] (*quod* 'what', *erat* 'was')

q.v. quod vide lit., 'which see' [a direction to refer to a highlighted subject in the same work which you are reading]

sc. scilicet lit., 'it is permitted to know' = that is to say, namely *(sci, lic)*

s.v. sub verbo under word [used in dictionaries and other reference books to refer you to another entry in the same work]

viz. videlicet lit., 'it is permitted to see' = namely, to wit [used to introduce examples or lists] *(vid, lic)*

See appendix II for Morpheme set 8.

EXERCISES

1. Find the word in the list below which <u>best</u> matches the dictionary definition given. Do <u>not</u> refer to dictionary at first. (You may do so when you are finished). Some of the words are decoys. Use no word more than once. Work from definition to word. Avoid multiple answers. (If you can't decide between two choices, give both and explain the problem for a chance at partial credit.)

1 heteronomous	2 licentious	3 polity	4 telegamic
5 probophily	6 autocratous	7 atmesis	8 peristaltic
9 parhomologous	10 delectation	11 inculpatory	12 theurgy
13 homotronic	14 malocclusion	15 gradiometric	16 apandrous
17 paratomy	18 perigonium	19 mesophilic	20 dolorifuge
21 parergon	22 anatopism	23 thearchy	24 parachromoparous
25 appetent	26 hypidiomorphic	27 toparch	28 synturgious
29 illicitness	30 metachronism	31 alegonymy	32 homeostasis

a. _____ Marked by the absence of legal or moral constraints.

b. _____ Improper closure of the teeth so that the cusps do not fit together.

c. _____ Possessing functionless male organs.

d. _____ Having only some constituents with distinct crystalline form (e.g. a rock).

e. _____ Civil order.

f. _____ Desiring eagerly.

g. _____ Thriving in an intermediate environment (e.g. of moderate temperature).

h. _____ A subordinate activity or work.

i. _____ A sac surrounding the reproductive organs in certain species.

j. _____ Reproduction by fission along a special division zone.

k. _____ The tendency in an organism to maintain a stable internal condition.

l. _____ A human act, process, power, or state of supernatural efficacy or origin.

m. _____ An error in a temporal sequence placing an event after its real date.

n. _____ A minor ruler or prince.

o. _____ Of or pertaining to involvement or implication in a charge of misconduct.

p. _____ Subject to external controls.

q. _____ Something that banishes or mitigates grief.

2. With your knowledge of the Latin morphemes, parse and gloss the underlined portions of the following Latin phrases and give a rough translation of each whole phrase. You may check most of your translations in a Latin-English dictionary or a dictionary of foreign phrases. (N.B.: all the words in b. and c. have ablative case inflection, indicating that the first word of your translation should be *with*.)

a. scientia est potentia   b. Deo volente   c. una voce
d. fugit hora*   e. pro tempore   f. sine loco
g. ex animo   h. cave canem   i. in flagrante delicto

3. The following words and phrases are taken from the field of law. Using an unabridged and/or legal dictionary (e.g. *Webster's Third New International Dictionary* and/or *Black's Law Dictionary*, your knowledge of Latin morphology and a glossary, briefly define, parse, and gloss each term.

a. probation   b. logomachy   c. mandamus
d. jurisdiction   e. impignoration   f. defenestration
g. mortuus sine prole

4. Fill in the blanks in each string of morphemes and other elements, then write out the complete word (or, as in c, two words) formed.

a. _____t i c   _____- i a   =   _____
    'putrid' [ADJ] 'blood'   =   'illness resulting from toxins in the
    'condition'   blood'
    [Use the allomorph of the morpheme meaning 'blood' which lacks an initial consonant.]

b. _____n   _____   =   _____

    'lung' 'inflammation'   = 'alternative term for *pneumonia*'

    [N.B.: do not use *pne/pneum* for 'lung'.]

c. prim _____   _____   _____   =   _____   _____
                                          °
    'first'[Lat. f sg] 'pregnancy' [Lat. f sg] = 'female pregnant for first time'

d. _____   =   _____

    'important point' [Lat. m/f sg] = 'pivotal point in an argument or discussion'

    [N.B.: root ends in sound which, combined with the following s̲ must be spelled x̲.)

*-*it* is a third person singular verb suffix.

e. _____ _____ = _____

'gland'   'tumor'   = 'tumor with glandular structure'

f. s i n e _____ e = _____

'without' 'care' = 'paid job requiring no work'

5. Gloss the underlined morphemes in the space provided.

a. <u>r h i n o l a r y n g</u> o l o g y   'study of disease of _____ & _____'

b. <u>l a c</u> t a t i o n   'production of _____'

c. c e r v i x (= <u>c e r v i c</u> + -s)   '_____ of body or _____'

12

Later Changes: From Latin to French to English

You may have noticed that the Latin morphemes encountered here sometimes resemble other words in English that are not treated as allomorphs of these morphemes. Sometimes these resemblances are between morphemes and their English glosses—e.g. *salv* meaning '<u>save</u>' [as in *salvage* 'saving from destruction']; *coc* [as in *precocious* 'having matured at an early age'] meaning '<u>cook</u>, ripen'. These resemblances are not coincidental. They usually occur because words have come to English both directly from Latin—especially in scholarly and scientific terminology—and indirectly, via French. The route of borrowing for most of the words from French was roughly

> Vulgar Latin > proto-Romance > Old French or Norman French > English.

Vulgar Latin was the everyday language of the common people of Rome and much of the Italian peninsula, not the standard, literary variety recorded in most writings of the time which we ordinarily mean when we refer to Latin. Vulgar Latin was the source of **Proto-Romance,** the unwritten spoken language of most of the later Roman Empire and its descendants, the Romance languages.

This chapter will identify some of the changes in form that led to this special variety of 'allomorphy', which will provide additional aids to memorizing and recognizing morphemes. The changes described sometimes took place in several stages and were thus often more complex than the ">" sign might suggest. The correspondences between Latin and English forms established here are general, however, and help to identify many French-Latin word pairs (i.e. doublets) found in English today.

159

LOSS OF INFLECTIONAL ENDINGS AND INDIVIDUAL SOUNDS

Even as the Romans were recording the literature that Western culture would take as a written standard for nearly two thousand years, many spoken varieties of Latin—i.e. Vulgar Latin—had come to look rather different in significant ways. By the time of proto-Romance the language would have been quite unintelligible to a contemporary of Julius Caesar. For our purposes, some of the most important changes involved inflectional endings. During the transition from Latin to French, two processes conspired to radically alter the tongue. The first was a morphological simplification in which the accusative case forms of nouns and adjectives supplanted the nominative and other case forms. The second was the loss of certain final consonants, most importantly *m*, together with a loss or change in the quality of (originally or newly) final vowels, which were typically unstressed. This explains why there is little trace of Latin inflectional suffixes like *-um, -em, -o, -at,* and *atem* in the words English has borrowed from French over the centuries. We should bear in mind, however, that unstressed vowels were also lost between Middle English (which, of course, contained many words from French) and Present-Day English. These changes together, then, leave both native English words (like *bake*) and French borrowings (like *cage*) with silent final vowels, the only remaining sign that they once had suffixes.

SPELLING VERSUS PRONUNCIATION

Because of the many differences between English spelling and pronunciation, it is important to observe that the Latin-English sound correspondences discussed here are mostly matters of spelling. In the example of *precocious,* above, both cs of the Latin word *precociosis,* which had a 'hard' (i.e. stop) [k] sound, are retained in the English word, but only in spelling. (In speech, of course, the English word is [prɪkošəs], which only preserves the first of the two [k] sounds in the Latin word.) For this reason we will focus primarily, though not exclusively, on the written forms of words.

OVERVIEW OF CONSONANT CHANGES

Most of the changes in consonants we have to contend with here are the result of some kind of partial or complete assimilation or deletion. We can characterize the phonetic changes affecting most consonants in very rough terms as follows:

Table 12.1 Sketch of Consonant Changes: Latin to French to English

in initial position	in medial position	in final position
t d̲ c̲ g̲ (rarely, b̲) > affricate > fricative if followed by a front vowel	stop > fricative > Ø if surrounded by vowels velar stop > i, y̲, or w̲ l̲ > u̲, or Ø after a vowel	consonant > Ø, particularly in consonant clusters

When an initial or medial consonant (i.e. one in the beginning or middle of a Latin word) is immediately followed by a front vowel like *i* or *e*, it will tend to take one or more steps along the following 'one-way street' toward French: stop > affricate > fricative > Ø. In this way, stops became either affricates or fricatives or Ø (i.e. nothing; they are deleted). This is at least partly a matter of assimilation in place of articulation; if a velar or alveolar stop occurs before a front vowel it may be drawn toward the open, roughly alveopalatal position of the highest part of the tongue for that vowel. By the same token, an affricate may open further when it occurs in the neighborhood of one or more vowels, becoming a fricative. For example, the [k] sound (written c̲) in the Latin word *centum* 'hundred (th)' first became [č]—as it remains in Italian *cento*—and eventually [s], as in English borrowings from French like the word *cent*.

Consonants in medial position, in particular those surrounded by vowels, often pass through some or all of the steps: stop > fricative > Ø. Fricatives, being more open than either stops or affricates, will, if they open further still, tend to disappear completely or become vowels (which are the most open of sounds). For example, the *t* in the Latin word *frater* 'brother' disappeared, yielding the word borrowed into English as *friar*. Velar stops in medial or final position also typically disappeared but could leave in their place a high vowel or a semi-vowel (i.e. i, y̲ or w̲) as in the development of Latin *fructus* and *vocalis* into English *fruit and vowel* respectively.

In final position, individual consonants tended to disappear, particularly if they occurred in clusters (i.e. groups of two or more consonants). For example, after the loss of the inflectional ending *-um*, Latin *profectum* ended in the cluster *ct*, from which the *c* was lost, ultimately providing the word *profit*.

OVERVIEW OF VOWEL CHANGES

For the same reasons that different dialects of English are most often distinguished by the sounds of their vowels rather than their consonants, the most subtle and complex sound changes since Latin have been those affecting vowels. In general, these changes can be characterized as vowel quality change (including diphthongization and monophthongization) and deletion. Vowel quality change typically involves the replacement of one vowel sound with another, as when the *i* in the first syllable of Latin *linguaticum* [lit. 'tongue thing'] becomes the *a* of *language*. **Monophthongization** is the replacement of a diphthong (a sequence of two vowel sounds) by a single vowel, which occurs in a change like *ae > e* in *aeternitas > eternity*. The reverse process is **diphthongization,** which occurs when a single vowel becomes a two vowel sequence, as seen in the change *venam > vein*. Deletion occurs when Latin loses the vowel in the second syllable (and thereby the whole syllable itself) as *malefacentia* 'wrongdoing' becomes *malfeasance*. (Deletion can occur in almost any position in a word. It is usually associated with a lack of stress in Latin.)

SOUND CHANGES IN DETAIL

The following lists show additional examples of sound changes. The Latin forms are shown on the left and the English forms that entered the language via French are on the right. (Latin verbs are cited in the first person singular form. Nouns are shown in their singular nominative or, when necessary for clarity, accusative case. Adjectives are given in their neuter singular nominative/accusative form.) In some instances the Latin and English forms have different meanings or display different affixes; nevertheless they do share one or more historical root morphemes and can be considered the same for our purposes. Because most words have changed sounds in more than one place, we highlight the letters being discussed in each case.

CONSONANT CHANGES

Affrication of Stops

Affrication is a familiar process frequently observed in rapid American English speech, where the first two words in a phrase like <u>Did you hear me?</u> are pronounced [d I ǰ ə] rather than [d I d y u]. This change involves partial assimilation of a stop to a neighboring semi-vowel. In Latin, affrication usually occurred before an <u>i</u> or <u>e</u>, but in many words the stop [k] (written <u>c</u> in Latin) is also affricated before <u>a</u>.

> <u>**t** or **d** > 'soft' **g** before i</u>
> viaticum   voyage
> linguaticum   language

coraticum	courage
ab + ante + aticum	advantage
ultraticum	outrage
judicem (< judex)	judge
vindicentia	vengeance

c > ch

cantus	chant
caput	chief
capitulum	chapter
caritas	charity

d > j before iu

diurnalis	journal

Much like the cases of affrication shown above but involving a more unusual change in place of articulation, from labial to alveopalatal, is

b or v > soft g (i.e. [ǰ])

cambiat	change
cavea	cage

Changes from Stop or Affricate to Fricative

In these changes, stops become fricatives with nearby or identical place of articulation.

b or p > v between vowels

prae + posit + um	provost
riparium	river
caballarium	cavalier

Assibilation

Assibilation is the process whereby stops (or affricates, which of course often come from stops) become **sibilants** (i.e. sounds like [s], [z], or [š]). This typically occurs when the stop stands before a mid- or high-front vowel in the Latin word.

t > 'soft' c or s

-ant-ia/-ent-ia	-ance/-ancy/-ence/-ency
eloquentia	eloquence
rationem	reason
palatium	palace
lectionem	lesson

'hard' c > 'soft' c or s before a front vowel

pacem (< pax)	peace
placeo	please
malefacentia	malfeasance

In words recently borrowed from French, we can see how some affrication proceeded to full assibilation, resulting in [š] or [ž], for example in

cantorix	chanteuse
caput	chef
rubeum	rouge

Vocalization

In the present context, the term 'vocalization' broadly refers to the change of a sound from a consonant into a vowel (or a semi-vowel) or the loss of a consonant in the environment of a vowel with some effect on that vowel.

c, g > y, i

fructus	fruit
conductum	conduit
facio	-(i)fy
paco	pay
religo	rely
crucifigo	crucify
frico	fray
legale	loyal
regale	royal
focarium	foyer

c > w

vocale	vowel

l, ll > u

altum	haute [ot], as in *haute cuisine, haute couture*
collocat	couch
bellitas	beauty
ultraticum	outrage

Deletion in Medial or Final Position

frater	friar
rotundum	round
cadentia	chance
sacristanum	sexton
periculosum	perilous
salvo	save
dignitatem	dignity

VOWEL CHANGES

Vowel Quality Changes

abbrevio	abridge
persona	parson
insulatum	isolate
species	spices
exemplum	sample

au > oi or oy

gaudium	joy
nausea	noise
claustrum	cloister

Diphthongization

a > ai before m, n, or l

clamor	claim
manus	maintain
vanum	vain
valeo	vail (as in *countervail*)

e > **ai** or **ei** before n

| teneo | retain |
| vena | vein |

a > **ea**

clar	clear (cf. *clear/clarity*)
rationem	reason
pacem	peace

Monophthongization

au > **o**

| pauso | pose |

Deletion

pietas	pity
exemplum	sample
signum	sign
musculum	muscle

Notice that sequences of vowels which either occurred in the Latin original or arose because of deletion of consonants are often reduced (i.e. one or more vowels in a sequence of vowels may be deleted). One can see that this occurred in a case like *securum* > *sure,* although it didn't always happen (cf. *native* > *naive*).

See appendix II for Morpheme set 9.

EXERCISES

1. Using the meanings of Latin and Greek morphemes you've learned or can find in a glossary, and the information on typical changes in the forms of words in Romance illustrated in chapter 12, give the English word borrowed from Old, Norman, Modern, or some other variety of French that comes from the Latin word shown. (Ignore portions of words given in parentheses.) The first two items are completed as examples. You may use the appendix to the *American Heritage Dictionary* (3rd ed.), or a similar source to confirm your answers.

	Latin	French > English
a.	tractum	trait
b.	musculum	muscle
c.	carnaticum (Hint: initial c does not > ch.)	_____
d.	abantio [< ab- + ante- + -o]	_____
e.	diversitatem	_____
f.	lacte	café au _____
g.	planum	_____
h.	magister	_____

(Hint: long sequences of vowels may be shortened.)

i. jurisprovidentia   _____
(Hints: intervocalic fricatives are less stable than medial stops; not all medial stops are lost.)

j. addirectio   _____

(Hint: the first i in the word was lost.)

k. catena   _____

2. Based on your knowledge of sound changes in the development from Latin to French as well as plausible semantic changes, fill in the blank spaces in the chart below with ten Latin-French pairs (i.e. doublet words or morphemes). Ignore parts in parentheses. Many of the words are decoys.

solid	fancy	fang	wide	capit(al)
invia(re)	capt(iare)	clam(or)	couch	emblem
chase	junct(ion)	cadence	employ	involve
choir	contin(ent)	chorus	envoy	rouge
fantasy	ruby	joint	claim	journey

| char(coal) | calm | implic(ate) | chance | rouse |
| contain | isolate | view | insulate | video |

	Latin	**French**
	video	view

3. Find the word in the list below which <u>best</u> matches each dictionary definition given. Don't use a regular dictionary but refer to Borror's *Dictionary of
Word Roots and Combining Forms* to identify unfamiliar morphemes. Some of
the words are decoys. Use no word more than once. Work from definition to
word. Avoid multiple answers. (If you can't decide between two choices, give
both choices and explain the problem.)

1 dynotrusion	2 cynodontia	3 degramic	4 metastasis
5 hypergamy	6 androgynous	7 tmesis	8 peristaltic
9 protuse	10 delectation	11 inculpatory	12 pantocrator
13 homeoregion	14 anthobrach	15 ectropion	16 ergatogyne
17 nephropathy	18 telegenic	19 epiopticon	20 mastobrach
21 ambiplasty	22 epipodium	23 symplectic	24 theurgy
25 illative	26 anthophyte	27 epiphonema	28 epiphilious

A. _____ An abnormal turning out of a part of the body (e.g. of an
eyelid).

B. _____ Pertaining to the grammatical case denoting movement into a
place or thing.

C. _____ Relating to or being an intergrowth of two different minerals.

D. _____ Marriage into a higher social class or caste.

E. _____ A division of Triassic Therapsida comprising a number of small carnivorous reptiles often with cusps on the teeth resembling those of certain mammals.

F. _____ A flowering plant.

G. _____ The omnipotent lord of the universe.

H. _____ An occult art by which one may evoke or utilize the aid of divine and beneficent spirits.

I. _____ A wingless queen ant resembling a worker.

J. _____ A summary argument concluding a discourse.

K. _____ A lateral ridge or fold along either side of the foot of various gastropods.

L. _____ The separation of the parts of a compound word by intervening words (e.g. of *another* in *a whole nother thing*).

4. The following words are taken from the field of philosophy. Using an unabridged dictionary and a glossary of morphemes, briefly define, parse, and gloss each term.

a. empiriological   b. monothelitism   c. encratism
d. theophany   e. metempsychosis   f. panentheism

5. Parse and gloss the following words, using their definitions as an aid and as a guide to associating their analyzed and actual current meanings.

a.   mýriopede

'arthropod with long, segmented body'

GLOSS _____

b.   senópia

'changes in lenticular elasticity, due to sclerosis, at a stage following presbyopia'

GLOSS _____

c.   ìchthyósis

'skin disorder characterized by rough, dry skin with plate-like hardenings'

GLOSS   _____

d.   complácency

'smugness'

GLOSS   *(com* = 'intensive')_____

e.   commúnion

'1. a Christian religious denomination; 2. the Eucharist'

GLOSS   _____

f.   coév/al

'isochronous'

GLOSS   _____   *(-al* = NOUN)

g.   altíloquent

'sesquipedalian'

GLOSS   _____

h.   éntropy

'total measure of energy (specifically, in the universe) not available for work'

GLOSS   _____

PROJECT

<u>Part 1:</u> Write a list of twenty unfamiliar terms from advanced textbooks or journal articles from the following disciplines: biology, zoology, medicine, chemistry,

physics, engineering, geology, literature, linguistics, rhetoric, mathematics, law, history, economics, philosophy, art, or another area approved by your instructor. (Consult with a specialized dictionary or an advisor in the chosen discipline to help identify important terms, if necessary.) If you have studied Latin elsewhere you are <u>strongly</u> encouraged to choose terms from Greek. Avoid terms containing proper names. All these words should be composed primarily of Latinate or Greek morphemes. All words should contain at least three syllables and more than half of the words should have four or more. All should contain <u>at least</u> one morpheme that you have not encountered before.

<u>Part 2:</u> For each term from part 1 approved by your instructor, write the following.

a. A full dictionary definition of the word.

b. A complete parsing of the word into its smallest morphemic components. (Confirm this by the use of a dictionary etymology of the English word, its parts, or its Latinate/Greek sources.) Meanings of many unfamiliar morphemes can be obtained from *The American Heritage Dictionary* (3rd ed.). You may also want to consult a dictionary of nomenclature from the discipline. In some cases, the use of a large Latin or Greek dictionary may be necessary to confirm the parsing.

c. A gloss of each morpheme in its <u>original</u> (i.e. earliest) Latin or Greek sense.

d. An identification of any allomorphy displayed by the morphemes and the names of the rules or processes (if any) which account for it.

e. An identification of the kinds of semantic change which have occurred (if any) from the original meanings of the components (i.e. morphemes or larger portions of the word) to their sense in the word in question.

f. An explanation of the compositional semantic structure of the word and any additional comments needed to explain its specific meaning as used in the discipline.

The following example indicates the minimum degree of exposition you should give each word.

a. **epexegesis** 'an explanation following a word or larger part of a text that limits its application or clarifies its meaning'

b. **ep / ex / ege / sis**

c. **epi-** 'on'; **ex-** 'out'; **hege** 'lead'; **-sis** 'NOUN: action of verb'

d. **epi-** is shortened to **ep-** before the initial vowel of **ex-** as a result of vowel truncation. **Hege** loses its **h** after a consonant.

e. **exege** 'lead out' shifts from a concrete, physical sense to an abstract one via metaphor in this word, where it comes to mean 'intellectually extract, deduce'. In a literary context the idea is one of 'pulling' something 'out' of a text as if it were a physical object 'containing' an idea or meaning. **epi-** also involves the spatial metaphor in shift from concrete location ('on top of') to the figurative 'additional' or 'supplemental'.

f. The compositional structure of the word is represented by brackets around the component morphemes and larger units as follows: **epi [[ex ege] sis]**. In other words, grouping its units from smallest to largest:

    i. **ex- + ege = exege** means 'lead out'
    ii. **-sis** is affixed to and modifies this verbal unit, making it a noun: **[exege] sis** 'the action of leading out';
    iii. **epi-** then modifies **exegesis** to mean 'a supplemental exegesis' or 'an exegesis added (here, to a text), making **epi [[exegesis]]** .

(N.B.: There is no actual reference to language, writing, interpretation, or meaning in the morphemes which make up the word.)

Appendix I, Part 1:
Morphemes to Glosses

ABBREVIATIONS AND SYMBOLS

Parts of speech: A = Adjective; N = Noun; V = Verb
Source languages: L = Latinate (i.e. from Latin, French, or occasionally, other Romance languages); G = from Greek; F = from French; L, G = both L and G; L/G = first allomorph(s) from L, other(s) from G; G/L = first allomorph(s) from G, other(s) from L;
Miscellaneous: ←derived from; rel. = related to; usu. = usually; neg. = negative; pass. = passive; interrog. = interrogative; inchoat. = inchoative (verbs of starting or becoming; chg. = change; sing. = singular.

morpheme	gloss	Morpheme set	source
a-/an-	not, without	2	G
-a	[feminine]		L,G
-a	[neuter plural]		L,G
ab-/abs-	from, away		L
-able	see *-ble*		L
abs-	see *ab-/abs-*		L
ac/acer/acerb	sharp, tip, extremities	6	L
acanth	spine, thorn		G
acer/acerb	see *ac/acer/acerb*		L
acet	vinegar		L
-ac	A, N		L,G
acou	hear		G
-acle	see *-cle*		L
acu	sharp		L
ad-	to, toward	4	L
-ad	N [group]		G

morpheme	gloss	Morpheme set	source
adelph	brother		G
aden	gland	8	G
adep/adip	fat		L
-ae	[feminine plural]		L
-ae	[feminine possessive]		L
-ae	[feminine dative]		L
aer	air		L,G
ag/eg/ig	act, do, drive	4	L
-age	N, A		F
ager	field	6	L
agog/agogue	teach, induce		G
agon	struggle, contest (< *ag* 'drive')		G
-al	A		L
al/all/allel	other	7	L, G
al/ol	nurture, grow	3	L
alb(in)	white	6	L
alg	pain	8	G
ali	wing	9	L
alt	high	4	L
am/amor/im	love	3	L
ambi-/amphi-	both		L/G
ambl	walk, go	4	L
amphi-	see *ambi-*		G
ampl	large		L
-an	A		L
an-	see *a-*		G
ana-	up, again, back	3	G
-ance/-ence	N [action of verb, present active]	2	F
-and/-end	N [future pass.] 'to be VERBed'		L
-ane	A		F
andr	male, man	4	G
anem	wind		G
angi	(blood) vessel		G
angin	painful spasm		L
angui	snake		L
anim	mind, spirit, (nonplant) life	2	L
ann/enn	year	3	L
-ant/-ent	A, N [VERBing, present] (cf. *-nt*, ch. 9)	2	L
ante-/anti-	old, before	3	L
anth/anthem	flower, collection		G
anthrop	human	1	G

morpheme	gloss	Morpheme set	source
anti-	against, opposite		G
apec/apic	tip	3	L
api	bee	9	L
apo-	away, from, off	4	G
apt/ept	fit, capable	3	L
aqu	water		L
-ar	A		L
ar/ard	burn, dry		L
arachn	spider	9	G
arbiter	judge		L
arbor	tree		L
arch	first, govern	4	G
ard	see *ar*		L
-ard	N [usu. with neg. connotation]		F
-arium	N [place, repository]		L
art	skill, manufacture		L
art/arthr	segment, joint		L,G
arter	artery		G
-ary/-ory	A, N	2	F
aster	star	6	G
-aster	N [agent, neg. evaluation]		L
-asthen	lack of strength (< *a-* + *sthen*)		G
-ate	N,A,V	2	L
atmo	air		G
aud	hear	6	L
aug	increase		L
aur	ear	8	L
auspec	foretell, protect (< *av* + *spec*)		L
auster	south, wind		L
auto/tauto	self, same	6	L/G
av	bird, fly	4	L
axill	armpit	8	L
bacch	orgiastic		G
bar/bary	weight		G
bas	bottom, low		L
bat	beat		L
bath/bathy	depth	6	G
batrach	frog		G
beat	blessed		L
bell	war	5	L
bene/bon	good, well	6	L

morpheme	gloss	Morpheme set	source
bi	two	5	L
bib	drink		L
bibl	book, Bible		G
bio	life	1	G
blast	embryonic, immature		G
bl	see *bol*		G
-ble	able to be done, suitable for		L
blephar	eyelid		G
bol/bl	throw, extend	3	G
bon	see *bene*		L
bov/bu/bos/bou	cow, milk	9	L,G
brach/brac	arm		G
brach/brachy	short	6	G
brev	brief, short		L
bronch	windpipe		G
bu	see *bov*		L
bucc	cheek		L
burs	pouch, money		L
cac	bad	1	G
cad/cas/cid	fall	4	L
calc	heel		L
calc	lime		L
calcul	pebble, count		L
cal/call	beautiful		G
can/cen	sing, intone		L
can/cyn	dog		L/G
cand	shine		L
cap/cep/caput/capit	head		L
cap/cep/cip/cup	take, contain	3	L
caps	box		L
caper	goat, impulse		L
car/carn	flesh	6	L
car	see *cer*		G
car	dear, expensive		L
car/carcin/canc	crab, cancer		L,G
card/cord	heart, agree	7	G/L
cas	see *cad*		L
cata-	down, away, back, opposite	3	G
caud/cod	tail	8	L
caus/cauter	burn		G
caut/cav	warm, beware		L
cav	hollow		L
ced/ceed/cess	go, let go	4	L
cens	judge, assess	5	L

morpheme	gloss	Morpheme set	source
cent	hundred(th)	5	L
center	center		L
cephal	head	5	G
cer/car/cr/ker/corn	horn, head, brain, neck		G,L
cer/cre/cr	to separate, judge	3	G,L
cere/cre	come forth, grow		L
cervic	neck, neck of uterus	8	L
chir	hand	9	G
chondr	cartilage		G
chrom	color, embellishment	1	G
chron	time	1	G
chrys	gold, yellow		G
chthon	earth, land		G
cid/cis	cut, kill	3	L
cil	eyelash, hair		L
cin	see *kin*		L
cin/con	ash, dust		L/G
circum-	around	1	L
cis	on the side of		L
cis	see *cid*		L
cit	summon, arouse		L
clam	cry out, call	9	L
clar	clear, bright		L
clav	key, locked	9	L
-cle	see *-le/etc.*		L
cli/cliv/clin	lean, lie, bed	6	L
clud	to close	4	L
co-	see *con-*		L
coc	ripen, cook		L
cod	see *caud*		L
col	live, inhabit, grow	9	L
col/coll	neck		L
col/cull	filter, clarify		L
coll	glue		G
com-	see *con-*		L
con	cone		G
con-/co-	together, with	3	L
contra-/counter-	against, facing	2	L
copro	dung, feces		G
cor/core	pupil (of eye)		G
corn	horn		L
coron	heart		L
corp/corpor	body, flesh	2	L
cortec	outer covering		L
cosm	universe, order, orna-ment	1	G
cost	side, coast		L

morpheme	gloss	Morpheme set	source
counter-	see *contra-*		F
cr	see *cer*		G
cras	disease; mixture		G
crat/crac	govern	5	G
cre	see *cer, cere*		L
crin	hair		L
cre/cred	believe, trust	6	L
crin	secrete		G
cruc	cross, important point	7	L
cry/crym	cold, freeze		G
crypt/cryph	secret, hidden	6	G
cub/cumb	lie down, remain	3	L
-cule	see *-le/etc.*		L
culp	fault, crime	2	L
cumb	see *cub*		L
cumul	heap		L
cup	desire		L
cup	see *cap*		L
cur	care	5	L
curs/curr	run	9	L
cuss	shake		L
cut	skin	8	L
cyan	blue		G
cyt	cell		G
dactyl	finger, digit		G
dam/damn/demn	loss, harm	6	L
de-	in reverse, away, down	1	L
deb	owe		L
dec	acceptable	7	L
decem/decim/deca	ten, tenth	5	L,G
dei/div	god, augury	3	L
dem	people	5	G
demi-	half	5	F
den/odon	tooth	9	L/G
dendr/dr/dry	tree	9	G
derm/dermat	skin	8	G
di/dich/dy/du	two	5	L,G
dia-	through, apart	3	G
diabol	devil < *(dia-* + *bol/bl)*		G
dic	speak, point	6	L
digit	finger, toe, number		L
dign	worthy, fitting		L
dipl	double	5	G
dis-/di-	apart, reversed		L
dit/don/dot/dos/dow/da/dat	give	6	L,G

morpheme	gloss	Morpheme set	source
doc/dog	teach	4	L/G
dol/dolor	suffer	6	L
dom	house, control		G,L
dorm	sleep		L
dors	back (of body or body part)		L
drom	run, course		G
duc	lead, draw, pull	2	L
dulc	sweet		L
dur	hard, lasting		L
dyn	power	9	G
-dynia	pain		G
dys-	bad		
e-	see *ex-*		L
ec-	see *ex-*		G
ec/oec	inhabit		G
eccles	church		G
ecto-	outside	1	G
-ectomy	act of cutting out (< *ec-* + *tom* + *-y*)		G
ed/es	eat	7	L
-ee	N [passive, agent]		F
ego	self, I		L,G
eid	see *vid*		G
-ell	see *-le/etc.*		L
em	take, buy		L
em	see *hem*		G
-eme	N [unit]		F
emet/emes	vomit		G
en-	see *in-/en-*		G
-ence	see *-ance*		G
encephal	brain (from *en-* + *cephal*)		G
-end	see *-and*		L
endo-	inside	1	G
ent	see *es*		L
-ent	see *-ant*	2	L
enter	intestine		G
entom	insect (from *en-* + *tom/ tm*)		G
eo	dawn, early		G
epi-	on, over	4	G
episi	vulva		G
equ	horse		L
equ/iqu	even, level	3	L
erg/urg/org	work	3	G

morpheme	gloss	Morpheme set	source
ero	physical love	4	G
err	wander, do wrong		L
eryth/erythr	red		G
es/ess/ent/ont	be, basic		L,G
-esc	see -sc		L
eso-	inward		G
esthet/esthes	perceive, feel	4	G
ess	see *es*		L
eth	custom		G
ethn	nation		G
eti/aeti	source, cause		G
etym	true		G
eu	well, good	4	G
ev	age, time	9	L
ex-/e-/ec-	out, away	4	L/G
exo-	outside		G
exter-/extern-	outside		L
extra-	outside	1	L
extro-	outside		L
fa/pha/phe	speak, spoken of	7	L/G
fac/fec/fic	do, make	3	L
fan	see *phan*		L
febr	fever		L
fel	cat		L
felic	happy		L
fer/pher/phor	bear, send, bring	7	L/G
ferr	iron		L
fet/foet	unborn child		L
fid	trust, bold		L
fid/fiss	split, divided		L
fil	thread, line		L
fil	offspring		L
fin	end, boundary		L
fla	blow	5	L
flor	flower		L
flu/fluc/fluv	flow, river	6	L
fod/foss	dig		L
formic	ant	9	L
frag/frang/fring	break	3	L
fran	see *phren*		F
frater	brother	7	L
fren	see *phren*		L
fru/frug	fruit, produce		L
frut	shrub		L
fug	flee	2	L

morpheme	gloss	Morpheme set	source
fund	base, bottom		L
furc	fork		L
fus	pour, melt, blend	3	L
galac	milk		G
gam	marriage, sexual union	1	G
gaster	stomach	8	G
ge	earth	7	G
gel	solidify, jelly, ice		L
gem/gemin	twin	7	L
ger	old person	7	G
ges/ger	carry, bring, offer, do		L
giga	giant, billion (10^9)		G
gingiv	gums		L
glob/glom	ball		L
gli/gle/glu/glut	gather, stick		G/L
gloss/glot/glott	tongue, speech	6	G
glyc/gluc	sweet		G
gn/gnos/gnor	know	6	G,L
gon/gen	angle, knee		G/L
gon/gen/gn	birth, type, origin	3	G,L
gnat	allomorph of *gon*/etc and *nat* 'birth'		L
grad/gred/gress	step, go	4	L
gran	grain		L
graph/gram	write, record	7	G
grat	thankful, pleased, kind	2	L
gravid	pregnant	8	G
greg	gather	2	L
gust	taste, enjoy		L
gyn/gynec	woman, female	6	G
gyr	ring, circle		L
hagio	sacred, saint		G
hal/sal	salt		G/L
hecto/hecato	hundred, many	5	G
hedon	pleasure		G
hedr	seat, side		G
heli	sun	4	G
helic	spiral		G
helminth	worm		G
hem/em	blood	8	G
hemer	day		G
hemi-/semi-	half	5	G/L
hepat	liver	8	G

morpheme	gloss	Morpheme set	source
hept/sept/septem	seven, seventh	5	G/L
herp/herpet/serp	creep, reptile	9	G/L
hes/her	to stick, hold back	6	L
hetero-	other, different	4	G
hex/sex	six, sixth	5	G/L
hiero	sacred		G
hipp	horse		G
hist	body tissue	8	G
hod	see *od*		G
hol	whole		G
hom	earthling, human being	2	L
homo-/homeo-	same	4	G
hor	hour, season, time	9	G
hum	earth, ground, low		L
hyd/hydr	water	6	G
hyper-/super-	over, above		G/L
hypno	sleep, trance		G
hypo-	under, below, partial	3	G
hyps	high, height		G
hyster	womb, neurotic disorder	8	G
-i	[masculine plural]		L
-i	[masculine possessive]		L
-i-	[filler]		L
-ia	land, state, medical condition	8	G,L
-ia	N [abstract]		G,L
-ia	[neuter plural]		L
-iac	N		G,L
-ial	see *-al*		L
-ian	see *-an*		L, G
iatr	treat, heal	1	G
-ible	see *-ble*		L
-ic	A, N	1	G,L
-ice	N		F
ichthy	fish	9	G
-icle	see *-cle*		L
icon	image		G
id/idi	same, self		G
id	see *vid*		G
-id	A		G
idio	individual, own (rel. id/idi)	1	G
ign	fire		L
-il/-ile	A		G

morpheme	gloss	Morpheme set	source
-in	N		G
in-	not	4	L
in-/en-	in, into	3	L/G
-ine	A		F
infra-	below, after	1	L
inguin	groin		L
insul	island		L
inter-	between, among	1	L
intra-	within	1	L
intro-	inwards		L
-io	classical form of -ion		L
-ion	N [action or result of VERBing]	2	F
-ise	alternate (usu. British form of -ize)		G
-ism	N [belief, practice]		G
iso-	equal	4	G
-ist	N [doing or associated with]		G
it	go		L
-it/-ite	N, A		L,G
-ite	native, follower, product		F
-itis	inflamation	8	G
-ity	N [quality of]		F
-ive	A, N	2	L
-ium	see -um		L
-ix	N, A[feminine]		L
-ize	V	1	G
jac/jec	throw, lay, lie, extend		L
jus/jur	judge, law, ritual	6	L
jug/jung	join		L
juven	young	7	L
kerat	horny, hard, cornea		G
kilo-	thousand	5	G
kin/cin	move		G
-la	see -le/etc.		L
lab	take, seize		G
lab	lip	8	G
lac	milk	8	L
lac	gap, basin		L
lacrim/lachrym	tear, tear duct	8	L
lagn	lust		G
lal	babble, talk		G

morpheme	gloss	Morpheme set	source
lamin/lamell	layer, blade		L
lapar	abdomen, abdominal wall		G
lapid	stone		L
laps	fall, expire		L
laryng	voice box, vocal cords	8	G
lat	carry	7	L
lat	wide, broad		L
later	side	9	L
latr	worship		G
lav	wash		L
-le/-ole/-cule/-cle/-lus/-la/-ell/-il/-ill	[diminutive] (cf. ch. 9)		L
leg	law, charge	2	L
leg/lig	pick, read	4	L,G
leg/lex	speak		L,G
len	soft, gentle		L
-lent	full of		L
leo/leon	lion		L,G
lep/lepr/lepid	scaly		G
leuk	see *luc*		G
lev	light, rise		G
lex	word		G
liber	weigh, consider	2	L
liber	book		L
liber	free		L
lic	permissible, unrestrained	4	L
lic	see *linqu*		L
lig	tie, bind	7	L
lign	wood	7	L
lim/limen/limin	threshold, border, shore		L
lin	flax		L
lingu	tongue		L
linqu/lic/liqu	leave		L
lip	fat, leave		G
liqu	fluid		L
liter	letter	2	G
lith/lite	stone	6	G
loc	place	5	L
locu	see *loqu*		L
log (related to leg, lex)	study, speak	1	G
loqu/locu	speak	7	L
luc/leuk	light, white, colorless, clear		L/G
lud	play		L
lumb	lower back, loins		L

morpheme	gloss	Morpheme set	source
lumen/lumin	light	5	L
lun	moon, madness		L
-lus	see -le/ect.		L
ly/lv/lu	loosen, dissolve		G/L
-ma [plural: -mata]	N [neuter]		G
mac	spot, stain		L
mach	batttle		G
macro-	long, large	1	G
magn	great, large	7	L
mal/male	bad	9	L
mamm	breast	8	L
man	remain		L
man	hand, handle	5	L
mand	order (< *man* 'hand' + *dat* 'given')		L
mani	intense desire		G
mant/manc	prophesy	9	G
mar	sea		L
mascul	male		L
mast	breast		G
mater/metr	mother, womb, surrounding material	7	L/G
math	learn, study		G
maxill	upper jaw		L
mea	go, pass, passage, meatus, passage		L
med	middle, near		L
mega/megal	great, million	6	G
mel	dark, black		G
melit/muls	honey, sweet		G
member	part of a whole		L
memor	remember		L
men	moon, month		L
men/min/mon	lead, project, threaten		L
men/mn/ment	think, mind	3	L, G
-ment	N		L
mer	share, part		G,L
merg/mers	sink, dip		L
meso-	middle	4	G
meta-	beyond	3	G
metr	uterus		G
micro-	small	1	G
milli-	thousand, thousandth	5	L
mim	copy, mime		G
min	little, inferior		L

morpheme	gloss	Morpheme set	source
min	see *men/min/mon*		L
mis	see *mit*		L
misc/mix	mix	6	L/G
mis	hate	1	G
mit/mis/miss	send, do		L
mod	moderate, control, manner		L
mono	one	5	G
-mony	N		L
mor	humor, manner, custom		L
morb	disease		L
morph	shape, form	1	G
mort	death		L
mot	move	2	L
muc/munc	moldy, sticky		L
mult	many		L
mun	common, public, gift	9	L
mus/mur/my/mys	mouse, muscle		L/G
mut	change, exchange		L
my	see *mus*		G
myc/myx	fungus	7	G
myel	spinal cord, bone marrow		G
myri	countless, ten thousand, numerous	5	G
myrme	ant		G
mys	see *mus*		G
myx	see *myc*		G
nan	dwarf, billionth		G
narc	sleep		G
nas/nar	nose	8	L
nat	swim		L
nat	source, birth, tribe	2	L
naut/nav	boat, seafaring	9	G, L
nav	see *naut*		L
-nd	see *-and*		L
nec	tie, bind, connect		L
nec/nic/necr	see *noc*		G
negr/nigr	black		L
neo	new, recent	4	G
nephr	kidney	8	G
neur	nerve		G
nihil/nil	nothing (cf. *nul/null*)	6	L
niter	nitrogen, salt compound		G
noc/nec/nic/necr	harm, death	3	L/G

morpheme	gloss	Morpheme set	source
noc/nyc	night	7	L/G
nod	knot		L
nom	law, system	1	G
nomen/onom/onomat/ onym	name	7	L/G
nov	new	2	L
noven/nona	nine, ninth	5	L/G
-nt	see -ant		L
nub	marry		L
nuc/nucle	nut, kernel (*nucle* from *nuc* + -*le*)		L
nul/null	nothing (cf. *nihil/nil*)	9	L
nunc	speak		L
nutr/nurt	nourish, care for		L
nyc	see *noc*		G
nymph	maiden, labia minora		G
-o-	[filler]		G
ob-	towards, against, down	4	L
ocl/ocell	eye	6	L
octo/octav	eight	5	G,L
od	song, performance		G
od/hod	path, way		G
oen	wine		G
-oid	A,N [resembling]	3	G
ol	smell		L
-ole	see -*le/etc.*		L
ol/ole	oil		L
olig	few, little		G
-oma	tumor, growth	8	G
-ome	mass, group		F
omni-	all	2	L
-on	N [neuter]		G
onc	mass, tumor		G
onom, onomat, onym	see *nomen*		G
ont	see *es*		G
oö	see *ov*		G
op/ophthalm	eye, see	8	G
ophi/ophid	snake		G
or	speak formally, pray		L
or	rise, appear		L
orb	circle		L
orch	testicle, orchid		G
org	see *erg*		G
orn/ornith	bird	9	G
orth	straight, correct	7	G

morpheme	gloss	Morpheme set	source
-ory	see -ary		L
-os	N [masculine singular]		G
os/osteo	bone	8	L/G
os/or	mouth, opening	8	L
-ose	full of, A [usu. neg. connotation]		L
osm	push, impel		G
osteo	see os/osteo		G
ot	ear		G
-ous/-os	A	2	L,G
ov/oö	egg	9	L/G
ox/oxy	sharp, sour	9	G
pac	bind, agreement, peace		L
pachy	thick		G
pall	pale		L
pal/pol	stake, spade		L
paleo/palaeo	old	7	G
pali/palin	again		G
palp	feel		L
pan-/pant-	all, overall		G
pap/pop	father, pope		L
par	part, equal		L
par	beget, produce	2	L
para-	beside, resembling	3	G
pater	father, country	7	G,L
path	feel, illness	1	G
pauc	few	5	L
pec	stumble, sin		L
pector	chest		L
pecu	wealth, property		L
ped/paed	child, teach	7	G
ped/pod/pus	foot	7	L
pel	push		L
pen/paen	almost		L
pen	lack, shortage		G
pen/pin	feather		L
pen/pun	punishment	6	L
pend	see pond		L
penta	five	5	G
pept/peps	digest, hydrolyze		G
per-	through, bad	2	L
peri-	around, close	1	G
pet	go, seek	2	L
petr	rock	2	G
pha	see fa		G

morpheme	gloss	Morpheme set	source
phag	eat	9	G
phall	penis		G
phan/phen/fan	show, appear		G
pharyng	throat		G
phas	speech		G
phe	see *fa*		G
phen	see *phan*		G
pher	see *fer*		G
phil	love, tendency	1	G
phleb	vein	8	G
phob	fear	8	G
phon	(speech) sound	1	G
phor	see *fer*		G
phot/phos	light	4	G
phras	speech		G
phren/fran/fren	diaphragm, heart, mind		G
phyl	tribe, class, race		G
phylac	guard	8	G
phyll	leaf	7	G
phys	nature		G
phys	bladder		G
phyt	plant	7	G
pig	paint		L
pil/pill	hair		L
pisc	fish		L
pithec	ape	9	G
plac	please, flat	9	L
plag/plagio	oblique, slanting		G
plas	form, mold		G
plat/platy	flat, broad		G
plaud/plod	clap, accept		L
ple/plec/plic	fold, tangle	6	L
pleb	common people		L,G
ple/plen	full, many	6	L
pleb	common people		L
pleg/ples	strike, stroke		G
plod	see *plaud*		L
plur	many, more	5	L
plut	wealth		G
pluvi	rain		L
pne/pneum	lung, respiration	8	G
pod	see *ped/pod/pus*		G
poe/poie	produce, create		G
pol	city, state	1	G
polio	gray (matter of brain/spinal cord)		G

morpheme	gloss	Morpheme set	source
poly	many	5	G
pom	fruit, apple	7	L
pon/pos	place, put	6	L
pond/pend	hang, weight, pay, con-sider	3	L
pop	see *pap*		L
por	passage, opening		L
port	carry		L
pos	see *pon*		L
pos	allomorph of *pot* 'be able, powerful'		L
post-	after, behind	1	L
poster	see post-		L
pot	be able, powerful	2	L
pot/pos	drink		G,L
potam	river		G
prae-	see *pre-*		L
prag	act, do	4	G
pre-	before	1	L
prec	entreat, pray		L
pred	prey	7	L
prehend/prehens	take, seize		L
presby	old		G
preter-	go by, beyond		L
prim/prin	first, foremost	5	L
pro-	forward, for	2	L,G
prob	test, find good	2	L
proct	anus and rectum		G
prol	offspring		L
proto	first, earliest	5	G
proxim	near		L
pseudo	false	1	G
psitt	parrot		G
psych	mind, spirit	1	G
psor	itch		G
pter	feather, wing	9	G
pto	fall		G
pty	spit		G
pu	see *py*		L
pub	mature		L
pug/pugn	fist, fight	6	L
pulmo	lung	8	L
pun	see *pen*		L
pur/purg	clean		L
pus	see *ped/pod/pus*		G,L

morpheme	gloss	Morpheme set	source
putr	see *py*		L
py/pu/putr	rot, decay		G/L
pyg	buttocks		G
pyr	fire, fever		G
qu-	[basis of relative/inter-rogative pronouns, etc.]		L
quadr/quater/quart	four, fourth	5	L
quin/quint	five, fifth	5	L
rach	spine, vertebrae		G
rad	spoke, ray		L
radic	root, basic		L
ram	branch		L
rap	seize, greed		L
re-/red-	again, back	2	L
reg/rig	rule, straight	4	L
ren	kidney		L
ret	net		L
retro-	reverse, back		L
rh/rrh/rrhag	flow		G
rhin	nose	8	G
rhizo	root	7	G
rid/ris	laugh		L
robus/robor	strong		L
rog	ask, take away	9	L
rub/ruf	red		L
-s	N [masculine, feminine]		L
s	be (as in *absent, present*)		L
sacer/secr	holy, priestlike	3	L
sal	see *hal*		L
sal/saul	jump	7	L
salv/salu	safe, healthy, salute	7	L
sanct	holy, official		L
sanguin	blood		L
sap	taste, perceive		L
sapr	rotten		G
sarc	flesh	8	G
sat	satisfy		L
saul	see *sal*		L
saur	lizard		G
-sc	[inchoat., begin action, chg. state]		L
sca/scal	climb, steps		L

morpheme	gloss	Morpheme set	source
scat	dung, feces (originally *skat*)		G
schis/schiz	split/divide		G
sci	know, discern	2	L
scia/skia	shadow, image, ghost		G
scler	hard	8	G
scop/scep	view, see (rel. *spec/spic*)		G
scrib	write		L
se-/sed-	apart	2	L
seb	hard fat		L
sec	cut, split	2	L
secu	see *sequ*		L
sed/sid/sess	sit		L
seism	shake		G
sem	sign, meaning		G
semi-	see *hemi-*		L
semen/semin	seed	3	L
sen	old	9	L
sent/sens	feel, think	4	L
sep	putrid, infected	8	G
sept, septem	see *hept*		L
sequ/secu	follow		L
ser	watery fluid		L
serp	see *herp*		L
serr	saw-toothed		L
serv	work for		L
sesqui	one and a half, one half more	5	L
sex	see *hex*		L
sicc	dry		L
silic	flint		L
sim	one		L
-sis	N [action, product, result]	4	G
sist	stand		L
sol	alone, single		L
sol	sun		L
solv/solu	loosen, unbind		L
som	body	9	G
somn	sleep	2	L
son	sound	5	L
sop/sopor	deep sleep		L
soph	wise, knowledge	9	G
soror	sister	7	L
spas	convulsion		G
spec/spic	look, see (rel. *scop/scep*)	3	L

morpheme	gloss	Morpheme set	source
spel	cave		G
sperm	seed		G
sphing	bind tight		G
sphyg	pulse		G
spir	breathe		L
spondyl	backbone, vertebra		G
spor	scatter, seed	7	G
squam	scale		L
stat/stet/stit	stand, condition	3	L
steat/stear	fat		G
steg/teg	cover, roof		G
stell	star		L
sten	narrow		G
sthen	strength		G
steth	chest		G
still	drop		L
stom	mouth, opening	8	G
strat	stretch, level, layer	9	L
stru/struc	build		L
styl	pillar, writing instrument	G	
sub-	under, down, secondary (rel. *hypo-*)	4	L
succ	juice, sap		L
sud	sweat		L
super-	above, excessive, beyond (rel. *hyper-*)	4	L
supra-	above, greater	1	L
syn-	with, together	4	G
-t-	[filler]		G
-t	[past pass. participle] (see ch. 9)		L
tac	silent		L
tach/tachy	fast	6	G
tact/tax	arrange, order	6	G,L
tag/teg/tig/tang/ting	touch, feel	3	L
taph	tomb, trench		G
taur	bull		L
tauto	see *auto*		G
teg	see *steg*		G
tele	far	4	G
telo-/teleo-	end, complete	9	G
temp/tempor	time, mix	2	L
ten/tend/tens	stretch, thin	4	L
ten/tin	hold, maintain	3	L

morpheme	gloss	Morpheme set	source
ter/terr	earth	6	L
tera/terat	monster, trillion (10^{12})		G
terg	back		L
tetra-/tessara-	four	5	G
thalass	sea		G
thanat	death		G
thaum	miracle		G
the	place, put	7	G
theo	god	1	G
therm	heat, temperature		G
thromb	clot	8	G
-tic	A		G,L
tom/tm	cut	3	G
ton	quality, pitch		G
top	place	1	G
tor	twist, drill		L
tot	whole		L
tox	poison		L
tract	pull		L
trans-/tra-	across, through	4	L
trem	shake		L
trep/trepan/tres	turn, bore through		G
tri/tris/trich/ter	three	5	G
trich	hair		G
troch	run, round object		G
trop	turn	9	G
troph/trop	nourish		G
trud/trus	thrust	4	L
tub	hollow		L
tuber	swelling		L
-tude	N		F
tum	swollen, agitated		L
tus/tund	deaden, blunt		L
-ty	N		F
-ule	see -le/etc.		L
ultim/ultra-	last, beyond		L
-um	N [neuter singular]		L
umb/umber	shade		L
un	one	5	L
und	wave		L
ung	oil, ointment		L
ungu	claw, nail		L
ur	tail		G
-ur/-ure	N		L/F

morpheme	gloss	Morpheme set	source
uran/ouran	heavens		G
urb	city		L
urg	see *erg*		G
-us	N [masculine]		L
uter	womb		L
uxor	wife	7	L
vac/van	empty, vain	6	L
vad/vas	go		L
vag	wander		L
vagin	sheath		L
val	strong, useful	7	L
van	see *vac*		L
var	change		L
vas/ves	vessel, blood vessel, duct	8	L
veh/vec	carry		L
ven	come, bring	2	L
ven	vein	8	L
venter	belly		L
ver	true	2	L
ver	see *vir/ver*		L
ver/verg/vers	turn	6	L
verb	word, verb		L
verd	green		L
verg	see *ver/verg*		L
verm	worm	9	L
via	through		L
vic/vinc	conquer	3	L
vid/vis/id/eid	see		L
vig/viginti/vic	twenty	5	L
vin/oen	wine	9	L/G
vinc	see *vic*		L
vir	man		L
vir/ver	green		L
vitr	glass		L
viv/vit	life	6	L
voc/vok	speak, call, voice	7	L
vol	will		L
volv	turn		L
vor	eat	3	L
xanth	yellow		G
xen	foreign	1	G
xer	dry		G
xyl	wood	9	G

morpheme	gloss	Morpheme set	source
-y	N	1	F,G,L
zo	animal	3	G
zyg	yoke		G
zym	ferment, catalyze		G

Appendix I, Part 2
Glosses to Morphemes

gloss	morpheme	Morpheme set	Source
A	-al		L
A	-an		L
A	-ane		F
A	-ar		L
A	-id		G
A	-il/-ile		G
A	-ine		F
A	-ous/-os	2	L,G
A	-tic		G,L
A,N	-ac		L,G
A,N	-ary/-ory	2	F
A,N	-ic	1	G,L
A,N	-ive	2	L
A,N [resembling]	-oid	3	G
A,N [VERBing, present]	-ant/-ent 2 (cf. -nt, ch. 9)		L
abdomen, abdominal wall	lapar		G
able to be done, suitable for	-ble		L
abnormal, bad	dys-		G
above, excessive, beyond	super-	4	L
above, greater	supra-	1	L
acceptable	dec	7	L
across, through	trans-/tra-	4	L
act, do	prag	4	G
act, do, drive	ag/eg/ig	4	L
after, behind	post-	1	L
again	pali/palin		G
again, back	re-/red-	2	L

gloss	morpheme	Morpheme set	Source
against, facing	contra-/counter-	2	L
against, opposite	anti-		G
age, time	ev	9	L
air	aer		L,G
air	atmo		G
all	omni-	2	L
all, overall	pan-/pant-		G
almost	pen/paen		L
alone, single	sol		L
angle, knee	gon/gen		G/L
animal	zo	3	G
ant	formic	9	L
ant	myrme		G
anus and rectum	proct		G
apart	se-/sed-	2	L
apart, reversed	dis-/di-		L
ape	pithec	9	G
arm	brach/brac		G
armpit	axill	8	L
around	circum-	1	L
around, close	peri-	1	G
arrange, order	tact/tax	6	G,L
artery	arter		G
ash, dust	cin/con		L/G
ask, take away	rog	9	L
away, from, off	apo-	4	G
babble, talk	lal		G
back (of body or body part)	dors		L
back	terg		L
backbone, vertebra	spondyl		G
bad	mal/male	9	L
ball	glob/glom		L
base, bottom	fund		L
batttle	mach		G
be (as in *absent, present*)	s		L
be able, powerful	pot/pos	2	L
be, basic	es/ess/ent/ont		L,G
bear, send, bring	fer/pher/phor	7	L/G
beat	bat		L
beautiful	cal/call		G
bee	api	9	L
before	pre-	1	L
beget, produce	par	2	L
believe, trust	cre/cred	6	L
belly	venter		L

gloss	morpheme	Morpheme set	Source
below, after	infra-	1	L
beside, resembling	para-	3	G
between, among	inter-	1	L
beyond	meta-	3	G
bind tight	sphing		G
bind, agreement, peace	pac		L
bird	orn/ornith	9	G
bird, fly	av	4	L
birth, type, origin	gon/gen/gn	3	G,L
black	negr/nigr		L
bladder	phys		G
blessed	beat		L
blood	hem/em	8	G
blood	sanguin		L
blood vessel	angi		G
blow	fla	5	L
blue	cyan		G
boat, seafaring	naut/nav	9	G,L
body	som	9	G
body tissue	hist	8	G
body, flesh	corp/corpor	2	L
bone	os/osteo	8	L/G
book	liber		L
book, Bible	bibl		G
both	ambi-/amphi-		L/G
bottom, low	bas		L
box	caps		L
brain (from *en-* + *cephal*)	encephal		G
branch	ram		L
break	frag/frang/fring	3	L
breast	mamm	8	L
breast	mast		G
breathe	spir		L
brief, short	brev		L
brother	adelph		G
brother	frater	7	L
build	stru/struc		L
bull	taur		L
burn	caus/cauter		G
burn, dry	ar/ard		L
buttocks	pyg		G
cac	bad	1	G
care	cur	5	L
carry	lat	7	L
carry	port		L

gloss	morpheme	Morpheme set	Source
carry	veh/vec		L
carry, bring, offer, do	ges/ger		L
cartilage	chondr		G
cat	fel		L
cave	spel		G
cell	cyt		G
center	center		L
change	var		L
change, exchange	mut		L
cheek	bucc		L
chest	pector		L
chest	steth		G
child, teach	ped/paed	7	G
church	eccles		G
circle	orb		L
city	urb		L
city, state	pol	1	G
clap, accept	plaud/plod		L
classical form of *-ion*	-io		L
claw, nail	ungu		L
clean	pur/purg		L
clear, bright	clar		L
climb, steps	sca/scal		L
clot	thromb	8	G
cold, freeze	cry/crym		G
color, embellishment	chrom	1	G
come forth, grow	cere/cre		L
come, bring	ven	2	L
common people	pleb		L
common people	pleb		L,G
common, public, gift	mun	9	L
cone	con		G
conquer	vic/vinc	3	L
convulsion	spas		G
copy, mime	mim		G
countless, 10,000, numerous	myri	5	G
cover, roof	steg/teg		G
cow, milk	bov/bu/bos/bou	9	L,G
crab, cancer	car/carcin/canc		L,G
creep, reptile	herp/herpet/serp	9	G/L
cross, important point	cruc	7	L
cry out, call	clam	9	L
custom	eth		G
cut	tom/tm	3	G
cut, kill	cid/cis	3	L
cut, split	sec	2	L

gloss	morpheme	Morpheme set	Source
dark, black	mel		G
dawn, early	eo		G
day	hemer		G
deaden, blunt	tus/tund		L
dear, expensive	car		L
death	mort		L
death	thanat		G
deep sleep	sop/sopor		L
depth	bath/bathy	6	G
desire	cup		L
devil (< *dia-* + *bol/bl*)	diabol		G
diaphragm, heart, mind	phren/fran/fren		G
dig	fod/foss		L
digest, hydrolyze	pept/peps		G
disease	morb		L
disease; mixture	cras		G
do, make	fac/fec/fic	3	L
dog	can/cyn		L/G
double	dipl	5	G
down, away, back, opposite	cata-	3	G
drink	bib		L
drink	pot/pos		G,L
drop	still		L
dry	sicc		L
dry	xer		G
dung, feces (originally *skat*)	scat		G
dung, feces	copro		G
dwarf, billionth	nan		G
ear	aur	8	L
ear	ot		G
earth	ge	7	G
earth	ter/terr	6	L
earth, ground, low	hum		L
earth, land	chthon		G
earthling, human being	hom	2	L
eat	ed/es	7	L
eat	phag	9	G
eat	vor	3	L
egg	ov/oö	9	L/G
eight	octo/octav	5	G,L
embryonic, immature	blast		G
empty, vain	vac/van	6	L
end, boundary	fin		L
end, complete	telo-/teleo-	9	G
entreat, pray	prec		L

gloss	morpheme	Morpheme set	Source
equal	iso-	4	G
even, level	equ/iqu	3	L
eye	ocl/ocell	6	L
eye, see	op/ophthalm	8	G
eyelash, hair	cil		L
eyelid	blephar		G
fall	cad/cas/cid	4	L
fall	pto		G
fall, expire	laps		L
false	pseudo	1	G
far	tele	4	G
fast	tach/tachy	6	G
fat	adep/adip		L
fat	steat/stear		G
fat, leave	lip		G
father, country	pater	7	G,L
father, pope	pap/pop		L
fault, crime	culp	2	L
fear	phob	8	G
feather	pen/pin		L
feather, wing	pter	9	G
feel	palp		L
feel, illness	path	1	G
feel, think	sent/sens	4	L
ferment, catalyze	zym		G
fever	febr		L
few	pauc	5	L
few, little	olig		G
field	ager	6	L
[filler]	-i-		L
[filler]	-o-		G
[filler]	-t-		G
filter, clarify	col/cull		L
finger, digit	dactyl		G
finger, toe, number	digit		L
fire	ign		L
fire, fever	pyr		G
first, earliest	proto	5	G
first, foremost	prim/prin	5	L
first, govern	arch	4	G
fish	ichthy	9	G
fish	pisc		L
fist, fight	pug/pugn	6	L
fit, capable	apt/ept	3	L
five	penta	5	G

gloss	morpheme	Morpheme set	Source
five, fifth	quin/quint	5	L
flat, broad	plat/platy		G
flax	lin		L
flee	fug	2	L
flesh	car/carn	6	L
flesh	sarc	8	G
flint	silic		L
flow	rh/rrh/rrhag		G
flow, river	flu/fluc/fluv	6	L
flower	flor		L
flower, collection	anth/anthem		G
fluid	liqu		L
fold, tangle	ple/plec/plic	6	L
follow	sequ/secu		L
foot	ped/pod/pus	7	L
foreign	xen	1	G
foretell, protect (< *av* + *spec*)	auspec		L
fork	furc		L
form, mold	plas		G
forward, for	pro-	2	L,G
rot, decay	py/pu/putr		G/L
four	tetra-/tessara-	5	G
four, fourth	quadr/quater/quart	5	L
free	liber		L
frog	batrach		G
from, away	ab-/abs-		L
fruit, apple	pom	7	L
fruit, produce	fru/frug		L
full of	-lent		L
full of, A [usu.neg.connotation]	-ose		L
full, many	ple/plen	6	L
fungus	myc/myx	7	G
gap, basin	lac		L
gather	greg	2	L
gather, stick	gli/gle/glu/glut		G/L
giant, billion (10^9)	giga		G
give	dit/don/dot/dos/dow/da/dat	6	L,G
gland	aden	8	G
glass	vitr		L
glue	coll		G
go by, beyond	preter-		L
go	it		L
go	vad/vas		L
go, let go	ced/ceed/cess	4	L
go, pass, passage, meatus, passage	mea		L

gloss	morpheme	Morpheme set	Source
go, seek	pet	2	L
goat, impulse	caper		L
god	theo	1	G
god, augury	dei/div	3	L
gold, yellow	chrys		G
good, well	bene/bon	6	L
govern	crat/crac	5	G
grain	gran		L
gray (matter of brain/spinal cord) polio		G	
great, large	magn	7	L
great, million	mega/megal	6	G
green	verd		L
green	vir/ver		L
groin	inguin		L
guard	phylac	8	G
gums	gingiv		L
hair	crin		L
hair	pil/pill		L
hair	trich		G
half	demi-	5	F
half	hemi-/semi-	5	G/L
hand	chir	9	G
hand, handle	man	5	L
hang, weight, pay, consider	pond/pend	3	L
happy	felic		L
hard fat	seb		L
hard	scler	8	G
hard, lasting	dur		L
harm, death	noc/nec/nic/necr	3	L/G
hate	mis	1	G
head	cap/cep/caput/capit		L
head	cephal	5	G
heap	cumul		L
hear	acou		G
hear	aud	6	L
heart	coron		L
heart, agree	card/cord	7	G/L
heat, temperature	therm		G
heavens	uran/ouran		G
heel	calc		L
high	alt	4	L
high, height	hyps		G
hold, maintain	ten/tin	3	L
hollow	cav		L

gloss	morpheme	Morpheme set	Source
hollow	tub		L
holy, official	sanct		L
holy, priestlike	sacer/secr	3	L
honey, sweet	melit/muls		G
horn	corn		L
horn, head, brain, neck	cer/car/cr/ker/corn		G,L
horny, hard, cornea	kerat		G
horse	equ		L
horse	hipp		G
hour, season, time	hor	9	G
house, control	dom		G,L
human	anthrop	1	G
humor, manner, custom	mor		L
hundred, hundredth	cent	5	L
hundred, many	hecto/hecato	5	G
image	icon		G
in reverse, away, down	de-	1	L
in, into	in-/en-	3	L/G
increase	aug		L
individual, own (rel. id/idi)	idio	1	G
inflamation	-itis	8	G
inhabit	ec/oec		G
insect (from en- + tom/tm)	entom		G
inside	endo-	1	G
intense desire	mani		G
intestine	enter		G
inward	eso-		G
inwards	intro-		L
iron	ferr		L
island	insul		L
itch	psor		G
join	jug/jung		L
judge	arbiter		L
judge, assess	cens	5	L
judge, law, ritual	jus/jur	6	L
juice, sap	succ		L
jump	sal/saul	7	L
key, locked	clav	9	L
kidney	nephr	8	G
kidney	ren		L
knot	nod		L
know	gn/gnos/gnor	6	G,L
know, discern	sci	2	L

gloss	morpheme	Morpheme set	Source
lack of strength (< *a-* + *sthen*)	-asthen		G
lack, shortage	pen		G
land, state, medical condition	-ia	8	G,L
large	ampl		L
last, beyond	ultim/ultra-		L
laugh	rid/ris		L
law, charge	leg/legitim	2	L
law, system	nom	1	G
layer, blade	lamin/lamell		L
lead, draw, pull	duc	2	L
lead, project, threaten	men/min/mon		L
leaf	phyll	7	G
lean, lie, bed	cli/cliv/clin	6	L
learn, study	math		G
leave	linqu/lic/liqu		L
letter	liter	2	G
lie down, remain	cub/cumb	3	L
life	bio	1	G
life	viv/vit	6	L
light	lumen/lumin	5	L
light	phot/phos	4	G
light, rise	lev		G
light, white, colorless, clear	luc/leuk		L/G
lime	calc		L
lion	leo/leon		L,G
lip	lab	8	G
little, inferior	min		L
live, inhabit, grow	col	9	L
liver	hepat	8	G
lizard	saur		G
long, large	macro-	1	G
look, see (rel. *scop/scep*)	spec/spic	3	L
loosen, dissolve	ly/lv/lu		G/L
loosen, unbind	solv		L
loss, harm	dam/damn/demn	6	L
love	am/amor/im	3	L
love, tendency	phil	1	G
lower back, loins	lumb		L
lung	pulmo	8	L
lung, respiration	pne/pneum	8	G
lust	lagn		G
maiden, labia minora	nymph		G
male	mascul		L
male, man	andr	4	G
man	vir		L

gloss	morpheme	Morpheme set	Source
many	mult		L
many	poly	5	G
many, more	plur	5	L
marriage, sexual union	gam	1	G
marry	nub		L
mass, group	-ome		F
mass, tumor	onc		G
mature	pub		L
middle	meso-	4	G
middle, near	med		L
milk	galac		G
milk	lac	8	L
mind, spirit, (nonplant) life	anim	2	L
mind, spirit	psych	1	G
miracle	thaum		G
mix	misc/mix	6	L/G
moderate, control, manner	mod		L
moldy, sticky	muc/munc		L
monster, trillion (10^{12})	tera/terat		G
moon, madness	lun		L
moon, month	men		L
mother, womb, surrounding mat'l	mater/metr	7	L/G
mouse, muscle	mus/mur/my/mys		L/G
mouth, opening	os/or	8	L
mouth, opening	stom	8	G
move	kin/cin		G
move	mot	2	L
N	-iac		G,L
N	-ice		F
N	-in		G
N	-ment		L
N	-mony		L
N	-tude		F
N	-ty		F
N	-ur/-ure		L/F
N	-y	1	F,G,L
N [abstract]	-ia		G,L]
N [action of VERBing, present]	-ance/-ence	2	F
N [action or result of VERBing]	-ion	2	F
N [action, product, result]	-sis	4	G
N [agent, negative evaluation]	-aster		L
N [belief, practice]	-ism		G
N [cutting out]($<$ ec- + *tom* + -y)	-ectomy		G
N [diminutive] (cf. Ch.9)	-le/-ole/-cule/-cle/-lus/-la/-ell/ -il/-ill		L

gloss	morpheme	Morpheme set	Source
N [doing or associated with]	-ist		G
N,A [feminine plural]	-ae		L
N,A [feminine singular]	-a		L,G
N,A [feminine sing. dative]	-ae		L
N,A [feminine sing. possessive]	-ae		L
N [future pass.] 'to be VERBed'	-and/-end		L
N [group]	-ad		G
N [masculine singular]	-os		G
N [masculine, feminine]	-s		L
N [neuter singular]	-um		L
N [neuter singular]	-ma [plural: -mata]		G
N [neuter singular]	-on		G
N [passive, agent]	-ee		F
N [place, repository]	-arium		L
N [quality of]	-ity		F
N [unit]	-eme		F
N [usu. with neg. connotation]	-ard		F
N,A	-age		F
N,A	-it/-ite		L,G
N,A,V	-ate	2	L
N,A [masculine plural]	-i		L
N,A [feminine singular]	-ix		L
N,A [masculine singular]	-us		L
N,A [masculine sing. possessive]	-i		L
N,A [neuter plural]	-a		L,G
N,A [neuter plural]	-ia		L
name	nomen/onom/onomat/onym	7	L/G
narrow	sten		G
nation	ethn		G
native, follower, product	-ite		F
nature	phys		G
near	proxim		L
neck	col/coll		L
neck, neck of uterus	cervic	8	L
nerve	neur		G
net	ret		L
new	nov	2	L
new, recent	neo	4	G
night	noc/nyc	7	L/G
nine, ninth	noven/nona	5	L/G
nitrogen, salt compound	niter		G
nose	nas/nar	8	L
nose	rhin	8	G
not	in-	4	L
not, without	a-/an-	2	G
nothing (cf. *nihil/nil*)	nul/null	9	L

gloss	morpheme	Morpheme set	Source
nothing (cf. *nul*/*null*)	nihil/nil	6	L
nourish	troph/trop		G
nourish, care for	nutr/nurt		L
nurture, grow	al/ol	3	L
nut, kernel (*nucle* from *nuc* + *-le*)	nuc/nucle		L
oblique, slanting	plag/plagio		G
offspring	fil		L
offspring	prol		L
oil	ol/ole		L
oil, ointment	ung		L
old	paleo/palaeo	7	G
old person	ger	7	G
old	presby		G
old	sen	9	L
old, before	ante-/anti-	3	L
on the side of	cis		L
on, over	epi-	4	G
one and a half, one half more	sesqui	5	L
one	mono	5	G
one	sim		L
one	un	5	L
order (<*man* 'hand' + *da* t'given')	mand		L
orgiastic	bacch		G
other	al/all/allel	7	L,G
other, different	hetero-	4	G
out, away	ex-/e-/ec-	4	L/G
outer covering	cortec		L
outside	ecto-	1	G
outside	exo-		G
outside	exter-/extern-		L
outside	extra-	1	L
outside	extro-		L
over, above	hyper-/super-		G/L
owe	deb		L
pain	-dynia		G
pain	alg	8	G
painful spasm	angin		L
painful spasm	angin		L
paint	pig		L
pale	pall		L
parrot	psitt		G
part of a whole	member		L
part, equal	par		L
passage, opening	por		L

gloss	morpheme	Morpheme set	Source
[past pass. participle] (see Ch.9)	-t		L
path, way	od/hod		G
pebble, count	calcul		L
penis	phall		G
people	dem	5	G
perceive, feel	esthet/esthes	4	G
permissible, unrestrained	lic	4	L
physical love	ero	4	G
pick, read	leg/lig	4	L,G
pillar, writing instrument	styl		G
place	loc	5	L
place	top	1	G
place, put	pon/pos	6	L
place, put	the	7	G
plant	phyt	7	G
play	lud		L
please, flat	plac	9	L
pleasure	hedon		G
poison	tox		L
pouch, money	burs		L
pour, melt, blend	fus	3	L
power	dyn	9	G
pregnant	gravid	8	G
prey	pred	7	L
produce, create	poe/poie		G
prophesy	mant/manc	9	G
pull	tract		L
pulse	sphyg		G
punishment	pen/pun	6	L
pupil (of eye)	cor/core		G
push	pel		L
push, impel	osm		G
putrid, infected	sep	8	G
quality, pitch	ton		G
rain	pluvi		L
red	eryth/erythr		G
red	rub/ruf		L
[relative/interrog. pronoun, etc.]	qu-		L
remain	man		L
remember	memor		L
reverse, back	retro-		L
ring, circle	gyr		L
ripen, cook	coc		L
rise, appear	or		L

gloss	morpheme	Morpheme set	Source
river	potam		G
rock	petr	2	G
root	rhizo	7	G
root, basic	radic		L
rotten	sapr		G
rule, straight	reg/rig	4	L
run	curs/curr	9	L
run, course	drom		G
run, round object	troch		G
sacred	hiero		G
sacred, saint	hagio		G
safe, healthy, salute	salv	7	L
salt	hal/sal		G/L
same	homo-/homeo-	4	G
same, self	id/idi		G
satisfy	sat		L
saw-toothed	serr		L
scale	squam		L
scaly	lep/lepr/lepid		G
scatter, seed	spor	7	G
sea	mar		L
sea	thalass		G
seat, side	hedr		G
secret, hidden	crypt/cryph	6	G
secrete	crin		G
see	vid/vis/id/eid		L
seed	semen/semin	3	L
seed	sperm		G
segment, joint	art/arthr		L,G
seize, greed	rap		L
self, I	ego		L,G
self, same	auto/tauto	6	L/G
send, do	mit/mis/miss		L
seven, seventh	hept/sept/septem	5	G/L
shade	umb/umber		L
shadow, image, ghost	scia/skia		G
shake	cuss		L
shake	seism		G
shake	trem		L
shape, form	morph	1	G
share, part	mer		G,L
sharp	acu		L
sharp, sour	ox/oxy	9	G
sharp, tip, extremities	ac/acer/acerb	6	L
sheath	vagin		L

gloss	morpheme	Morpheme set	Source
shine	cand		L
short	brach/brachy	6	G
show, appear	phan/phen/fan		G
shrub	frut		L
side	later	9	L
side, coast	cost		L
sign, meaning	sem		G
silent	tac		L
sing, intone	can/cen		L
sink, dip	merg/mers		L
sister	soror	7	L
sit	sed/sid/sess		L
six, sixth	hex/sex	5	G/L
skill, manufacture	art		L
skin	cut	8	L
skin	derm/dermat	8	G
sleep	dorm		L
sleep	narc		G
sleep	somn	2	L
sleep, trance	hypno		G
small	micro-	1	G
smell	ol		L
snake	angui		L
snake	ophi/ophid		G
soft, gentle	len		L
solidify, jelly, ice	gel		L
song, performance	od		G
sound	son	5	L
(speech) sound	phon	1	G
source, birth, tribe	nat	2	L
source, cause	eti/aeti		G
south, wind	auster		L
speak, point	dic	6	L
speak formally, pray	or		L
speak	leg/lex		L,G
speak	loqu/locu	7	L
speak	nunc		L
speak, call, voice	voc/vok	7	L
speak, spoken of	fa/pha/phe	7	L/G
speech	phas		G
speech	phras		G
speech sound	phon	1	G
spider	arachn	9	G
spinal cord, bone marrow	myel		G
spine, thorn	acanth		G
spine, vertebrae	rach		G

gloss	morpheme	Morpheme set	Source
spiral	helic		G
spit	pty		G
split, divided	fid/fiss		L
split/divide	schis/schiz		G
spoke, ray	rad		L
spot, stain	mac		L
stake, spade	pal/pol		L
stand	sist		L
stand, condition	stat/stet/stit	3	L
star	aster	6	G
star	stell		L
step, go	grad/gred/gress	4	L
stomach	gaster	8	G
stone	lapid		L
stone	lith/lite	6	G
straight, correct	orth	7	G
strength	sthen		G
stretch, level, layer	strat	9	L
stretch, thin	ten/tend/tens	4	L
strike, stroke	pleg/ples		G
strong	robus/robor		L
strong, useful	val	7	L
struggle, contest (< *ag* 'drive')	agon		G
study, speak	log (related to leg, lex)	1	G
stumble, sin	pec		L
suffer	dol/dolor	6	L
summon, arouse	cit		L
sun	heli	4	G
sun	sol		L
sweat	sud		L
sweet	dulc		L
sweet	glyc/gluc		G
swelling	tuber		L
swim	nat		L
swollen, agitated	tum		L
tail	caud/cod	8	L
tail	ur		G
take, buy	em		L
take, contain	cap/cep/cip/cup	3	L
take, seize	lab		G
take, seize	prehend/prehens		L
taste, enjoy	gust		L
taste, perceive	sap		L
teach	doc/dog	4	L/G
teach, induce	agog/agogue		G

gloss	morpheme	Morpheme set	Source
tear, tear duct	lacrim/lachrym	8	L
ten, tenth	decem/decim/deca	5	L,G
test, find good	prob	2	L
testicle, orchid	orch		G
thankful, pleased, kind	grat	2	L
thick	pachy		G
think, mind	men/mn/ment	3	L,G
thousand	kilo-	5	G
thousand, thousandth	milli-	5	L
thread, line	fil		L
three	tri/tris/trich/ter	5	G
threshold, border, shore	lim/limen/limin		L
throat	pharyng		G
through	via		L
through, apart	dia-	3	G
through, bad	per-	2	L
throw, extend	bol/bl	3	G
throw, lay, lie, extend	jac/jec		L
thrust	trud/trus	4	L
tie, bind	lig	7	L
tie, bind, connect	nec		L
time	chron	1	G
time, mix	temp/tempor	2	L
tip	apec/apic	3	L
to close	clud	4	L
to separate, judge	cer/cre/cr	3	G,L
to stick, hold back	hes/her	6	L
to, toward	ad-	4	L
together, with	con-/co-	3	L
tomb, trench	taph		G
tongue	lingu		L
tongue, speech	gloss/glot/glott	6	G
tooth	den/odon	9	L/G
touch, feel	tag/teg/tig/tang/ting	3	L
towards, against, down	ob-	4	L
treat, heal	iatr	1	G
tree	arbor		L
tree	dendr/dr/dry	9	G
tribe, class, race	phyl		G
true	etym		G
true	ver	2	L
trust, bold	fid		L
tumor, growth	-oma	8	G
turn	trop	9	G
turn	ver/verg/vers	6	L
turn	volv		L

gloss	morpheme	Morpheme set	Source
turn, bore through	trep/trepan/tres		G
twenty	vig/viginti/vic	5	L
twin	gem/gemin	7	L
twist, drill	tor		L
two	bi	5	L
two	di/dich/dy/du	5	L,G
unborn child	fet/foet		L
under, below, partial	hypo-	3	G
under, down, secondary	sub-	4	L
universe, order, ornament	cosm	1	G
up, again, back	ana-	3	G
upper jaw	maxill		L
uterus	metr		G
V	-ize	1	G
V[inchoat., begin action, chg.state]	-sc	L	
vein	phleb	8	G
vein	ven	8	L
vessel, blood vessel, duct	vas/ves	8	L
(blood) vessel	angi		G
view, see (rel. *spec/spic*)	scop/scep		G
vinegar	acet		L
voice box, vocal cords	laryng	8	G
vomit	emet/emes		G
vulva	episi		G
walk, go	ambl	4	L
wander	vag		L
wander, do wrong	err		L
war	bell	5	L
warn, beware	caut/cav		L]
wash	lav		L
water	aqu		L
water	hyd/hydr	6	G
watery fluid	ser		L
wave	und		L
wealth	plut		G
wealth, property	pecu		L
weigh, consider	liber	2	L
weight	bar/bary		G
well, good	eu	4	G
white	alb(in)	6	L
whole	hol		G
whole	tot		L
wide, broad	lat		L

gloss	morpheme	Morpheme set	Source
wife	uxor	7	L
will	vol		L
wind	anem		G
windpipe	bronch		G
wine	oen		G
wine	vin/oen	9	L/G
wing	ali	9	L
wise, knowledge	soph	9	G
with, together	syn-	4	G
within	intra-	1	L
woman, female	gyn/gynec	6	G
womb	uter		L
womb, neurotic disorder	hyster	8	G
wood	lign	7	L
wood	xyl	9	G
word	lex		G
word, verb	verb		L
work	erg/urg/org	3	G
work for	serv		L
worm	helminth		G
worm	verm	9	L
worship	latr		G
worthy, fitting	dign		L
write	scrib		L
write, record	graph/gram	7	G
year	ann/enn	3	L
yellow	xanth		G
yoke	zyg		G
young	juven	7	L

Appendix II:
Morpheme Sets 1 to 9

Learn the following **morphemes** (i.e. word components or elements) and their **glosses** (i.e. thumbnail definitions or basic meanings). Focus on the first two columns of the list. The **mnemonic** (i.e. memory-aiding) words given in the third column illustrate the use of each element in a fairly common English word. These mnemonics are intended to give you a frame in which you can easily learn both the form and meaning of the morpheme. For example, the word *philanthropy*, which is a <u>noun</u> *(-y)* with the basic meaning '<u>love</u> *(phil)* for <u>human</u> *(anthrop)* beings'—in particular as expressed by giving large amounts of money to charity, is especially useful. It gives you a single word frame for three different morphemes in the first list below. The other example words (in the fourth column) show other occurences of the morpheme; you can use these as substitute or additional mnemonics. You will probably learn these and other morphemes and glosses most rapidly if you drill using

a. flash cards (i.e. small or cut index cards) with the morpheme written on one side and its gloss on the reverse so that each will spark your recollection of the other—this is the most widely preferred method—or
b. the following pages by themselves, covering the morpheme or gloss column and trying to recall each item by looking at the gloss or morpheme column beside it —or
c. some method of your own design which produces the same (or even better) results.

Drill until you can give both the gloss or glosses for each morpheme and the morpheme for each individual gloss from memory alone.

We will be concerned primarily with the five major categories of words (i.e. parts of speech) in this and morpheme list: nouns, verbs, adjectives, prepositions, and adverbs. The meanings of these terms are basically defined and illustrated by the words in boldface type in the sentences below.

NOUN: labels an actual or abstract thing that may act as subject or object of a verb. E.g. That **dog** <u>is barking again</u>; <u>Only Leigh's</u> **pride** <u>was injured</u>; **Running** <u>is supposed to be good exercise</u>.

VERB: details activity, process or state of being or becoming in a construction with a subject or object noun. E.g. <u>Tony</u> **slapped** <u>the wall</u>; <u>Jan</u> **wears** <u>running shoes every day</u>; <u>On Monday I</u> **learned** <u>how sick she</u> **was**.

ADJECTIVE: modifies (i.e. further specifies or labels) a noun. E.g. <u>Pat is **tall**</u>; <u>They have an **old**</u> **wooden** <u>fence</u>; <u>Jess is **wiser**</u> than I am.

PREPOSITION: marks a spatial relationship, usually with regard to something labelled by a noun. E.g. <u>The key is **on** the table</u>; <u>She stood **in** the box</u>; <u>It came **to** a conclusion</u>.

ADVERB: (1) manner or direction in which a verb is performed. E.g. <u>Sandy **slowly** walked toward</u> <u>the door</u>; <u>Kim watched **silently**</u>; <u>I ran **around** the house</u>; <u>The clouds floated **away**</u>. (2) modifies an adjective. E.g. <u>I became **completely** frantic</u>; <u>That was **rather** nice of them</u>. (3) comments on an entire sentence, usually from the speaker's perspective. E.g. **Surely** <u>Sam won't go</u>; <u>Julie</u> **probably** <u>went</u>.

MORPHEME SET 1

Use the mnemonic and/or the other example words illustrating form and meaning to learn the following word elements (morphemes) and their glosses (thumbnail definitions).

morpheme	gloss	mnemonic(s)	other example words
-ic	A,N	chronic, topic	photographic, neurotic, psychic, historic
-ize	V	vocalize	Americanize, extemporize, psychologize
-y	N	astronomy	sympathy, privacy
anthrop	human	anthropology	anthropomorphic, philanthropy
bio	life	biology	macrobiotic, biography, bioluminescent
cac	bad	cacophony	caconym, cacodemonic
chrom	color	monochrome	chromosome, chromatic
chron	time	chronic	diachronic, chronometer, anachronistic
circum-	around	circumnavigate	circumference, circumpolar, circumspect
cosm	universe, order, ornament	cosmic, cosmopolitan, cosmetic	macrocosm, microcosm, cosmogony, cosmonaut, cosmecology
de-	in reverse, away, down	detract, decend	decode, denote, demand, deoxygenate, deport, destruction
ecto-	outside	ectoderm	ectoplasm, ectoparasite, ectomorph
endo-	inside	endogamy	endoscopy, endopsychic, endomorph
extra-	outside	extraordinary	extraterrestrial, extramarital, extraneous
gam	marriage, sexual union	monogamy, gamete	bigamy, epigamic, gamosepalous, exogamous, gamophyllous, gamogenesis
iatr	treat, heal	psychiatry	iatrogenic, geriatric, pediatrician
idio	individual, own	idiom, idioisyncracy	idiopathy, idiomorphic, idiosyncracy, idiolect, idiochromatic
infra-	below, after	infrared	infrastructure, infralapsarian
inter-	between, among	internal, interior	international, interfere, interject, intercalate
intra—	within	intramural	intravenous, intravert
log	study, speak	logic, eulogy	logorrhea, anthropology, analogy, prologue

morpheme	gloss	mnemonic(s)	other example words
macro-	long, large	macro-economics	macrocephalic, macrocyte, macro(command)
micro-	small	microscope	microcosm, microbe, microphotography
mis	hate	misogamy	misogyny, misology
morph	shape, form	morpheme	polymorphous, ectomorph, endomorph, morphology
nom	law, system	astronomy	autonomy, binomial
path	feel, illness	pathology	empathy, sympathy, pathos, pathetic
peri-	around, close	perimeter	periscope, perihelion
phil	love, tendency	Anglophile, hemophilia	philosophy, philanthropy, philately
phon	sound, speech sound	telephone	phonetic, euphony, cacophony, phonics, phonology, symphonic, aphonia
pol	city, state	politics	monopoly, police, political, metropolis, megalopolis
post-	after, behind	postwar, posterior	posterity, post partum, postpose, post-prandial
pre-	before	prehistoric	preadolescent, pre-washed
pseud	false	pseudonym	pseudopod, pseudoscience
psych	mind, spirit	psychiatry	psychic, psychotic
pyr	fire, fever	pyromaniac	pyrotechnics, pyrometer, pyrite, antipyretic
supra-	above, greater	suprastructure, supranormal	supralittoral, supraspinous, supraordinate, supramolecular
theo	god	theology	polytheism, theocracy, theogony, atheist
top	place	topography	topical, topology, toponym
xen	foreign	xenophobia	xenon, xenogamy, xenoplastic

MORPHEME SET 2

Learn the following morphemes, their meanings, and alternate forms indicated after a slash (e.g. a-/an-).

element	meaning	mnemonic(s)	other example words
a-/an-	not, without	amoral, anarchy	agnostic, apathy, anhydrous, an-aerobic
anim	mind, spirit, life	animate	animadversion, animosity, unan-imous
ab-/abs-	from, away	abreact, abstract	abolish, abdicate, abstruse, ablative, absolute
-ary/-ory	A,N	temporary, sensory	tertiary, mortuary, granary, auditory, oratory

-ate	N,A,V*	delegate, irate, navigate novitiate	precipitate, prelate, roseate
contra-/counter-	against, facing	contraceptive, counterpart	contradict, contrapositive, counterpoint, counterproductive
corp/corpor	body, flesh	corpuscle, corpse	corpulent, corpus, corps, corporal
culp	fault, crime	culprit	culpable, mea culpa, exculpate
duc	lead, draw, pull	duct, conduct, induce	produce, educate, deduct
-ence/-ance	N	penance, science	exuberance, intransigence
-ent/-ant	A,N	parent, protestant	proponent, incumbent, defiant, tenant
fug	flee	fugitive	fugacious, centrifuge, fugue
grat	thankful, kind	grateful	gratuity, disgrace, ingratiate, ingrate, gratis
greg	gather	congregation	egregious, gregarious, segregate
hom	earthling, human	hominid	homo erectus, homicide
-ion	N	nation	action
-ive	A,N	elusive, laxative	permissive, missive, gerundive
leg	law, charge	legal, allege	legislature, relegate, legacy
liber	weigh, consider	deliberate	equilibrium, Libra
liter	letter	literal	literary, literati, transliterate
mot	move	motion	motility, motive, emotion
nat	source, birth, tribe	innate, native, nation	natal, nativity, neonatal
nov	new	novelty	innovate, novitiate, novice, nova
omni-	all	omniscient	omnipotent
-ous	A	porous	poisonous, ridiculous, pompous
par	beget, produce	parent	post partum, parturition, oviparous
per-	through, bad	pervade, pernicious	perspicacity, perturb
pet	go, seek	centripetal petition	impetus, appetite
petr	rock	petrify	petroglyph, petroleum
pot	be able, powerful	potential, potent	omnipotent, impotent
pro-	forward, for	proceed, pro-war	provide, procure, produce
prob	test, find good	probe	approbation, probity, reprobate
re-/red-	again, back	review, redundant	re-appoint, redolent
sci	know, discern	omniscient, conscious	prescient, scilicet, plebiscite, adscititious
se-/sed-	apart	separate	select, sedition, seduce, segregate
sec	cut, split	secant	section, sector, transect, sect, secateur
somn	sleep	insomniac	somnolent, somnambulent
tempor	time	temporary	temporal, contemporary, extemporaneous
ven	come, bring	intervene	contravene, ventive
ver	true	verify	veritable, veracity

MORPHEME SET 3

Learn the following morphemes, their meanings, and alternate forms.

morpheme	meaning	mnemonic(s)	other example words
al/ol	nurture, grow	alma mater, abolish	alumnus, exalt, alimentary, adolescent
am/im/amor	love	paramour, amateur, amatory	amity, inimical
ana-	up, again, back	anachronism,	anaclastic, analeptic, anacardium, anabolic, analog
ann/enn	year	per annum, perennial	annals, millennium, centennial
ante-/anti-	old, before	anterior, anticipate	ante-bellum, antedate, antecedent, antiquity
apec/apic	tip	apex, apical	apiculate, apicfixed
apt/ept	fit, capable	aptitude, inept	adapt, adept
bol/bl	throw, extend	parabola, emblem	hyberbole, metabolism, problem, parable
cap/cep/cip/cup	take, contain	captive, except, incipient, recuperate	principle, precept, percipient, occupy
cata-	down, away, back, opposite	cataclysm, catapult	catalyst, catalepsy, catalog, catacomb
cer/cre/cr	separate, judge	discern, critic	criterion, secern, secret, secrete
cid/cis	cut, kill	homicide, incision	patricide, excise, circumcise, concise
con-/co-	together, with	convene, co-author	concomitant, concord, coterminous
cub/cumb	lie down, remain	incubate, incumbent	concubine, recumbent
dei/div	god, augury	deity, divinity	deification, divine, deism, diva
dia-	through, apart	diameter, dialysis	diathesis, dialogue, diopter, diaphoresis, diapositive
equ/iqu	even, level	equity, iniquity	equanimity, equidistant, equal, equator, equation
erg/urg/org	work	energy, metallurgy, organ	demiurge, organon, ergative, georgic, liturgy
fac/fec/fic	do, make	factory, defect, artificial	perfect, prefect, fact, factotum, factor, facsimile, deficit, suffice, artifice
frag/frang/fring	break	fragile, frangible, infringe	diffract, fragile, refrangent, fracture
fus	pour, melt, blend	effusive, fuse, fusion	infuse, infusion, refuse, affusion, fusile, diffusion

morpheme	meaning	mnemonic(s)	other example words
gon/gen/gn	birth, type, origin	gonad, genesis, benign	theogony, gentry, indigenous, gene, agnate, pregnant
hypo-	under, below, partial	hypodermic	hypalgia, hypothermia, hypothesis, hypogeal, hypophysis
in-/en-	in, into	invade, enclose	inception, encase
men/mn	think, mind	mental, amnesia	memento, dementia, mnemonic
meta-	beyond	metaphysics, metamorphosis	metaphor, metalanguage, method
noc/nec/nic/necr	harm, death	innocuous, internecine, pernicious, necrophilia	innocent, noxious, nectar, nectarine, obnoxious, necrosis
-oid	resembling [A,N]	android	spheroid, pterygoid, adenoids
para-	beside, resembling	parallel, paramedic	paranormal, paragraph, parody
pond/pend	hang, weigh, pay, consider	depend, appendix, expend, ponder	pendulum, preponderate, vilipend
sacer/secr	holy, priestlike	sacred, consecrate	sacerdotal, execrate
semen/semin	seed	semen, inseminate	seminal, disseminate, seminary
spec/spic	look, see	despicable, spectacle	inspect, spectrum, retrospect
sta/stat/stet/stit	stand, condition	static, status	obstetrician, institute, stationary, stet, prostitute, constitution, statute, ecstasy
tag/teg/tig/tang/ting	touch, feel	contagion, integer, contiguous, tangent, contingent	tangible, tax, contact, contingency
ten/tin	hold, maintain	tenable, continuous	tenure, tenacious, tenacity, retention
tom/tm	cut	anatomy, tmesis	atom, microtome, entomology, epitome, tmema
vic/vinc	conquer	victor, invincible	evict, evince, convince, conviction
vor	eat	voracious	omnivore, carnivore
zo	animal	zoology	protozoon, diazo, zoomorphic, azoic

* *Note:* This morpheme is pronounced [et] (rhyming with late) when it occurs in any verb (e.g. *relegate, abdicate*) as well as in a few adjectives (e.g. *irate*) and nouns (e.g. *reprobate*). In most nouns (e.g. *novitiate, prelate*) and most adjectives (e.g. *celibate*), however, it is pronounced [ᵊt] (i.e. it rhymes with the last syllable of *rocket* or *mallet*).

MORPHEME SET 4

Learn the following morphemes, their meanings and alternate forms. (Note: Entries such as *ten(d)/tens* indicate that the morpheme may occur with or without the letters enclosed in the parentheses. In other words, *ten(d)/tens* is an abbreviation for *ten/tend/tens*.)

morpheme	meaning	mnemonic(s)	other example words
-ity	N [name of quality]	stupidity	alacrity, mostrosity, femininity, paucity
-sis	N [name of action or its result]	stat + -sis > stasis	tmesis, analysis, symphysis, thesis, metastasis, phthisis, praxis
ad-	to, toward	adapt	it, abbreviate, adduce, affect, annul, arrive, attract
ag/ig	act, do, drive	agent, navigate	agenda, action, agile, exigent, intransigent, exiguous
alt	high	altitude	altimeter, altiloquence, altithermal
ambl	walk, go	perambulator	ambulatory, amble, somnambulist
andr	male, man	android	polyandry, androgyny, apandrous
apo-	away, from, off	apology	apocrypha, apostasy, apoplectic, apotheosis, apogee
arch	first, govern	archtype, anarchy	archaeopteryx, archaeology, oligarchy, archbishop, archive
av	bird, fly	avian, aviator	avicolous, aviculidae, avine
cad/cas/cid	fall	cadence, casual	incidence, coincide, recidivism, incident, occident
ced/ceed/cess	go, let go	concede, proceed, process	cede, secede, antecedent, intercede, excess
clud/clus	to close	seclude	occlude, recluse, conclude
dog/doc	teach	doctrine, dogma	doctor, doxology, docile, orthodox, docent
epi-	on, over	epitome	epitaph, epigram, epibiotic, epicene
ero	physical love	erotic	Eros, autoerogenous, erogenous, erotica
esthet/esthes		perceive, feel	anesthetic, synesthesia, esthetics, kinesthetic
eu	well, good	euphoria	eulogy, euthanasia, eugenic, euphony, euphemism, euphuism
ex-/e-/ec-	out, away	extend, educe, ecstatic	exact, egregious, tonsilectomy, appendectomy
grad/gred/gress	step, go	gradient, ingredient, regress	retrograde, gradual, ingress, egress
heli	sun	heliocentric	helium, perihelion, aphelion, heliolatry
hetero-	other, different	heterosexual	heterodox, heterogeneous, heterodont, heterodyne, heteronomy

morpheme	meaning	mnemonic(s)	other example words
homo-/ homeo-	same	homosexual, homeostasis	homologous, homogeneous, homeopathy
in-	not	incompatible, ignorant	inequity, illegal, impossible, irreverent
iso-	equal	isometrics	isosceles, isopathy, isobar
leg/lig	pick, read	elect, legible	selection, elegant, legend, lectern, diligent, eligible
lic	permissible, unrestrained	illicit, licentious	license, scilicet, licet
meso-	middle	mesosphere	mesomorph, mesobiotic, mesopotamian, mesolithic
neo	new, recent	neo-Fascist, neologism	neonomian, neogamy, neophyte, neoteny, neonatal
ob-	towards, against, down	object, obstacle, oppress	occlude, obdurate, obit, obreption, obloquy, oppose, obstruct
phot/phos	light	photon, phosphor	aphotic, phose, photosynthesis, photosphere, photoprotein
prag	act, do	pragmatic, practice	practicable, apraxis, practicum
reg/rig	rule, straight	regular, regent, incorrigible	rex, regal, regimen, regulus, regina, regime, dirigible
sent/sens	feel, think	sentient, sensory	sententious, sentinel, sensual, consensus, insensate
sub-	under, down, secondary	subhuman, subclass	subreption, success, suffuse, suborn
super-	above, excessive	superhuman, superfluous	superimpose, supernumerary, superior
syn-	with, together	synchronize	sympathy, syllogism, symphony, synergy, systolic
tele	far	telephone	telemetry, telepathy, telesthesia, telekinesis, telegnostic
ten/tend/tens	stretch, thin	extend, tenuous, tensor	sile, extenuate, tendon, tend
trans-/tra-	across, through	trans-Atlantic, transparent, traverse	transaction, transfigure, translucent, traduce, tradition, trajectory, travesty
trud/trus	thrust	protrude, intrusive	extrude, intrude, abstruse

MORPHEME SET 5

morpheme	meaning	mnemonic(s)	other example words
bell	war	belligerent	antebellum, bellicose, rebellion, bellipotent

morpheme	meaning	mnemonic(s)	other example words
bi	two	bisexual	biennial, bifurcation, bisect, bipedal, bilingual
cens	judge, assess	censor	censure, census, censorious, cens, censorate
cent	hundred, hundredth	century, centimeter	bicentennial, percent, centesimal, centgener
cephal	head	encephalitis	microcephaly, acephalous, cephalalgia
crat/crac	govern	democratic	plutocracy, autocratic, meritocracy, aristocrat
cur	care	curator	curate, sinecure, procuration
decem/decim/deca	ten, tenth	decade, decimal	decimate, decuple, decagon, decemvirate
dem	people	democracy	pandemic, endemic, demiurge, demographic
demi	half	demigod	demisemitone, demimonde, demi-sec
di/dich/dy/du	two	dioxide, dichotomy, dyad, dual	diptera, dichogamy, dyarchic, duplex
dipl	double	diploid	diploid, diplopia, diplococcus
fla	blow	inflate	flatus, sufflation, afflatus, flatulent
hecto/hecato	hundred, many	hecatomb, hectometer	hectare, hectoliter
hemi/semi	half	hemisphere, semicircle	hemimorphic, hemimetabolism, semifinal, semiconductor
hept/sept/septen	seven, seventh	heptagon, septuagenarian	heptad, septennate
hex/sex	six, sixth	hexagon, sextet	hexameter, sextuplets
kilo	thousand	kilogram	kilometer, kilowatt, kilocycle
loc	place	local	locus, allocate, collocation
lumen/lumin	light	lumen, luminous	lumen, luminary, illuminati
man	hand, handle	manual, manipulate	emancipate, manumission, manicure
milli	thousand(th)	millennium, millimeter	millisecond, millipede, millenarian
mono	one	monologue	mononucleosis, monomania, monomorphic, monotonous
myri	countless, numerous, 10,000	myriad, myriameter	myrioscope, myriarch, myrianida

morpheme	meaning	mnemonic(s)	other example words
noven/nona	nine, ninth	novendial, nonagenarian	novena, novenary, November, nones, nonagon, nonage
octo/octav	eight	octopus, octave	octavo, octahedron, octagon
pauc	few	paucity	paucal, pauciloquence, paucifolious
penta	five	pentagon	pentagram, pentacle, pentameter
plur	many, more	plurality, plurilateral	plurennial, pluripotentiality
poly	many	polygon	polyphonic, polygamy, polysemy
prim/prin	first, foremost	primary, principal	primogeniture, prima donna, principle
proto	first, earliest	prototype, protozoa	protopathic, protoplasm
quadr/quater/quart	four, fourth	quadrangle, quaternary, quarter	quadrilateral, quatrefoil, quartet
quin/quint/quinqu	five, fifth	quintet, quintessence	quinta, quintain, quinquennium
sesqui	one and a half, one half more	sesquicentennial, sesquilateral	sesquipedalian, sesquiquadrate
son	sound	sonic	sonority, dissonant, assonant, sonnet
tetra/tessara	four	tetrachloride	tetragrammaton, tetrahedron, tetrad
tri/tris/trich/ter	three	triple, trichotomy, ternary	triskaidekaphobia, triptych, tertiary
un	one	union	unary, uniform, unisexual
vig/viginti/vic	twenty	vigintillion, vicennial	vigesimal, vicenary

MORPHEME SET 6

morpheme	meaning	mnemonic(s)	other example words
ac/acer/acerb	sharp, tip, extremities	acid, acrid, acerbic	acuity, acromegaly, exacerbate
agr	field	agriculture	agriology, agrostology, agronomy
alb/albin	white	albumen, albino	albescent, albedo, albumin
aster	star	asteroid	asterism, astral, asteriated
aud	hear	auditory	subaudition, audit, audiology

morpheme	meaning	mnemonic(s)	other example words
auto/tauto	self, same	autonomy, tautology	autolysis, automaton, tautonym, tautophony, autodidact
bath/bathy	depth	bathysphere	bathos, bathyal, bathochrome
bene/bon	good, well	benediction, bonus	benefactive, bonhomie, debonair
brach/brachy	short	brachy	brachylogy, brachycephalic
car/carn	flesh	carnal	carnelion, carnivorous, incarnation, carrion
cli/cliv/clin	lean, lie, bed	client, recline, proclivity	clinograph, declivity, cline, clitoris
cre/cred	believe, trust	credo, miscreant	credendum, incredulous
crypt/cryph	secret, hidden	crypt, apocrypha	cryptogenic, cryptogamic, cryptonym
dam/damn/dem/ demn	loss, harm	damage, indemnity	indemnify, damnable, condemn
dec/dic/deic	speak, point	index, dictate, deictic	dictum, interdict, juridical, malediction, deixis, benediction, jurisdiction, syndic
dit/don/dot/	give	edit, donate, antidote	addition, donor, dosology, epidote
dos/dow/da/dat		dose, endow, data	dowry, condone, dative, tradition, perdition, data
dol/dolor	suffer	condolences	dolorific, condole, indolent
flu/fluc/fluv	flow, river	fluid, fluctuate, fluvial	confluence, effluvium, flux, influence
gloss/glot/glott	tongue, speech	gloss, polyglot, glottis	epiglottis, glossolalia, bugloss, glottal, glossary, diglossia
gn/gnos/gnor	know	cognition, agnostic, ignorant	gnosis, gnostic, prognosticate, ignoramus, diagnostic, prognosticate
gyn/gynec	woman, female	androgyne, gynecology polygyny, gynecocracy	
hes/her	to stick, hold back	adhesive, coherent	hesitate, cohesive, inhere
hyd/hydr	water	dehydrate	hydatid, hydrography, hydrolysis
jus/jur	judge, law, ritual	judge, justice, jury	adjure, abjure, adjudicate, jurisprudence, juridical
lith/lite	stone	megalith, albolite	lithotriptor, neolithic, dendrolite, lithotomy
mega/megal	great, million	megalith, megaton	megalomania, megabyte
misc/mix	mix	miscellany, mixture	miscegenation, permixture, commixture, promiscuous
nihil/nil	nothing	annihilate, nil	nihilism, nihil obstat
ocl/ocell	eye	ocular, ocellus	monocle, oculomotor, ocellated
pen/pun	punish	penal, punitive	impunity, penology
ple/plec/plic	fold, tangle	duplex, implicate	explicate, quintuple, plexus,

morpheme	meaning	mnemonic(s)	other example words
			plexiglass
ple/plen	full, many	replenish, plenty	plethora, plenary, replete, pleonasm
pon/pos	place, put	postpone, propose	impone, interpose, postiche, apposite
pug/pugn	fist, fight	pugilist, pugnacious	impugn, oppugn, repugnance
tach/tachy	fast	tachometer	tachygraphy, tachylite, tachistoscope
tact/tax	arrange, order	tactic, syntax	hypotactic, taxonomy, taxidermy, taxon, taxis
terr	earth	extraterrestrial	terra cotta, Mediterranean, terrevert, terran, terra incognita, inter, disinter
vac/van	empty	vacuum, vanish	vacuity, evacuate, evanescent, vanity
ver/verg/vers	turn	convert, converge, converse	verge, divergence, extraversion, inverse, adverse, obverse, perversity
viv/vit	life	vivid, vital	convivial, vita, curriculum vitae, viva, vivacious, viviparous, vitamin

MORPHEME SET 7

morpheme	meaning	mnemonic(s)	other example words
al/all/allel	other	alias, allomorph	alibi, alter, allele, allopathy, allelocatalytic
card/cord	heart, agree	cardiac, cordial	electrocardiogram, endocardium, misericord
cruc	cross, important point	crucify, crucial	crux, cruciform, crucible, cruciate, excruciating
dec/decor	acceptable	decent, decorum	indecent, decorous, decorist, decor
ed/es	eat	edible, obese	comestible, edacious, esurient, esculent
fa/pha/phe	speak, spoken of	famous, aphasia, euphemism	ineffable, blaspheme, phatic, emphasis, dysphasia
fer/pher/phor	bear, carry, send, bring	fertile, transfer, refer, metaphor	peripheral, pheromone, phosphor, differ; words ending in: -phoresis (transmission), -pheresis (removal), -phoria (mental state)
frater	brother	fraternity	fratricide, fraternal

morpheme	meaning	mnemonic(s)	other example words
ge	earth	geology	perigee, apogee, geode, georgic, epigeal, Gaea
gem/gemin	twin	Gemini	bigeminal, trigeminus, gemellus, geminate
ger	old person	geriatric	gerontogeous, gerontomorphosis, gerontology
graph/gram	write, record	telegraph, telegram	tetragrammaton, pantograph, graphite, epigram, diagram, digraph
juven	young	juvenile	rejuvenate, juvenal
lat	carry	translate	ablation, collate, illation, superlative, dilatory, prolate, elate, prelate
lig	tie, bind	ligament, oblige	ligate, ligature, alligation, colligate, religion
lign	wood	ligneus	lignify, lignite, lignescent
loqu/locu	speak	soliloquy, elocution	circumlocution, interlocutor, obloquy, grandiloquence, colloquium, colloquial
magn	great, large	magnify	magnanimous, magniloquent, magnum, magnitude
mater/metr	mother, womb, surrounding stuff	maternal, matrix	matrilineal, metritis, metrorrhagia, metropolis, endometrium, dura mater, matter, material
myc	fungus	mycology	streptomycin, mycosis
noc/nyc	night	nocturnal, nyctophobia	equinox, nocturn, noctule, nyctitropism
nomen/onom/ onomat/ onym	name	nominate, onomatopoeia, antonomasia, pseudonym	nomenclature, patronymic, nominal, onomastic, synonym, antonym, eponym
orth	straight, correct	orthopedic, orthodox	orthographic, orthogonal, anorthite, orthotic
paleo	old	paleolithic	paleontology, paleoclimatic, paleobotany
pater	father, country	paternal, expatriate	perpetrate, patron, repatriate, sympatric, patriarchal, patrilocal, patron
ped/paed	child, teach	pediatric, encyclopaedia	pedology, pedodontia, pedo, orthopedic, pedogogy, paedomorphism, paedogenic
ped/pod/pus	foot	pedal, podiatry, platypus	centipede, cephalopod, octopus, expedite
phyll	leaf	chlorophyll	phyllotaxis, heterophyllous, phylloid, phyllophagous
phyt	plant	phytogenic	phytolite, thallophyte, phytoplankton, neophyte
pom	fruit, apple	pomegranate	pomade, pome, pomiferous, pomology, pomaceous

morpheme	meaning	mnemonic(s)	other example words
pred	prey	predator	depredation, predacious, predatory
rhizo	root	rhizome	mycorrhiza, rhizopod, rhizophagus
sal/saul	jump	salient, assault	resilience, salacious, saltitory, saltation, saltigrade
salv/salu	safe, healthy	salvation, salubrious	salutary, salvable, salubrity, salutatorian, salute, salvo
soror	sister	sorority	sororial, sororicide, sororate
spor	scatter, seed	diaspora, sporozoan	sporadic, sporogenesis, sporophyll, sporophore, sporophyte
the	place, put	epithet, thesis	prosthesis, antithesis, diathesis, parenthetical, thetic, anathema
uxor	wife	uxorial	uxoricide, uxorious, uxorilocal
val	strong, useful	valor, valid	valence, convalesce, prevalent, valetudinarian
voc/vok	speak, call, voice	vocation, revoke	vociferous, invoke, vocative, convoke, evoke

MORPHEME SET 8

morpheme	meaning	mnemonic(s)	other example words
aden	gland	adenoids	adenoma, adenomyxoma, adenopathy
alg	pain	analgesic	neuralgia, nostalgic, algolagnia, algogenic
aur	ear	aural	auricle, aurilave, auris, auristillae
axill	armpit	axillary (hair)	axilla, axillae, axillar, cervicoaxillary
caud/cod	tail	caudate, coda	caudal, longicaudate, caudiform, caudad
cervic	neck, neck of uterus	cervix	cervical, cervicoaxillary, cervicodynia
cut	skin	cuticle	subcutaneous, cutis, cuticula
derm/dermat	skin	hypodermic	dermatitis, taxidermy, dermopterous, pachyderm
gaster	stomach	gastrointestinal	gastropod, gastritis, gastronome, gastrula
gravid	pregnant	gravidity	prima gravida, gravid, multigravida
hem/em	blood	hemoglobin, anemia	hemostat, hematology, hematoma, hemophilia
hepat	liver	hepatitis	hepatoma, hepatolysis, hepatotomy

morpheme	meaning	mnemonic(s)	other example words
hist	body tissue	histology	histanoxia, histoma, histogenesis, histoteliosis
hyster	womb, neurotic disorder	hysterectomy, hysteria	hysterolysis, hysteropathy, hysterics, hysterical
-ia	land, state, medical condition	utopia, pneumonia	Albania, neuralgia, exophthalmia
-itis	inflamation	hepatitis	neuritis, endocarditis, phlebitis, pleuritis
lab	lip	labium	labret, labiomental, labiocervical, labiomancy
lac	milk	lactose	lactation, galaxy, lactiferous, lactein
lacrim/lachrym	tear, tear duct	lacrimase, lachrymose	lacrimatory, lachrymator
laryng	voice box, vocal cords	laryngitis	larynx, laryngectomy, laryngophony
mamm	breast	mammal	mammogram, mammoplasty, mammae
nas/nar	nose	nasal, nares	narial, nasturtium, nasopharynx, nariform
nephr	kidney	nephritis	epinephrine, nephrostomy, nephron, nephrocele
-oma	tumor, growth	carcinoma	glaucoma, melanoma, fibroma
op/ophthalm	eye, see	optics, ophthalmology	autopsy, biopsy, isomatropia, myopic, exopthalmic
os/osteo	bone	ossify, osteoporosis	os, osseous, ossuary, osteomyelitis
os/or	mouth, opening	osculate, oral	oratory, oscillate, osculant, oscitation, oracle
phleb	vein	phlebitis	phleborrhagia, phlebostasis, phlebotomy, phlebosclerosis
phob	fear	phobia	Russophobia, claustrophobia, agoraphobia, hydrophobia
phylac	guard	prophylactic	anaphyliaxis, phylacteries, phylaxin
pne/pneum	lung, respiration	pneumonia	apnea, dyspnea, pneumatic, pneumothorax
pulmo	lung	pulmonary	pulmolith, pulmometer
rhin	nose	rhinocerous	rhinitis, oxyrhine, rhinoplasty
sarc	flesh	sarcophagus	sarcoma, sarcopoietic, sarcosome
scler	hard	arteriosclerosis	sclera, sclerosant, sclerokeratitis
sep	putrid, infected	antiseptic	sepsometer, septicemia, sepsis
stom	mouth, opening	stoma, colostomy	stomatitis, stomach, anastomosis, cyclostome
thromb	clot	thrombosis	prothrombin, thrombus, thrombocyte, thromboembolism

morpheme	meaning	mnemonic(s)	other example words
vas/ves	blood vessel, duct	vasectomy, vesicle	vas, vasodilator, vascular, vesica
ven	vein	intravenous	vena, venose, venomotor, veno-stasis

MORPHEME SET 9

morpheme	meaning	mnemonic(s)	other example words
ali	wing	aliform	ala, alar, alary, alate, alula, aliped, aliferous
api	bee	apiary	apiculture, apian, apiarist
arachn	spider	arachnid	arachnoid, arachnean, arachnodactyly, arachnophobia
bov/bu/bos/bou	cow, milk	bovine, butter, boustrophedon	bovate, bovid, butyric, bucolic, bulimia, ovibos, bulimia
chir	hand	chiropractor	chiropodist, enchiridion, chiromancy, chiroptera
clam/claim	cry out, call	clamor, reclaim	clamant, declaim, acclaim, conclamation, clamorous
clav	key, locked	clavier, conclave	enclave, clavichord, clavicle, autoclave, claviger, exclave
col	live, inhabit, grow	colony, cultivate	culture, arboricole, horticulture, saxicole, arenicolous
curs/curr	run	cursor, current	discursive, excursive, curriculum, incursion, precursor, cursory
den/odon	tooth	dental, periodontal	mastodon, edentate, dentition, odontoid, orthodonture, trident
dendr/dr/dry	tree	rhododendron, druid, hamadryad, dryad	dendrochronology, dendrite, philodendron, dendriform
dyn	power	dynamo	dyne, dynasty, aerodyne, dynamic
ev	age, time	medieval	coeval, primeval, longevity
formic	ant	formic, formicary	formica, formic acid, formication,
herp/herpet/serp	creep, reptile	herpes, herpetology, serpent	herpetism, serpentine, serpigo, serpolet, serpula
hor	hour, time, season	horology, horoscope	horologe, horologer, horometry
ichthy	fish	ichthyology	ichthyornis, ichthyosis, ichthyism, ichthyopsida

morpheme	meaning	mnemonic(s)	other example words
ly/lv/lu	loosen, dissolve	analysis, electrolyte, dissolve, solution	lyotropic, electrolysis, dialysis, electrolyte, solvent, dissolute
mal/male	bad	malefactor	malicious, maleficent, malaprop, malice, malign, malevolent
mant/manc	prophesy	necromancy	mantic, chiromantic, praying mantis, ceromancy
mun	common, public, gift	municipal, remunerate	munificent, commune, immune, communicate
naut/nav	boat, seafaring	nautical, naval	Argonaut, astronaut, navigate, nautilus, nave, nausea, navicular
nul/null	nothing	annul	null, nullify, nullity
orn/ornith	bird	ornithology	ornithomancy, ornithosis, notornis
ov/oö	egg	oval, oöcyte	ovary, ovate, ovoid, ovule, ovulate, ovum, oögamous, oölogy, oölite
ox/oxy	sharp, sour, oxygen	oxymoron, oxalic	oxygen, oxycephaly, paroxysm, oxytone, oxyacetyline, amphioxus
phag	eat	sarcophagus	bacteriophage, anthropophagy, phagocyte, dysphagia
pithec	ape	australopithecus	pithecanthropus, pithecan, pithecological, Dryopithecus
plac	please, flat	placate, placid	placebo, placenta, placable, placoid
pter	feather, wing	pterodactyl, helicopter	archaeopteryx, pteridophyte, pteridology, apterous
rog	ask, take away	interrogate	supererogatory, rogatory, surrogate, abrogate, prerogative, subrogate
sen	old	senility	senescent, senator, senectitude, senopia
som	body	psychosomatic	chromosome, soma, somatic, somatogenic, somatotype, acrosome
soph	wise, knowledge	sophisticated, philosophy	sophist, sophomore, Theosophy, sophistry, gastrosoph
strat	stretch, level, layer	prostrate, stratum	stratify, stratigraphy, stratus, substrate
telo-/teleo-	end, complete	telic, teleology	teleorganic, telencephalon, telesis, teleostome, telephase
trop	turn	heliotrope	trope, tropism, entropy, phototropic, anatropous, tropotaxis

morpheme	meaning	mnemonic(s)	other example words
verm	worm	vermicelli	vermiform, vermouth, vermin, vermicular, vermifuge
vin/oen	wine	vino, oenology	vinegar, vinaceous, viniculture, oenophile, oenomel, oenotherapy
xyl	wood	xylophone	xylem, xyloid, xylograph, xylose, xylophagous

Further Reading and Research Tools

SOURCES OF INFORMATION ON COMPLEX MORPHOLOGY AND VOCABULARY

The morphemes assigned in each chapter may be supplemented by others found in the glossary (see appendix I). The following elaborated dictionaries of morphemes may also be useful for reference to morphemes not found in the glossary.

Borror, Donald J. 1960. *Dictionary of Word Roots and Combining Forms.* Palo Alto, CA: Mayfield Publishing Co.

Hogben, Lancelot. 1969. *The Vocabulary of Science.* NY: Stein and Day.

Smith, Robert W. L. 1966. *Dictionary of English Word-Roots; English-Roots and Roots-English, with Examples and Exercises.* Totowa, NJ: Littlefield, Adams.

Other works on specific categories of English word elements include the following:

Suffixes and Other Word-final Elements of English. 1982. Detroit: Gale Research.

Prefixes and Other Word-Initial Elements of English. 1984. Detroit: Gale Research.

Supplementary advanced vocabulary for specific subject fields is organized in thesauruslike fashion in the following work:

Urdang, Laurence, Anne Ryle, and Tanya H. Lee. 1986. *-Ologies and -Isms.* Detroit: Gale Research.

Lists of English words from Latin, Greek, and other sources can be found in the following works:

Urdang, Lawrence. and Frank R. Abate. 1991. *Dictionary of Borrowed Words.* New York: Wynwood Press.
Mawson, C. O. Sylvester. 1987. *The Harper Dictionary of Foreign Terms.* New York: Harper & Row.

In addition to the books listed, there exist numerous useful specialized dictionaries, glossaries, and encyclopedias that treat vocabulary and serve as guides to the nomenclature and terminology of specific fields.

ETYMOLOGICAL DICTIONARIES

The most comprehensive of all historical treatments of English is the renowned *The Oxford English Dictionary* (OED). Now in its second edition and available in computer-accessible form, it is without doubt the single most valuable source available on English etymology. The printed version of the dictionary exists in both its original twelve-volume format and a photographically reduced two-volume edition (sold with a good magnifying glass!). (The first edition of the OED was followed by four supplementary volumes of material incorporated in the second edition.) Other recommended etymological dictionaries include the following:

The American Heritage Dictionary of the English Language. 3rd ed. 1992. Boston: Houghton Mifflin. (This is a regular desktop dictionary that is especially strong on deep etymology.) It is also available on Macintosh and PC disks.
Onions, C. T., ed. 1966. *The Oxford Dictionary of English Etymology.* Oxford: Clarendon Press. (This dictionary contains abridged material from the first edition of the OED.)
Partridge, Eric. 1966. *Origins: A Short Etymological Dictionary of Modern English.* New York: Macmillan.

SOURCES ON RELEVANT AREAS OF LINGUISTICS

The student may want to refer to the following introductory works for additional information and reading in the various subdisciplines of linguistics discussed in this book.

General Linguistics

Burling, Robbins. 1992. *Patterns of Language: Structure, Variation, Change*. San Diego: Harcourt Brace Jovanovich.

Clark, Virginia P.; Paul A. Eschholz, and Alfred E. Rosa. 1994. *Language: Introductory Readings*. 5th ed. New York: St. Martin's Press.

Crystal, David. 1987. *The Cambridge Encyclopedia of Linguistics*. Cambridge: Cambridge University Press.

Finegan, Edward, and Niko Besnier. 1989. *Language: Its Structure and Use*. San Diego: Harcourt Brace Jovanovich.

Fromkin, Victoria, and Robert Rodman. 1993. *An Introduction to Language*. 5th ed. New York: Holt, Rinehart and Winston.

History of English

Baugh, Albert, and Thomas Cable. 1993. *A History of the English Language*. 4th ed. Englewood Cliffs, NJ: Prentice-Hall.

Claiborne, Robert. 1983. *Our Marvelous Native Tongue*. New York: Times Books.

Millward, C. L. 1989. *A Biography of the English Language*. New York: Holt, Rinehart and Winston.

Pyles, Thomas, with a revision by John Algeo. 1993. *The Origins and Development of the English Language*. 4th ed. New York: Harcourt Brace Jovanovich. (There is also a useful companion workbook for this volume.)

Phonetics

Ladefoged, Peter. 1993. *A Course in Phonetics*. 3rd ed. New York: Harcourt Brace Jovanovich.

Usage and Rhetoric

Bolinger, Dwight L. 1980. *Language, the Loaded Weapon: The Use and Abuse of Language Today*. London: Longman.

Eschholz, Paul A. and Alfred E. Rosa. 1985. *Language Awareness*. 4th edition. New York: St. Martin's Press.

Quinn, Jim. 1980. *American Tongue and Cheek*. Middlesex, Eng.: Penguin Books.

Sociolinguistics and Dialectology

Cassidy, Frederick J., ed. 1985. *The Dictionary of American Regional English*. Cambridge, Mass.: Belknap Press of Harvard University Press.

Trudgill, Peter. 1983. *Sociolinguistics: An Introduction to Language and Society.* Harmondsworth, Eng.: Penguin Books.

Wardhaugh, Ronald. 1992. *An Introduction to Sociolinguistics.* 2nd ed. Oxford: Basil Blackwell.

Wolfram, Walt. 1991. *Dialects and American English.* Englewood Cliffs, N.J.: Prentice-Hall.

Language and Culture

Bonvillain, Nancy. 1993. *Language, Culture, and Communication: The Meaning of Messages.* Englewood Cliffs, N.J.: Prentice-Hall.

Language Change, Historical Linguistics, and Language Classification

Aitchison, Jean. 1991. *Language Change: Progress or Decay?* 2nd ed. Cambridge: Cambridge University Press.

Baldi, Philip. 1983. *An Introduction to the Indo-European Languages.* Carbondale, Ill.: Southern Illinois University Press.

Buck, Carl D. 1933. *A Comparative Grammar of Greek and Latin.* Chicago: The University of Chicago Press.

Buck, Carl D. 1949. *A Dictionary of Selected Synonyms in the Principal Indo-European Languages; A Contribution to the History of Ideas.* Chicago: The University of Chicago Press.

Ruhlen, Merritt. 1987, rpt. 1991. *A Guide to the World's Languages.* Stanford, Calif.: Stanford University Press.

Latin and Greek Grammar and Vocabulary

Ehrlich, Eugene. 1985. *Amo, Amas, Amat, and More: How to Use Latin to Your Own Advantage and to the Astonishment of Others.* New York: Harper & Row.

Gildersleeve, B. L., and Gonzalez Lodge. 1895. *Latin Grammar.* 3rd ed. New York: Macmillan; rpt. New York: St. Martin's Press, 1984.

Glare, P.G.W., ed. 1968–82. *Oxford Latin Dictionary.* Oxford: Oxford University Press.

Liddle, Henry G., and Robert Scott. 1843, rpt. 1968. *A Greek-English Lexicon.* Oxford: Oxford University Press.

Smyth, Herbert W. 1956. *Greek Grammar.* Cambridge, Mass.: Harvard University Press.

Wodehouse, S. C. 1910. *English-Greek Dictionary. A Vocabulary of the Attic Language with a Supplement of Proper Names Including Greek Equivalents for Names Famous in Roman History.* London: Routledge & Kegan Paul (rpt. 1979).

Changes from Latin to French to English

Pope, M.K. 1952. *From Latin to Modern French.* Manchester, Eng.: Manchester University Press.

Spelling

Cummings, D. W. 1988. *American English Spelling.* Baltimore: The Johns Hopkins University Press.

Index

-*a*, 123, 126, 129

a-, 34–35

-*a/-ae*, 123–24

Abbreviated form, 154

Abbreviation, 95–96. *See also* Semantic change or shift

Abbreviations of Latin words and phrases, 154

Ability, morphemes expressing, 130

Ablative absolute constructions, 153

Ablative case, 148–49

Ablaut, 51, 142–43

Abstract meaning, 103. *See also* Semantic change or shift

Abstraction, morphemes expressing, 129–30

Acceptability. *See* Standard; Usage

Accusative case, 148–49, 160, 162

Acronyms, 41–42

Action, morphemes expressing, 129–30

Active (in verbs), 126, 142

ad-, 101

Adam, 136

Adam's apple, 64. *See also* Larynx

Adjective, 7, 30–33, 36, 50, 92, 116, 122, 126–26, 148, 160, 162

  extended to use as a noun, 92

  -forming suffix -*y*, 32

  -forming suffixes, 32, 130

  phrase, 153

Adverbs, 31, 116

Affixes, 129, 162

Affricate, 60, 63, 65, 122, 161

Affrication, 162, 164

Afghanistan, 137

African languages, 23

African varieties of English. *See* English: African varieties of

agent, 126

Agent, morphemes expressing, 130

Airflow in articulation, 58–64

Albanian, 138

Alfred the Great, 18

Allomorph, 48–53, 57, 68, 73–74, 76, 78–80, 91

  longer, 79

Allomorphy, 47–49, 56, 69, 82, 91, 93, 127, 143, 159

  idiosyncratic or unpredictable, 47–53, 73

  regular or predictable, 73–83

  shared, 48

Alternation, 51–53, 80. *See also* Allomorphy

Alveolar, 59, 61–65, 67, 69, 79, 122

Alveolar ridge, 59–60, 63

Alveolar stop, 161

Alveolum, 59

Alveopalatal, 60, 63–65, 122, 161

Amelioration, 102. *See also* Semantic change or shift

American dialects. *See* English: American, dialects of

American English. *See* English: American

American Indian languages, 23

Americanisms. *See* English: Americanisms in

Analogy, 39–40